AAUSC 2009 Volu

MW00565475

Principles and Practices of the *Standards* in College Foreign Language Education

Virginia M. Scott, Editor

Eva Dessein and Rachel Nisselson, Editorial Assistants

HEINLE
CENGAGE Learning™

Australia • Brazil • Japan • Korea • Mexico • Singapore • Spain • United Kingdom • United States

HEINLE
CENGAGE Learning™

AAUSC 2009 Volume:
Principles and Practices of the
***Standards* in College Foreign**
Language Education
Virginia M. Scott, Editor

Publisher: Beth Kramer

Editorial Assistant: María Colina

Marketing Manager:
Mary Jo Prinaris

Marketing Coordinator:
Janine Enos

Marketing Communications
Manager: Stacey Purviance

Content Project Manager:
PrePress PMG

Senior Art Director: Linda Jurras

Print Buyer: Amy Rogers

Permissions Editor:
Mardell Glinski Schultz

Photo Manager:
Jennifer Meyer Dare

Cover Designer: PrePress PMG

Compositor: PrePress PMG

For product information and
technology assistance, contact us at **Cengage Learning
Customer & Sales Support, 1-800-354-9706**

For permission to use material from this text or product,
submit all requests online at **www.cengage.com/permissions**
Further permissions questions can be emailed to
permissionrequest@cengage.com

Library of Congress Control Number: 2009937267

ISBN-13: 978-1-4282-6288-1

ISBN-10: 1-4282-6288-1

Heinle
20 Channel Center
Boston, MA 02210
USA

Cengage Learning is a leading provider of customized learning solutions with office locations around the globe, including Singapore, the United Kingdom, Australia, Mexico, Brazil, and Japan. Locate your local office at **international.cengage.com/region**

Cengage Learning products are represented in Canada by Nelson Education, Ltd.

For your course and learning solutions, visit **www.cengage.com**.

Purchase any of our products at your local college store or at our preferred online store **www.ichapters.com**.

Printed in the United States of America
1 2 3 4 5   14 13 12 11 10

ED042

Contents

American Association of University Supervisors and Coordinators and Directors of Language Programs

Abstracts

HEATHER WILLIS ALLEN
In Search of Relevance: The Role of the *Standards* in the Undergraduate Foreign Language Curriculum

Beyond the *Standards'* influence on K-12 language education policy and continued discussions of their relevance and application to foreign language (FL) instruction and assessment, the tangible impacts of the *Standards* in shaping curriculum and classroom instruction have not been wide-ranging in university-level FL departments. This chapter identifies and discusses three factors that have contributed to the reception of the *Standards* in higher education and, more specifically, in terms of the advanced undergraduate FL curriculum. Based on the discussion of these factors, I respond to the question of whether the *Standards* provide a framework adequate for addressing the critical challenge facing university-level FL programs today of the meaningful integration of language and content across the curriculum. Ultimately, I argue that although the *Standards* continue to serve as an important document within a historical continuum of pedagogical change, they fail to provide principled guidance for university-level FL departments struggling to identify pathways or approaches to inform how curricula are articulated.

KATHERINE ARENS
Teaching Culture: The *Standards* as an Optic on Curriculum Development

This chapter offers an experiment in defining what it means to teach culture, based on the *Standards for Foreign Language Learning in the 21st Century* (2006). Traditional postsecondary FL classrooms all too often define "culture" as a set of facts; the *Standards* suggest that culture may be profitably defined as a field of cultural practices, signifiers, and knowledge. In consequence, a curriculum may be developed stressing how learning a culture means not only acquiring its knowledge base but also the strategic competencies needed to function within it. Defining culture as a pragmatic field structured like a language but functioning in more dimensions requires that any curriculum be targeted at a particular site or region within which a group acts and defines itself as culturally literate through communication, pragmatic practices (behaviors, institutional functions), and a characteristic knowledge base.

To make this case, I first offer a rereading of the *Standards* to redefine learning language as learning culture. I then provide examples of how such a rereading of the *Standards* can be implemented to structure curricula fostering various forms of culture literacy. The experiment proposed here argues that the *Standards* apply to a more encompassing model for learning, especially for teaching and learning culture as a set of semiotic systems revealed in the pragmatic choices made by members of a cultural community in a particular field of culture. My experiment, therefore, challenges how the *Standards* have been read and implemented overall.

ELIZABETH BERNHARDT, GUADALUPE VALDÉS, AND ALICE MIANO
A Chronicle of *Standards*-Based Curricular Reform in a Research University

In 1995, Stanford University embarked upon curricular renewal in all major foreign languages. This curricular renewal was motivated by the university senate's concern that campuswide internationalization could not come about without a serious commitment to language teaching and learning. That commitment was then institutionalized in the Stanford Language Center. The Center was charged with encouraging excellence in language teaching, establishing and maintaining performance standards, providing professional development opportunities for the teaching staff, and developing a research program about language teaching and learning. At the heart of the renewal process established by the Language Center was a professional development program focused on Oral Proficiency Interview (OPI) certification that helped the teaching staff to acquire a common framework and professional language upon which to engage and interact. Also key was a focus on the *Standards* as blueprints for program development. This chapter narrates the process the staff negotiated over several years of development, using the 1st- and 2nd-year Spanish programs as the specific instance of *Standards*-based curriculum development. Appended to the chapter is the curricular document that includes objectives for interpersonal, presentational, and interpretive language based on a quarter system calendar for 2 years of instruction. In addition, the chapter chronicles how the *Standards*-based curriculum had both a washback and a feedback effect on staff-development and knowledge of language assessment. Finally, the chapter maps a future path, noting the shortcomings of current assessment procedures for analyzing presentational language, and proposing an alternative.

LISA DEWAARD DYKSTRA
Reconceptualizing the Goals for Foreign Language Learning: The Role of Pragmatics Instruction

The the *Standards for Foreign Language Learning in the 21st Century* (2006) and the 2007 MLA report, *Foreign Languages and Higher Education: New Structures for a Changed World*, have put forth recommendations for language education in the United States. Both documents lament the dearth of competent speakers of languages other than English and both advocate for a change to the current system. However, in this chapter I argue that neither model is sufficient. After a thorough analysis of the *Standards* and the MLA report, I present a review of the literature on interlanguage pragmatics and argue that the inclusion of pragmatics instruction can aid in the personal transformation necessary for true competence in the second language. Pragmatics study provides a starting point for the deconstruction of the original self by presenting often conflicting patterns of a paradigm that to learners appears to be self-evident as well as uniform across cultures, namely what constitutes politeness—the building block of interaction that serves as a frame for all discourse. When politeness is found to be distinct across cultures, the sense of a foundation of communication gives way and the native culture, and with it the self, are challenged. The inclusion of pragmatics can result in a different self than before, an amplified self with varying sets of workable frames for interaction. It is in this way that meaningful entrance into and interaction with the target culture can take place. The *Standards* and the MLA report come up short precisely because they do not adequately address this important component of language.

EILEEN KETCHUM MCEWAN
Incorporating the *Standards* Into a 3R Model of Literary and Cultural Analysis

Although useful for providing directions and continuity for foreign language programs at the high school and university levels, the *Standards for Foreign Language Learning in the 21st Century* (2006) seem to overlook the specific skills of literary analysis, a traditional focus for many college-level language programs. This chapter attempts to address that oversight by offering a 3R Model of Literary and Cultural Analysis (Recognize-Research-Relate). The 3R Model combines literary, linguistic, and cultural acquisition within a general analytical model that fulfills the *Standards'* Five Cs of foreign language learning. Based on research in schema theory and reader-response theories, the 3R Model helps students identify literary and linguistic elements that seem representative of a target culture, research the target culture through various resources to arrive at a multifaceted view of that culture, and apply the newly developed background knowledge to the text for a more culturally informed reading. Specific examples taken from Francophone literature provide a detailed presentation of the three steps of the model, accompanied by suggestions for using the model with other languages and levels of linguistic competency, thereby demonstrating its wide-ranging application within postsecondary language programs.

ANA OSKOZ
Using Online Forums to Integrate the *Standards* Into the Foreign Language Curriculum

This chapter reports on the work conducted in a foreign language (FL) program at the University of Maryland Baltimore County that integrates both in-class and online discussions to reflect on students in and interpret various documents and experiences. In particular, this study focuses on students in one class of Intermediate Spanish I who used asynchronous online interactions to explore, analyze, and reflect on cultural topics. Five groups of students' online discussions were collected and analyzed through the framework of the 5 goals of the *Standards*. Subsequent quantitative analysis of the data showed that the online forums can become springboards for students to share, debate, and interpret information; to gain knowledge and understanding of other cultures; to reflect and make connections to additional bodies of knowledge; to compare and contrast the target culture with their own; and to participate in multilingual and multicultural communities. Pedagogical suggestions to enhance the value of the discussion boards are provided at the end of the chapter.

JUNE PHILLIPS
Strengthening the Connection Between Content and Communication

This chapter presents some of the underlying concepts that informed the development of the *Standards for Foreign Language Learning in the 21st Century*, especially those that concern achieving communicative and content goals in all levels of language courses. It proposes that a firm understanding of the contexts embedded in the three modes of communication—Interpersonal, Interpretive, and Presentational—establishes an instructional orientation that is more informative for teaching/learning than the four skills alone provided. Using the communicative modes as the starting point for a solid base of cultural or interdisciplinary content (including literary sources) results in learning that has strong intellectual content in the humanities rather than rote learning and manipulative language practice. To facilitate this merging of communication and content, a series of templates are offered that instructors can use so that questions are asked at the planning stage that are appropriate to the content area. This scan of content with potential for student learning is then matched with communicative tasks appropriate to the proficiency level of students. The templates help to establish a mindset for instructors so that new materials can be explored with minimal materials development time and also take advantage of contemporary events, student interests, and opportunities for curricular enrichment.

JEAN MARIE SCHULTZ
A *Standards*-Based Framework for the Teaching of Literature Within the Context of Globalization

The 2007 MLA report, *Foreign Languages and Higher Education: New Structures for a Changed World*, calls into question many of the current practices in language teaching, their underlying philosophies, and even the structure of departments of foreign languages and literatures in light of the impact of increased globalization, which privileges the development of "translingual" and "transcultural" competence. Particularly at stake is the traditional role of literature in the foreign language curriculum, a role made all the more problematic within the context of the *Standards for Foreign Language Learning in the 21st Century* (2006), which are ambivalent as to how literary texts should figure into the foreign language classroom. Although three of the *Standards*' Five Cs—Cultures, Comparisons, and Communication—have generated new paradigms for the incorporation of literature in the language classroom, very little research has been done in terms of Communities and Connections. This chapter explores why these two standards seem to have been passed over within the pedagogical literature and examines how they can figure prominently into a reconfigured foreign language curriculum that advances the goals of the *Standards* as well as those of the 2007 MLA report. The chapter further explores how literature can be repositioned within interdisciplinary practices that might serve to create new kinds of connections within the global arena, as well as how literature helps provide students access to new foreign language communities. Finally, the chapter concludes by illustrating the theoretical discussion with the description of an intermediate French language course designed specifically to meet the needs of students interested in Global Studies.

H. JAY SISKIN
A Great Rattling of Dry Bones: The Emergence of National Standards in the Early 20th century

The founding of the MLA in 1883 signaled a victory for modern languages in their struggle to gain academic recognition. Greek and Latin were dealt yet another blow to their prestige when "modern language men" persuasively argued that French and German had the same virtues that the classicists had arrogated to themselves, namely a rich literature, efficacy in mental discipline, and an aid to mastering other disciplines. Indeed, the modern languages could go one step further, claiming their practical value in contemporary society. At the same time, waves of immigration were bringing about increased growth in high school enrollments and a more diverse student body, causing concern among many educators. At the 1891 meeting of the National Council of Education in Toronto, the chair of the Committee on Secondary Education, James H. Baker, complained that "the present condition of affairs [as regards high school curricula] is chaotic and that it may be improved in many respects" (Baker, cited in "Report of the committee of 10" *School Journal*, 1895, p. 718).

Such was the historical moment that motivated a series of reports evaluating the place of modern languages in the curriculum, the best ways to teach them, and above all, standards of achievement for entrance into college. In this chapter, I will examine two of these reports—the *Report of the Committee of Ten* and the *Report of the Committee of Twelve*—as well as the formation of the College Board. I will emphasize their importance for standard setting, articulation, and assessment in the context of the educational culture of the times.

ROBERT M. TERRY
The National Standards at the Postsecondary Level: A Blueprint and Framework for Change

For years we have looked for the one right way to teach foreign languages. Many different methods, techniques, and approaches have surfaced, but none has yet provided us with *the* way. The most recent phenomenon to appear is the *Standards for Foreign Language Learning in the 21st Century*. While still not affording us the answer, since their 1996 appearance the *Standards* have had a noticeable impact on foreign language teaching: New state frameworks, new curricula, new textbook series, and a new focus on performance in the classroom, as outlined in the Five Cs (Communication, Cultures, Connections, Comparisons, Communities).

Another challenging yet exciting C is now facing those of us who teach at the college/university level: Change. The challenge is in convincing colleagues why change is necessary and why they should change. We all should read the 2007 Modern Language Association report, *Foreign Languages and Higher Education: New Structures for a*

Changed World. Although this report does not mention the *Standards*, there is a striking overlap of both the spirit and the tenets set forth originally in that 1996 document.

The two-tiered structure that typically exists between the humanists and language specialists, as the MLA report calls them, must be addressed and must evolve for our own common interests. Our goals need to be restructured to produce linguistically and culturally competent users and not rivals to native speakers. It is time for a change. The national standards provide us with the tested and proven blueprint and roadmap that we need.

Introduction

Virginia M. Scott, Eva Dessein and Rachel Nisselson, Vanderbilt University

> *All students can be successful language and culture learners,*
> *and they must have access to language and culture study*
> *that is integrated into the entire school experience...*
>
> (*Standards*, p. 7).

In the 10 years since the *Standards for Foreign Language Learning in the 21st Century* were published, they have received limited attention by those engaged in college-level foreign language teaching and learning. Although preparation of K-12 teachers generally requires familiarity with both national and state standards documents, college-level teachers are by and large unaware of or uninformed about them. Moreover, graduate students preparing for college-level teaching often encounter only superficial mention of the *Standards*[1] in their methods courses or during supervised teaching. We hope that this volume will contribute to the ongoing professional discourse about the *Standards* among college foreign language teachers and graduate students who are preparing for careers in the academy. We are grateful to Carl Blyth, the series editor for AAUSC Issues in Language Program Direction, as well as the members of the editorial board, for working with us on this important project. We would also like to thank Beth Kramer at Heinle Cengage Learning and Sathyabama Kumaran at PreMedia Global for working with us during the final stages of production. Above all, we owe a debt of gratitude to the contributors to this volume whose insights and perspectives will no doubt play a significant role in shaping our continuing conversations about the *Standards*.

Looking Back Ten Years

In her introduction to the 1999 volume, *Foreign Language Standards: Linking Research, Theories, and Practices,* June Phillips sets an optimistic tone for the success of the *Standards for Foreign Language Learning in the 21st Century*. She argues that both the design of the content standards and the efforts made to achieve strong national consensus place the standards for world languages on a firm foundation.[2] The Five Cs and 11 standards (see Appendix A) were, indeed, endorsed by national, regional, and state foreign language organizations; in 2002, the Foreign Language Standards Collaborative was also accepted for membership in the National Council for Accreditation of Teacher Education (NCATE). This widespread endorsement of the *Standards* is remarkable and, as Phillips notes, "virtually every state's standards strongly align with the national ones" (1999, p. 2). This optimism is echoed in the executive summary of the project, which states that "[t]he resulting document represents an unprecedented consensus among educators, business leaders, government, and the community on the definition and role of foreign language instruction in American education" (para. 1). Since the publication of the *Standards*, most elementary, middle, and high school foreign language teachers in public schools across the United States have been implementing them.

Although the *Standards* initially targeted K-12 foreign language learners, they were quickly expanded to include postsecondary learners. Aware of the impact that the new standards would likely have on college-level language learning, the *ADFL Bulletin* published 17 opinion papers in the fall 1999 and winter 2000 issues to stimulate and enrich the discussion of the *Standards*. Several of these comments, made in response to the 1996 publication of *Standards for Foreign Language Learning: Preparing for the 21st Century*, remain particularly salient to our discussion today. For example, Jeannette Bragger and Donald Rice (1999) predicted that K-12 foreign language learning and teaching was likely to change significantly in the ensuing decade but that a transition to standards education across K-16 would take many years. Scott McGinnis (1999) noted that although they should be viewed as a challenge to our sense of professionalism rather than as a threat, standards or any form of performance assessment imposed from the outside is often viewed by college and university faculty members as "tantamount to a surrender of some sort of academic freedom" (p. 80). Thomas Beyer (2000) expressed a realistic concern that was certainly shared by many others, stating "[e]ven though I wish to support the Standards, I recognize that many of us were not trained and do not feel qualified to do what the Standards require" (p. 60). James Davis (2000) and Joan Kelly Hall (2000) argued that teacher training is the answer to any long-term transformation of foreign language learning. Finally, Sheri Spaine Long (1999) noted that the standards project was one among several "megatrends"—another important one being instantaneous digital access to foreign culture—that would steer us to the common ground of culturally based foreign language education (p. 74). The views expressed in these commentaries resonate today, leading us to wonder what, if anything, is different now, 10 years later.

Standards Today

Assessing the influence of the *Standards* document on foreign language teaching and learning during the past decade would be impossible. The language of the *Standards* has become part of the discourse in the profession to varying degrees and every school and college has been touched in some way. What is clear, however, is that their effect on college-level foreign language education has been haphazard at best. Some programs have participated in the national conversation about standards, whereas others have remained unaffected. Rather than assuming college and university foreign language teachers are disinterested, or that they are elitist intellectuals disinclined to adapt their teaching to standards imposed from the outside, this lack of attention is more likely attributable to various complex, systemic issues. First, and most obvious, the disjuncture between K-12 and college education is a wide-reaching dilemma in the American educational system; for most academic subjects there is little intentional articulation between high school and college. Second, this disjuncture is exacerbated by the variety of college programs: public versus private institutions, 4-year liberal arts colleges versus research universities. Third, foreign language programs within one single institution may be housed in different departments, each with distinct curricular offerings and learning goals. Finally, some institutions separate foreign language teaching from foreign literature/culture teaching, often creating additional problems related to coherence and articulation. These issues, and others we may have overlooked, are impediments to any intentional focus on the *Standards for Foreign Language Learning in the 21st Century* among college foreign language teachers.

In their 1999 article Bragger and Rice pose three critical questions that remain pertinent to our discussion about the *Standards*: Who are the change agents? When and how will the changes occur? What kind of changes will be needed? These questions will serve to organize our assessment of current and future discussions about the *Standards* in college-level foreign language education.

Who are the change agents?

The future of the national standards in college foreign language education lies in engaging all faculty members who teach foreign languages and literatures in constructive discussions that focus on shared concerns. Doris Kadish (2000) notes that standards-based curricular revisions were implemented at the University of Georgia primarily because, as she says, "[w]e happen to have a number of faculty members who are interested in issues relating to foreign language education, including officers of the AATSP and AATF, the authors of a leading textbook, and several applied and theoretical linguists" (p. 49). Although her situation may not be typical, she attributes their success with the *Standards* to having a critical mass of faculty members "interested in issues related to foreign language education" (p. 49). We would argue that all our colleagues, regardless of what they teach, are fundamentally interested in foreign language education. Moreover, we believe that the key to engaging them in discussions about the *Standards* lies in focusing on the rights and responsibilities of all students to become members of a 21st-century global community. In other words, we must make the case that concentrating our efforts on the very few gifted students who show promise as near-native users of the target language (and who are most like us) is misguided. Any discussions about standards should focus on students—on whom we teach—rather than on culture clashes among teachers. We can all be change agents if we agree that "all students can be successful language and culture learners" (*Standards*, p. 7).

When and how will the changes occur?

The executive summary of the *Standards* document states that the "*Standards for Foreign Language Learning* will not be achieved overnight; rather, they provide a gauge against which to measure improvement in the years to come" (para. 3). The kind of changes that will prove lasting must account for a gradual, recursive process that is not subject to deadlines. New generations of teachers will become increasingly familiar with the *Standards*, and best practices will emerge gradually as more research links the theoretical principles of the standards to learning and teaching.

One of the critical issues we must address in any discussion of how changes may occur involves acknowledging that the language of the *Standards* can be an impediment. Most foreign language teachers have little difficulty understanding what it means to teach "reading," "writing," "listening," or "speaking." However, as Phillips (1999) notes, teachers need to "think modes or domains, not skills" (p. 7). For applied linguists this notion may be easy to grasp; for those who do not read or talk about language teaching, however, this kind of language can be unfamiliar and perhaps even alienating. Understanding the *Standards* may be, therefore, closely related to one's membership in the discourse community of foreign language teachers.

To explore the challenges that teachers may face, we interviewed five graduate teaching assistants (TAs) at our institution who were only marginally familiar with the *Standards*.[3] We consider the views of graduate students to be especially critical in this conversation because they will be the change agents of the future. Both native and non-native speakers of English as well as novice and more experienced TAs were included. We gave them an overview of the Five Cs (Appendix A) and an excerpt from the *Standards* document (pp. 27–38). Their reactions to the excerpt ranged from extremely positive to rather unconvinced. In fact, individual TAs often experienced this range of reactions themselves. For example, when referring to the excerpt from the *Standards* document Jonathan Wade stated,

> It's beautiful, it's nice, but this would have to be the intro to something that's going to show me how it's done. It is abstract until you see it in practice. I would want to see this [*Standards*] book as something that's going to show me how other professors have done this or how students have learned in this way.

Echoing these thoughts, Angela Archambault spoke of the seductive quality of the *Standards* but expressed doubt as to the reality of their application. "When I read it," she commented, "I had the impression that I was reading a travel brochure that was trying to seduce me to come and promote the Five Cs. But I'd like more follow-through…What's the proof? What's the concrete evidence for teachers?" Lucas Faugère's comments were perhaps the most interesting in that he seemed unable to fully understand the excerpt. He said,

> For me it [the *Standards* document] remains an abstraction, an abstract language ... that is problematic to tie to what we are doing daily in the classroom. It stands as an ideal ... that we should strive for. There's a gap between the conceptual level and the pedagogy. It's hard to translate these concepts into pedagogy.

Only Ingo Kieslich seemed both convinced by the underlying principles of the *Standards* and relatively satisfied by what the document offers. In fact, he bristled at the idea of more specific information about the pedagogical applications of the *Standards*. He revealed, "I'm not sure I would actually want more as far as a pedagogical approach is concerned…The danger is ending up with a bombastic textbook that provides everything but the teacher." Overall, the TAs' comments encapsulate the criticism of the *Standards* often voiced by college foreign language teachers—that they are too abstract and/or insufficiently prescriptive.

Ultimately, this conversation with graduate students helped us understand that, as with other kinds of theoretical discourse, it can take time to acquire the language and assimilate the concepts outlined in the *Standards*. Rather than being able to "teach" the *Standards*, we must give our colleagues and novice teachers opportunities to familiarize themselves with both the language and the theoretical principles. Phillips (2007) states that "the standards were not developed to be a secret code of the profession; rather, they were written to communicate with a larger audience" (p. 268). Although transparency may have been the intent of the task force, we think that viewing learning and teaching through the discourse lens of standards is a gradual process. Just as it took time to understand what "proficiency-oriented teaching" meant, it will also take time for our colleagues who teach at the college level to wrap their minds around the theoretical principles and goals outlined in the Five Cs. Moreover, as Carmen Chaves Tesser (2000) notes, the language of the *Standards* may eventually serve to bring us together:

> The Standards for foreign language learning in general and the language-specific Standards in particular provide us with a common language, a useful vocabulary, and an emerging common culture to allow us a better understanding of our individual roles and of our individual fields. The Standards are not a threat to the integrity of our fields of endeavor whether we pursue analyses of literary texts and other cultural aesthetic products or whether we pursue the analyses of second language acquisition and other cultural connections. The Standards give us a (pre)text, a common ground on which to map our interest and academic pursuits. (Tesser, 2000, p. 79)

What kind of changes will be needed?

In her 1999 article Phillips noted that teachers will need to "dedicate themselves to intensive work with the theoretical principles that form the basis for standards-driven learning" (p. 3). Although this suggestion may be legitimate, most teachers will unlikely take the necessary time to familiarize themselves with the pertinent theories regarding second language learning and teaching. Furthermore, the *Standards* raise several important questions about second language development that have yet to be fully explored. For example, even though the *Standards* state that English may be used—"It is also important to remember that students can use critical thinking skills in beginning language classes by conducting some tasks in English" (p. 35)—there is no clear sense in the profession regarding when or how much it should be used.

In addition, many foreign language teachers wrestle with the complex issues related to the role of grammar in second language development. In particular, there is no common understanding of the importance of accuracy, especially regarding speaking. Another related issue involves the question of holding students to a native-speaker standard in the target language. Recent research calls into question the very notion of the native speaker and points to learning goals that are predicated on a more realistic conception of second language use (Cook, 1999, 2002; Kramsch, 2002; Levine, 2001; Scott, 2010; Train, 2002). Finally, the question that has caused most concern relates to the role of literature in the foreign language curriculum. Because the *Standards* make little or no mention of literature per se, it remains essential to explore the role it plays in developing the "interpretive mode" (*Standard 1.2*) or in promoting "an understanding of the relationship between the products and perspectives of the culture studied" (*Standard 2.2*). Richard Kern's (2003) literacy-based curriculum, founded on the idea that learners should be prepared to interpret multiple forms of language use, both oral and written, involves all Five Cs and serves as a good example of work in this area. Virginia Scott and Julie Huntington's (2007) research on the role of literature in developing the Interpretive mode provides another example of relevant research in this area. In the end, studies that explore questions raised by the *Standards* must precede any clear understanding of what kind of changes will be needed.

Looking Forward

The contributions in this volume, divided into three parts, will serve to stimulate the ongoing discussion about standards in college-level foreign language education. Part 1, entitled "Historical Perspectives: Past, Present, and Future," begins with a chapter by Jay Siskin that reviews the long and elaborate history of developing standards for foreign language learning and teaching in the United States. This chapter makes it clear that "the Standards did not develop out of thin air" (Siskin, 1999, p. 87) and are not a new cult of innovation, but rather a result of long-standing professional conversations. Robert Terry, who served as associate editor of the 1999 volume, *Foreign Language Standards: Linking Research, Theories, and Practices*, draws on his history with the standards project and adds a sixth C: Change. In this second chapter he argues that we must convince our colleagues in colleges and universities that standards offer an exciting opportunity to transform our profession. Terry also makes the case that the 2007 MLA report, *Foreign Languages and Higher Education: New Structures for a Changed World*, supports the spirit and the principles that were part of the original 1996 *Standards* document. In the third chapter June Phillips, who has played a vital role in the standards project from the beginning, offers insight into ways that the three modes of communication—Interpersonal, Interpretive, and Presentational—form the basis of an understanding of teaching that goes beyond a four-skills approach. She argues that the communicative modes can be the starting point for a strong intellectual engagement in other areas of the humanities, such as culture, literatures, and other cross-disciplinary studies. In the fourth chapter Heather Allen takes a critical view, underscoring the limited impact the *Standards* have had on college-level foreign language education. She ultimately sees their value principally as contributing to an ongoing professional dialogue about overarching goals and instructional approaches to inform how and what we teach.

Part 2, "Curricular Reform: Shifting Paradigms," is composed of three chapters. In the first, Elizabeth Bernhardt, Guadalupe Valdés, and Alice Miano recount how the Stanford Language Center used both the *Standards* and the Oral Proficiency Interview (OPI) as conceptual frameworks for curricular reform and professional development. The Stanford model is an example of a program that has successfully integrated the *Standards*, both in terms of overarching goals and everyday instruction. In the next chapter, Lisa Dykstra proposes a new model for foreign language learning based on pragmatics instruction, which has as its goal the transformation of the learner into a multilingual self. Trained in the pragmatic elements of the target culture, particularly politeness conventions, this multilingual self is truly able to interact with other cultures. Dykstra's chapter provides a thorough review of literature on interlanguage pragmatics and outlines how pragmatics instruction addresses the *Standards* goal areas of communication and culture. In the final chapter of this part, Ana Oskoz demonstrates how Web-based applications allow for an integration of the *Standards* while maintaining a focus on grammar instruction. She highlights one program in which an intermediate Spanish class used these forums to address all of the Five Cs in a collaborative, constructivist, and learner-centered environment. Oskoz also provides useful suggestions for instructors interested in implementing a similar program.

Part 3 "Literature and Culture: Closing Divides" is composed of three chapters. In the first, Jean Marie Schultz responds to the charges set out in the 2007 MLA report by proposing ways to use the Communities and Connections standards as a flexible framework for a globalized approach to the teaching of literature. She argues that these two Cs have been overlooked and can serve as a way to reposition literature within interdisciplinary practices. Using the example of an intermediate French language class at the University of California at Santa Barbara, she shows how this approach can be used to promote critical language awareness as well as transcultural and translingual competencies. In the second chapter, Eileen McEwan notes that the *Standards* do not address literary analysis, a skill she considers particularly important at the college level. She proposes a 3R (recognize-research-relate) model to complement the Five Cs of the *Standards*. Drawing on examples from Francophone texts, she shows how her model can strengthen the rigorousness of the *Standards* to match a college-level curriculum. In the final chapter Katherine Arens presents a curriculum with culture at its core. Through a rereading of the *Standards*, she suggests that a language-based culture curriculum ought to teach not only language but also create a space within which individuals exercise identity and agency with respect to the target culture. According to Arens, the standards project has the potential to lead us past existing linguistic models by modeling precisely how this kind of "translinguistic and transcultural" language learning might be staged and practiced.

Finally, the chapters in this volume offer historical perspectives and critical responses to the *Standards*; they also illustrate ways the *Standards* can be used to shape college-level curricula. Like Hiram Maxim (2004), we believe that the *Standards* are "one of the most comprehensive attempts to date for envisioning and coordinating FL education across educational levels" (p. 79). Moreover, this volume represents a collaborative effort between a professor of both language and literature (Virginia Scott) and two graduate students whose academic interests combine languages and literatures (Eva Dessein and Rachel Nisselson). The interactions we have had during the editorial process have enriched our understanding of the *Standards* immeasurably, and we have every reason to believe that this volume will contribute in significant ways to this important national dialogue.

Notes

1. Throughout this volume when the word "*Standards*" is capitalized and in italics it refers to the published document, *Standards for Foreign Language Learning in the 21st Century* (1999, 2006).

2. An 11-member task force representing the 4 national language organizations (the American Council on the Teaching of Foreign Languages, the American Association of Teachers of French, the American Association of Teachers of German, and the American Association of Teachers of Spanish and Portuguese) collaborated on the standards project.

3. We would like to thank the following people for participating in our conversation about *Standards*: Angela Archambault (native English speaker, Ph.D. student in French), Lucas Faugère (native French speaker, M.A. student in French and English), Ingo Kieslich (native German speaker, Ph.D. candidate in German), Jessica Riviere (native English speaker, Ph.D. student in German), and Jonathan Wade (native English speaker, Ph.D. in Spanish).

References

Beyer, T. R., Jr. (1999). What standards? Standards—so what? *ADFL Bulletin, 31*(2), 59–60.

Bragger, J. D. & Rice, D. B. (1999). The implications of the *Standards* for higher education. *ADFL Bulletin, 31*(1), 70–72.

Cook, V. (1999). Going beyond the native speaker in language teaching. *TESOL Quarterly 33*, 185–209.

Cook, V. (Ed.). (2002). *Portraits of the L2 user*. Clevedon, UK: Multilingual Matters.

Davis, J. J. (2000). From where I sit: The Standards and university instruction. *ADFL Bulletin, 31*(2), 61–63.

Hall, J. K. (2000). A proposal for governance of pre-K—12 teacher preparation. *ADFL Bulletin, 31*(2), 64–66.

Kadish, D. Y. (2000). The challenge we face: Applying national standards to the college foreign language curriculum. *ADFL Bulletin, 31*(2), 49–52.

Kern, R. G. (2003). Literacy and advanced foreign language learning: Rethinking the curriculum. In H. Byrnes & H. H. Maxim (Eds.), *Advanced foreign language learning: A challenge to college programs* (pp. 2–18). AAUSC Issues in Language Program Direction. Boston, MA: Heinle.

Kramsch, C. (2002). The privilege of the non-native speaker. In C. Blyth (Ed.), *The sociolinguistics of foreign-language classrooms* (pp. 251–262). AAUSC Issues in Language Program Direction, Boston. MA: Heinle.

Levine, G. S. (2004). Co-construction and articulation of code choice practices in foreign language classrooms. In C. M. Barrette & K. Paesani (Eds.), *Language program articulation: Developing a theoretical foundation* (pp. 110–130). AAUSC Issues in Language Program Direction. Boston, MA: Heinle.

Long, S. S. (2000). Common ground: K-12 standards and higher education. *ADFL Bulletin, 31*(2), 72–74.

Maxim, H. H. (2004). Articulating foreign language writing development at the collegiate level: A curriculum-based approach. In C. M. Barrette & K. Paesani (Eds.), *Language program articulation: Developing a theoretical foundation* (pp. 78–93). AAUSC Issues in Program Direction. Boston, MA: Heinle.

McGinnis, S. (1999). RE: *Standards. ADFL Bulletin, 31*(1), 80–81.

Phillips, J. K. & Terry, R. M. (Eds.). (1999). *Foreign language standards: Linking research, theories, and practices.* Lincolnwood, IL: National Textbook Company.

Phillips, J. K. (1999). Standards for world languages—on a firm foundation. In J. K. Phillips & R. M. Terry (Eds.), *Foreign language standards: Linking research, theories, and practices* (pp. 1–14). Lincolnwood, IL: National Textbook Company.

Phillips, J. K. (2007). Foreign language education: Whose definition? *The Modern Language Journal, 91*, 266–268.

Scott, V. M. (2010). *Double talk: Deconstructing monolingualism in classroom second language learning.* New York: Prentice Hall.

Scott, V. M. & Huntington, J. A. (2007). Literature, the interpretive mode, and novice learners. *The Modern Language Journal, 91*, 3–14.

Siskin, H. J. (1999). The national standards and the discourse of innovation. *ADFL Bulletin, 31*(1), 85–87.

Standards for foreign language learning: Preparing for the 21st century. (1996). Yonkers, NY: National Standards in Foreign Language Education Project.

Standards for foreign language learning in the 21st century. (1999, 2006). National Standards in Foreign Language Education Project. Lawrence, KS: Allen Press.

Standards for foreign language learning in the 21st century. Executive summary. http://www.actfl.org/files/public/StandardsforFLLexecsumm_rev.pdf

Tesser, C. C. (2000). Moving from debate to dialogue: The standards and articulation. *ADFL Bulletin, 31*(2), 78–79.

Train, R. W. (2002). The (non)native standard language in foreign language education: A critical perspective. In C. Blyth (Ed.), *The sociolinguistics of foreign-language classrooms* (pp. 3–39). AAUSC Issues in Language Program Direction. Boston, MA: Heinle.

Appendix A
Standards for Foreign Language Learning

Communication
Communicate in Languages Other Than English

Standard 1.1: Students engage in conversations, provide and obtain information, express feelings and emotions, and exchange opinions.

Standard 1.2: Students understand and interpret written and spoken language on a variety of topics.

Standard 1.3: Students present information, concepts, and ideas to an audience of listeners or readers on a variety of topics.

Cultures
Gain Knowledge and Understanding of Other Cultures

Standard 2.1: Students demonstrate an understanding of the relationship between the practices and perspectives of the culture studied.

Standard 2.2: Students demonstrate an understanding of the relationship between the products and perspectives of the culture studied.

Connections
Connect With Other Disciplines and Acquire Information

Standard 3.1: Students reinforce and further their knowledge of other disciplines through the foreign language.

Standard 3.2: Students acquire information and recognize the distinctive viewpoints that are only available through the foreign language and its cultures.

Comparisons
Develop Insight Into the Nature of Language and Culture

Standard 4.1: Students demonstrate understanding of the nature of language through comparisons of the language studied and their own.

Standard 4.2: Students demonstrate understanding of the concept of culture through comparisons of the cultures studied and their own.

Communities
Participate in Multilingual Communities at Home and Around the World

Standard 5.1: Students use the language both within and beyond the school setting.

Standard 5.2: Students show evidence of becoming life-long learners by using the language for personal enjoyment and enrichment.

Part One

Historical Perspectives: Past, Present, and Future

Chapter 1

A Great Rattling of Dry Bones: The Emergence of National *Standards* in the Early 20th Century

H. Jay Siskin, Cabrillo College

Introduction

In May 1932, Professor Peter Hagboldt contributed a piece to the *Modern Language Journal*, attempting to put into perspective the battles raging at the time concerning "the best method." The contemporary reader will recognize the wisdom of his words and realize that they apply not only to methodology but also to seemingly novel pedagogical frameworks and proclamations:

> Each generation produces its own guides. Unfortunately some of these guides believe themselves to be prophets with entire new and revolutionary thoughts and theories. [...] They do not realize that their new ideas are as ancient as our remotest forefathers and as revolutionary as those of a Tory. Frequently [...] they are young teachers who have either had not time to gather experience or no desire to read and digest the literature dealing with that which has been thought, practiced, and accomplished in the past. (Hagboldt, 1932, p. 625)

Despite Hagboldt's overstatements, his pronouncement is not without merit. It is well worth "digesting the literature" to situate current practice within an historical continuum. In this way, we may distinguish revolution from evolution, and, hopefully, demarginalize the work of our "remotest" forefathers and foremothers. With these goals in mind I will examine the earliest efforts to create national standards and articulations between high school and college.

The Struggle for Standards

The Modern Language Association (MLA) was founded in the last decades of a century marked by a fervent optimism in the forward movement of science and technology. In 1895, H. Schmidt-Wartenberg, professor of Germanic Philology at the University of Chicago, and secretary of the Central Division of the MLA, proclaimed that the founding of the MLA was the "main event" in the history of foreign language teaching in the United States. At the turn of the new century, Thomas R. Price, professor of English at Columbia University, scarcely avoided hyperbole during his presidential address to the attendees of the MLA meeting during December of 1900:

> As teachers of the modern languages, in our survey of our own Association and of the American university system, we must all feel a certain warmth of exhilaration. The progress that our favorite studies have been making is so splendid. Within that period of forty years which the memory of older men among us can now cover, and, for the younger men, in each of the periods into which those forty years could be divided, there has been, in a steady current of progress, so vast an improvement in our methods of instruction, so vast an increase in the magnitude of our work, in the number of our pupils, in the size and qualification of our professorial force. In the national movement of thought and theory in education, we have shared, indeed, with the physical sciences in popular favour; and even as compared with the physical sciences themselves, the growth of instruction in the modern languages has been, I think, the more rapid and the more impressive. Excluded at first, or hardly recognized, as a factor in liberal education, they have now made good their position, in all grades of instruction, in school and college and university. (Price, 1901, p. 77)

Modern languages had indeed made good their position in school and postsecondary education. That achievement—accomplished by three distinguished national committees: the Committee of Ten, the Committee of Twelve, and the Committee on College Entrance Requirements—took years of investigations, debates, and committee reports devoted to methods, outcomes, standards, articulation, and testing. As a concrete outcome, the College Entrance Examination Board was created and institutionalized. The genesis of these committees and their influence on the establishment of national standards for high school graduation and college entrance are the focus of this chapter.

The Committee of Ten

The late 19th century witnessed what many considered unplanned and uncontrolled growth in the high school curriculum. Moreover, different colleges prescribed different entrance requirements, making it more difficult to prepare students for postsecondary education. Wilson Farrand, headmaster of the Newark Academy, decried this situation in his inaugural address as president of the Schoolmasters' Association of New York:

> Princeton requires Latin of candidates for one course, but not for the others. Yale demands it of all, Columbia of none. Princeton names five books of Caesar and four orations of Cicero; Yale names four books of Caesar and three books of Virgil.... Yale calls for Botany, Columbia for Physics and Chemistry, Princeton

for no science. Princeton and Columbia demand both German and French, while Yale is satisfied with either. On the other hand, while Princeton and Columbia demand only American History, Yale calls also for that of England.... (Ferrand, 1895, as cited in Fuess, 1950, p. 17)

Furthermore, educators questioned the desirability or feasibility of a single curriculum, particularly in light of the large numbers and greater diversity of the student population.

At the 1891 meeting of the National Council of Education in Toronto, the chairman of the Committee on Secondary Education, James H. Baker, presented a report entitled "Uniformity in Requirements for Admissions to College." Its purpose was "to show that the present condition of affairs [as regards high school curricula] is chaotic and that it may be improved in many respects" (Baker, cited in "Report of the committee of 10" *School Journal*, 1895, p. 71). The council recommended that a committee be appointed, to consist of representatives from universities, colleges, high schools, and preparatory schools, and charged with investigating the problems of secondary and higher education.

Thirty individuals responded to the council's invitation to participate in such a conference, which was held in Saratoga, New York, the following year. Over the course of a 3-day session, the attendees formulated a plan that Columbia Professor Nicholas Murray Butler, in his capacity as chairman of the Committee of Conference between Colleges and Secondary Schools, presented to the National Council of Education. The report called for the formation of an executive committee of ten, to be accorded "full power to call for [...] conferences [of secondary and college teachers] during the academic year 1892–1893; that the results of the conferences be reported to said executive committee for such action as they deem appropriate; and that the executive committee be requested to report fully concerning their action to the council."[1]

Headed by Charles W. Eliot, president of Harvard University, the Committee of Ten itself was composed of teachers from secondary schools, preparatory schools, colleges, and universities. The choice of Charles W. Eliot as chair was a keen strategic move. He was active in the National Education Association (NEA) and wielded considerable influence not only in postsecondary education but in elementary and high schools as well. He was well known as an educational reformer; among other progressive positions, Eliot espoused an elective system at Harvard and advocated electivism as far down as the later elementary grades (Kliebard, 2004, p. 10). Eliot made no class distinction between students preparing for college and those for whom a high school diploma represented the end of formal studies. For Eliot, "the right selection of subjects, along with the right way of teaching them, could develop citizens of all classes endowed in accordance with the humanist ideal—with the power of reason, sensitivity to beauty, and high moral character" (Kliebard, 2004, p. 10). Eliot's influence is discernable not only in the work of the Committee of Ten but in subsequent developments in college entrance examinations as well. The members of the Committee of Ten first met in November 1892, in New York. The members in turn created nine committees—referred to as *Conferences*—including one that investigated "other modern languages," that is, modern languages other than English. The conferences were charged with making recommendations in 11 areas of concern; these concerns were formulated as questions intended to guide, but not necessarily organize, the conferences' final report. Inquiries covered topics such as the starting point for the study of a particular subject, the selection of topics, and curricular design.

The conferences met at different locations during a 3-day period beginning December 28, 1892; their final report was adopted a year later. Twenty-seven thousand copies of the *Report of the Committee of Ten on Secondary School Studies* were distributed free of charge; the second edition, containing an index, a table of contents, and an introduction by N. A. Calkins, chairman of the Board of Trustees of the NEA, was published by the Bureau of Education in Washington in 1894. In his introductory remarks, Calkins deemed the *Report* "the most important educational document ever issued in the United States" (Bureau of Education, 1894, p. iii). He characterized the spirit of the text as distinctly moderate and conservative, perhaps a rhetorical strategy to render some of the more innovative recommendations less threatening. Although the report of the Other Modern Languages Conference does contain some "radical" ideas,[2] the recommendations for the elementary and advanced high school curriculum differed little from then-current practice. In fact, they nearly duplicated those of the Commission of Colleges in New England on Admission Examinations.

Among the 11 inquiries taken up by the committee and its conferences, questions 6, 9, and 10 are the most relevant for this chapter, insofar as they sought to determine the prerequisite high school curriculum for college admission.[3]

> *Question 6:* In what forms and to what extent should the subject enter into college requirements for admission? Such questions as the sufficiency of translation at sight as a test of knowledge of a language, or the superiority of a laboratory examination in a scientific subject to a written examination on a text-book, are intended to be suggested under this head by the phrase "in what form."
>
> *Question 9:* Can any description be given of the best method of teaching this subject throughout the school course?
>
> *Question 10:* Can any description be given of the best modes of testing attainments in this subject at college admission examinations?

Recommendations of the Committee of Ten

Course of Study

The following are the outcomes expected in the primary modern language at the end of the high school course of study. These goals are only language specific when enumerating grammar items (point a) and reading goals, that is, number of pages to be covered (point b):

> *Advanced German—(a)* Proficiency in more advanced grammar. In addition to a thorough knowledge of accidence, of the elements of word-formation, and of the principal values of prepositions and

conjunctions, the scholars must be familiar with the essentials of German syntax, and particularly with the uses of modal auxiliaries and the subjunctive and infinitive modes. (*b*) Ability to translate ordinary German. It is thought that pupils can acquire this ability by reading, in all, not less than seven hundred duodecimo pages.

Advanced French—(*a*) Proficiency in more advanced grammar. In addition to a thorough knowledge of accidence and of the values of prepositions and conjunctions, the scholars must be familiar with the essentials of French syntax—especially the use of modes and tenses—and with the more frequently recurring idiomatic phrases. (*b*) Ability to translate standard French. It is thought that pupils can acquire this ability by reading, in all, not less than one thousand duodecimo pages.

The final two points are generic for both languages:

(*c*) Ability to write in French/German a paragraph upon an assigned subject chosen from the works studied in class. (*d*) Ability to follow a recitation conducted in French/German and to answer in that language questions asked by the instructor (pp. 99–100).

Prescribed methods of instruction borrow heavily from a preexisting document, the *Synopsis of French and German Instruction for 1890,* in the high schools of Boston. Activities and recommendations included:

- Translation from German and French, with the goal of developing translation at sight.
- Rapid reading; the authors decry the "mistaken idea of thoroughness" as a waste of time, recommending that all passages of an abstract or technical nature should be skipped or translated by the instructor: "not a moment should be lost in contending with difficulties that have no necessary connection with the language" (pp. 100–101). Frequent reviews of reading material are to be avoided; rather, new texts should be introduced to stimulate students' interest and enlarge their vocabulary.
- Practice in pronunciation, conversation, and composition should be provided. This recommendation is barely elaborated. The authors appear to consider translation into the foreign language as a first step in acquiring pronunciation and conversational skills. The target language is to be used as much as possible beginning in the first-year course. Desired outcomes were modest: "In the first year the pupil can catch by ear the names of familiar things and many common phrases; during the second he ought to form sentences himself; and in the third the recitations should, if the instructor has a practical command of French or German, be conducted mainly in that language" (p. 101).
- The deferment of grammar instruction until 3 months into the course. The preliminary period should be devoted to sight-reading. The instructor should point out important points of grammar as they occur; in theory, the pupil would be acquiring the "inflections of the language"

through reading and translation. After 3 months have passed, the instructor may devote attention to grammar in its more abstract form.

- Limited use of the Natural Method. The conference did not seek to condemn this method but asserted that its success depends upon favorable conditions and teachers "peculiarly adapted" to that method of instruction.

As an afterthought, the conference noted that its recommendations could apply to Spanish or any other modern language that might be introduced into the curriculum.

College Requirements

College requirements are dispatched in three short paragraphs. It was advised that college examinations for admission should coincide with high school requirements for graduation. They should consist essentially of a sight translation from German or French into English and a written translation from English into the modern language.

Curriculum Design

One of the broader implications of the *Report* related to curricular design. The Committee of Ten recommended that the modern languages have equal status for college entry as the classical. The committee outlined four model curricula, whose principal difference was the type of language prescribed: The *classical* curriculum contained three languages, including Greek and Latin; *the Latin-scientific* included two languages, one of them modern; the *modern languages* curriculum called for two modern languages; and the *English* contained one language, either modern or classical. In practical terms, a classical language was not an absolute necessity for college preparation, whereas three curricula prescribed a modern language (cf. Ravitch, 1995, p. 171).

Report of the Committee of Ten: Reception

The findings of the Committee of Ten were eagerly anticipated by the educational community. The *Educational Review* of 1893 heralded the significance of the forthcoming report and raised expectations for its positive influence on curriculum and articulation:

> No committee appointed in this country to deal with an educational subject has ever attracted so much attention as this one, and everywhere confidence is felt that the result of its deliberations will be wise and practical. It is not too much to expect that the leading colleges and the best secondary schools will be guided by its recommendations, and that in consequence a long step will have been taken toward providing this country with something like a systematic organization of secondary education. Every branch of the educational system, higher and lower, will feel the good effects of this long-desired reform. (as cited in Knight, 1952, p. 94)

The following year, the same journal noted that all the magazines having "a large constituency of intelligent and cultivated readers"—the *Nation*, *Harper's Weekly*, and the *Atlantic Monthly*, as examples—had given considerable attention to the *Report*. The critiques were nuanced, but flattering: "The great importance and significance of the report is recognized by them all" (*Educational Review*, 1894, as cited in Knight, p. 97).

Outlook predicted that the *Report* would "profoundly modify secondary education in the United States, greatly to the advantage of our entire educational system" ("An important report," 1894). The writer noted the progressive credentials of the committee and its recommendations, reassuring the readers, however, that none appeared overly extreme or radical. Nevertheless, the *Report* would shake up the educational establishment: "It would be idle to deny, however, that when the schools and colleges come to put in practice the recommendations made in this report—as many of them will and as all of them should—there will be a great rattling of dry bones" ("An important report," 1894).

It did not take long, however, for the critics of the *Report* to become more vocal, indeed bellicose. In an 1894 article entitled "A big question for teachers," the *New York Times* announced the then upcoming meeting of the NEA in Asbury Park, where a "deep-seated pedagogic war" was in the works. There was no "open outbreak" as yet, but rather "a deliberate formation of the lines of battle." The stakes were nothing less than "the very life of the present high-school system of the United States." Opponents, who were designated as "conservatives," maintained that adopting the recommendations of the *Report* would be "the most revolutionary proceeding in modern education." The *Times* article also recorded the defense of the *Report* issued by the Reverend James MacKenzie before an audience of between two to three thousand teachers. Among the objections to the committee's work was the charge that the proposed system was created by college men, who sought to "set in motion machinery which would make the high school training simply a thing designed to furnish a uniform variety of raw material for the freshmen classes of colleges." The *Report* had lost sight of the needs of the high school student. MacKenzie rebutted by noting that 70% of the men and women who prepared the preliminary work of the *Report* were high school teachers. This and other criticisms were attributed to ignorance, especially in those communities where "old methods, low aims and small school appropriations were the ruling elements." MacKenzie's conclusion praised the *Report* as "the first classic in American pedagogic literature."

The *Times* report concluded with membership reaction. Among the discussants was Dr. A. F. Nightingale, assistant superintendent of the Chicago high schools. He spoke with "the vigor of a typical Chicago man, putting a degree of force into what he said that was unusual in this meeting of pedagogues, where a quiet style of oratory prevails." An important concern of Nightingale was the displacement of Latin by the modern languages

> I therefore deprecate the force and fervor of that movement, now gaining strength, which would permit some modern language to usurp the place which rightly belongs to Latin, and for which there is no adequate alternative. ("A big question," 1894)

Other discussants voiced more objections such that the secretary of NEA expressed doubt whether a majority of teachers would endorse the *Report* should it come to a vote. The discussion ended without resolution.

Formation of the Committee on College Entrance Requirements

The topic was again taken up at the NEA in Denver, where William Carey Jones, professor of Latin at the University of California, delivered a paper entitled "What Action Ought To Be Taken by Universities and Secondary Schools to Promote the Introduction of Programmes Recommended by the Committee of Ten?" summarized in the *School Journal* of 1895.[4] Carey noted that although the committee recommended closer relationships between secondary schools and colleges, it provided no system for developing them. He urged the formation of a committee composed of representatives from universities and high schools to devise plans to promote a "federation" of educational institutions (p. 246). Such a committee was assembled near the close of the meeting and was subsequently enlarged to become the Committee on College Entrance Requirements, to be chaired by the outspoken Chicago man, A. H. Nightingale. The work of this committee was later subsumed by the *Report of the Committee of Twelve*, as described next.

The Committee of Twelve

The NEA, represented by Nightingale and Charles H. Thurber of Colgate (New York) Academy, addressed the 1896 Modern Language Association meeting, seeking a broader professional response to the question of college entrance requirements. The MLA in turn created its own committee, charging it with the task of drawing up model preparatory courses in French and German, and making recommendations concerning their practical management (cf. *Report of the Committee of Twelve*, 1901, p. 1). During the 1896 meeting of the MLA, it was resolved:

> That a committee of twelve be appointed: (*a*) To consider the position of the modern languages in secondary education; (*b*) to examine into and make recommendations upon methods of instruction, the training of teachers, and such other questions connected with the teaching of the modern languages in the secondary schools and the colleges as in the judgment of the committee may require consideration.

> That this committee shall consist of the present president of the association, Prof. Calvin Thomas,[5] as chairman, and eleven other members of the association, to be named by him.

> That the association hereby refers to this committee the request of a committee of the National Educational Association for coöperation in the consideration of the subject of college entrance examinations in French and German. (Thurber, 1896, p. xxii)

The committee's first act was to send out a questionnaire to 2,500 teachers, to determine the status of secondary instruction in French and German at the national level. The committee also sought to "elicit opinions with respect to a number of more or less debatable questions which, as was thought, would be likely to arise in the course of the committee's deliberations" (*Report of the Committee of Twelve*, 1901, p. 2). The *Report* does not reproduce these questions; this lack of detail conforms to the committee's goal of providing clear, practical, and concise advice, thereby avoiding "a learned essay, weighted down with historical lore, statistical tables and exhaustive bibliographies" (p. iv).

The oft-quoted picture that emerged was one of "somewhat chaotic and bewildering conditions" (p. 3). Given this complexity, the committee delayed its report until the 1898 MLA conference. Moreover, the committee refined its mission: Rather than dictate radical changes in the American system (or lack of system), it focused on adapting the report to the prevailing conditions. The more modest goals of the committee became

> to describe a certain number of grades of preparatory instruction, corresponding to courses of different length; to define these grades as clearly as possible in terms of time and work and aim, and to make a few practical recommendations with regard to the management of the instruction—recommendations having as their sole object the educational benefit of the pupil.... (Modern Language Association [MLA], 1901, p. 4)

It was thought that the combined authority of the study's sponsors—the MLA and the NEA—would transform the committee's recommendations into a national norm. Moreover, colleges would be not only willing but also "glad" to reformulate their requirements in terms of the national standards (p. 4).

Methodology became a key factor in the committee's deliberations. The members noted sharp differences of opinion among respondents; before advising teachers how to teach, the committee resolved to reexamine the entire issue in the context of recent contributions to the field, "to the end that their final recommendations might be as free as possible from any vagaries of personal prejudice" (p. 5). As a consequence, the *Report* contains a lengthy review of methodology, presenting both the advantages and shortcomings of the Grammar Method, the Natural Method, the Psychological Method (i.e., Gouin and his followers), the Phonetic Method (outlined by Viëtor), and the Reading Method. The committee's recommended national standards clearly favored reading and sight translation. These standards were organized into three benchmarks, or "grades," intended to provide unified norms of instruction, thereby facilitating articulation between secondary schools and the colleges:

> For the purpose of simplifying the relation between the colleges and the secondary schools and for the purpose of securing greater efficiency and greater uniformity in the work of the schools it is hereby proposed that there be recognized, for the country at large, three grades of preparatory instruction in French and German, to be known as the elementary, the intermediate, and the advanced, and that the colleges be invited to adopt the practice of stating their requirements in terms of the national grades. (MLA, 1901, p. 43)

Although the committee strove to make a distinction between outcomes and "seat time," it nevertheless postulated that the elementary level would correspond to 2 years of the language, at the rate of four recitations[6] per week; the intermediate level, 3 years; and the advanced, 4 years. The *Report* concludes with model courses at the three levels of instruction and sample examination for admission to college. The following are the outcomes for the elementary courses, along with examination activities in French. German activities were similar in content. These give a clear idea of the ambitious goals of the committee and by inference, the necessity of focusing those goals on reading and translation.

THE ELEMENTARY COURSE IN GERMAN

The Aims of the Instruction

At the end of the elementary course in German the pupil should be able to read at sight, and to translate, if called upon, by way of proving his ability to read, a passage of very easy dialogue or narrative prose, help being given upon unusual words and constructions; to put into German short English sentences taken from the language of every-day life or based upon the text given for translation, and to answer questions upon the rudiments of the grammar [...]. (p. 46)

The Elementary Course in French

At the end of the elementary course the pupil should be able to pronounce French accurately, to read at sight easy French prose, to put into French simple English sentences taken from the language of everyday life, or based upon a portion of the French text read, and to answer questions on the rudiments of the grammar [...]. (p. 75)

Sample Examination Activities: French

I. Translate into English:
   Un jeune homme plein de passions, assis sur la bouche d'un volcan, et pleurant sur les mortels dont à peine il voyait à ses pieds les demeures, n'est sans doute, ô vieillards! qu'un objet digne de votre pitié; mais quoi que vous puissiez penser de René, ce tableau que toute ma vie j'ai eu devant les yeux une création à la fois immense et imperceptible, et un abîme ouvert â (sic) mes côtés.

II. CHATEAUBRIAND
   (a) Write the five principal parts of the three verbs [...]: vus, sortir, descend.
   (b) Write a synopsis of the conjugation (first person singular of each tense) of se réjouir and savoir.
   (c) Write the inflection of: the present indicative of boire and faire; the future of pouvoir; the present subjunctive of prendre.
   (d) Write the forms of the demonstrative pronouns.
   (e) In what ways may the use of the passive voice be avoided in French?

III. Translation into English:
    (a) Here is the pen, shall I send it to her? No; do not send it to her; give it to me.
    (b) Cats and dogs are domestic animals.
    (c) You must give them some white bread and good coffee, if they have none.
    (d) The old man is very well this evening, although he has worked all day.
    (e) We have just searched for your gloves, but we do not find them in the room where you left them a quarter of an hour ago.
    (f) Why do we weep for mortals whose life and character we scarcely know? We always have them before our eyes. Whatever we may think of them, they are surely worthy of our pity. (p. 87)

The Report of the Committee of Twelve was unanimously adopted by the MLA at its 1899 meeting in New York (Henneman, 1900, p. 37). The Central Division of the MLA likewise adopted the report, issuing a resolution that nothing less than the elementary course should be accepted for college entrance (Hatfield, 1899, p. lxxx).

The recommendations of the Committee of Twelve were incorporated textually into the *Report of Committee on College Entrance Requirements*.

Creation of the College Board

Two of the active participants in the formation of the Committee of Ten—Nicholas Murray Butler of Columbia and Charles Eliot of Harvard—had an even more ambitious agenda. Speaking before the 1894 meeting of the New England Association of Colleges, Eliot proposed the formation of a board of examiners to conduct admission examinations throughout the United States. The certified results would be valid at all New England colleges and anywhere else that chose to accept them. Eliot's proposal went nowhere: "I hardly think that the proposition was regarded by the Association of Colleges as one seriously to be taken up. At any rate it was not taken up" (cited in Fuess, 1950, p. 16).

The 1899 *Report of the Committee of Twelve* created additional impetus for some sort of assessment procedure. The committee rejected the idea that all colleges formulate the same entrance requirements or that all schools provide the same courses of study. Rather, the committee recommended that the colleges state their entrance requirements in terms of national "constants" or units and that the schools build their curricula from the units designed in accordance to these specifications.[7] This recommendation allowed both flexibility of programs and uniformity of standards, in harmony with Eliot's vision.

The time was ripe to reintroduce the idea of a common examination for college admission. The occasion was a meeting of the Association of Colleges and Secondary Schools of the Middle States and Maryland, held on December 2, 1899, in Trenton. On the agenda was a discussion of "Uniform College Admissions Examinations." Butler had decided to present a resolution calling for the establishment of a college admissions board. President Eliot, although not a member of the organization, took a night train to Trenton to offer support and encouragement to Butler. Butler's brief presentation resulted in a highly contentious exchange. At a particularly difficult turn, President Eliot rose and delivered a persuasive rebuttal to Butler's critics. A vote was taken and the organization declared itself unanimously in favor of the establishment of a board of examiners, which evolved into the College Entrance Examination Board. Later, Butler reflected: "This might never have happened if President Eliot had not come down from Cambridge to support the proposal and make that kind of speech" (Butler, as cited in Fuess, 1950, p. 26).[8] The College Entrance Examination Board of the Middle States administered its first examinations in June 1901. Among the subjects tested were French, German, Greek, and Latin. Spanish was added the following year. The exams incorporated the standards set by the MLA, that is to say, those endorsed by the *Report of the Committee of Twelve* (Ravitch, 1995, p. 172).

The *Report of the Committee of Twelve* did not age well. The very standards underpinning the college entrance examinations were soon considered in need of reform. Writing 13 years later, Krause (1913) recalls that the *Report of the Committee of Twelve* was meant only as a "beginning effort," rather than a "perfect finality." The Committee's intention was that this provisional document be revised based on advances in knowledge and the accumulation of experience. This has not happened:

> Unfortunately, however, the committee put its approval upon old methods, upon indirect teaching of modern languages and getting at literature quickly. This one factor alone and more than all others has brought about the condition of affairs as we find them now: we see the old-time, self-complacent methodologists supposedly with the mighty, far-reaching report as their guide, persisting in the *laissez-faire* attitude. (Krause, 1913, p. 70)

Krause insists that a revised version of the *Report* become a categorical imperative, "for times have changed and demand an adjustment to our more enlightened environment" (p. 71).

Likewise, a committee was appointed at the 1909 meeting of the Central Division of the Modern Language Association in Iowa City to consider revising the *Report*. Its conclusions, presented at the 1910 meeting of the Association in St. Louis, favored revision. Advances in knowledge rendered the *Report* outmoded; it no longer represented the consensus of public opinion; and its emphasis on reading and an early study of literature was counterproductive: "it has encouraged poorly prepared teachers to turn out poorly prepared students" (pp. xlix–l).

The MLA accepted the committee's conclusions and adopted the resolution formulated by the chair of the Germanic Section, Hermann Almstedt. The resolution expressed "an urgent request that a similar joint committee be appointed at once to cooperate in the work of revision of the *Report of the Committee of Twelve*, so that at next year's union meeting the revised *Report* may be acted upon" (MLA, 1901, p. 1). The documentary trail is lost at this point, but it may be inferred from later references to the *Report* that it persisted in its original form and still had a cadre of supporters. In 1919, the editor of the *Modern Language Journal* deemed it "obsolescent" (Editorial comment, p. 137). Mitchell (1931) calls it "outworn" (p. 116) and laments its continuing influence, whereas Geddes (1933) asserts that "Even today, after thirty-three years, the findings of that report are practically incontrovertible" (p. 29). There was also a larger, political signifi-cance of the *Report*: It was brandished as a weapon of the conservatives in their battle against the reformers. Its importance in the preparation of the college en-trance examinations enshrined the status quo. Henceforth, the ability to translate and master grammatical rules became the principal criteria for college admission (cf. Powers et al., 1971, p. 18).

These early efforts at setting standards and creating articulation were based on extensive research, discussion, and collegial collaboration. The committees' goals were ambitious, and the results deemed to be momentous. Yet within two decades, they were condemned as inadequate and outmoded. The Committee of Ten and the Committee of Twelve have been lost in our disciplinary "amnesia." As a result, the current discussion of standards and articulation ignores over a century of thoughtful reflection. Musumeci (1997) decries our ignorance of the past and the insights it can bring to present-day concerns: "Deprived of the wis-dom that the measure of time and historical perspective affords, these profession-als are blind to the difference between the ephemeral and the durable, between the gimmicky and the effective" (pp. 4–5).

The contributions to this volume address the *Standards for Foreign Language Learning in the 21st Century* from various linguistic and pedagogical frameworks. As we read them, let us reflect upon past efforts at setting standards to determine what lessons can be drawn from the ephemeral reports of the last century that will ensure enduring standards for the new millennium.

Notes

1. The council further requested that the directors of the National Education As-sociation provide appropriate funding for the newly formed Committee of Ten, a request that the NEA exceptionally granted (Fuess, 1950, p. 14).

2. Radical recommendations included longer sequences of study—the introduc-tion of elective languages courses in the grammar schools beginning at age 10; and the study of up to three modern languages by the end of high school. Note that these desiderata are still being expressed among language profes-sionals to this day.

3. Indeed, this document represents one of the earliest attempts at articulation. Harvard's president Eliot noted this in an address before the American Institute of Instruction (July 11, 1894; cited in Fuess, p. 16):

   On the whole the greatest promise of usefulness which I see in the Report of the Committee of Ten lies in its obvious tendency to promote cooperation among school and college teachers, and all other persons intelligently inter-ested in education, for the advancement of well-marked and comprehensive educational reforms.

4. Carey later became the first professor of Law at Berkeley. He was instrumental in the founding and administration of Boalt Hall.
5. Calvin Thomas was professor of Germanic Languages at Columbia University.
6. The typical length of a recitation was 45 minutes (cf. Pringle, 1922, p. 160; Brown, 1909, p. 158).
7. These units became subsequently known as Carnegie units, after the Carnegie Foundation for the Advancement of Teaching specified that a unit corresponds to a course of five periods each week over one academic year (Ravitch, 1995, p. 172).
8. For a more detailed discussion of the establishment and accomplishments of the College Entrance Examination Board, see Ravitch, (1995), pp. 171–172 and Fuess (1950), pp. 11–17.

References

A big question for teachers. (1894, July 13). *New York Times*, p. 8.
An important report. (1894, January 13). *Outlook 49*(2), p. 58.
Bureau of Education. (1894). *Report of the Committee of Ten on secondary school studies*. New York: American Book Company.
Editorial Comment. (1919). *The Modern Language Journal, 4*, 132–137.
Fuess, C. M. (1950). *The college board: Its first fifty years*. New York: Columbia University Press.
Geddes, J. (1933). The old and the new. *The French Review, 7*(1), 26–38.
Hagboldt, P. (1932). The best method. *The Modern Language Journal, 16*, 625–631.
Hatfield, J. T. (1899). Discussion of some questions raised by the report of the Committee of Twelve. *PMLA, 14*(4), pp. lxxx–lxxxi.
Henneman, J. B. (1900). The seventeenth annual meeting of the Modern Language Association. *Modern Language Notes, 15*(2), pp. 33–38.
Kliebard, H. (2004). *The struggle for the American curriculum, 1893–1958*. New York: RoutledgeFalmer.
Knight, E. W. (1952). *Fifty years of American education: A historical review and critical appraisal*. New York: Ronald Press.
Krause, Carl A. (1913). The trend of modern language instruction in the United States. *Educational Review, 45*, 237–248.
MacKenzie, J. C. (1894, August 2). The course for academies and high schools recommended by the Committee of Ten. *The Independent*, p. 7.
Mitchell, S. L. (1931). Spanish in the junior college. *Hispania, 14*(2), 115–120.
Modern Language Association of America. (1884). *Proceedings at New York, 1*(December 29, 30, 1884), pp. i–vii.
Modern Language Association. (1901). *Report of the Committee of Twelve of the Modern Language Association of America*. Boston: D. C. Heath & Co.
Musumeci, D. (1997). *Breaking tradition: An exploration of the historical relationship between theory and practice in second language teaching*. San Francisco: McGraw-Hill.
National Education Association. (1899). *Report of Committee on college entrance requirements*. Chicago: University of Chicago Press.
Powers, J. R., Brooks, N., Gaarder, A. B., Goding, S. C., Latimer, J. F., Nionakis, J. P., et al. (1971). Professional responsibilities. In J. L. Dodge (Ed.), *Northeast conference on the teaching of foreign languages* (pp. 15–50). Middlebury: Northeast Conference on the Teaching of Foreign Languages, Inc.
Price, T. R. (1901). The new function of modern language teaching. *PMLA, 16*, 77–91.

Ravitch, D. (1995). The search for order and the rejection of conformity: Standards in American education. In D. Ravitch & M. A. Vinovskis (Eds.), *Learning from the past* (pp. 167–190). Baltimore: Johns Hopkins Press.

Recommended by Committee of Ten: What action out to be taken by universities and secondary schools to promote their introduction. (Synopsis of a paper by Professor William Carey Jones). (1895, September 21). *The School Journal, 50*(27), p. 246.

Report of the Committee of Ten. (1895, June 29). *The School Journal, 50*(27), p. 718.

Schmidt-Wartenberg, H. (1895). The central division of the Modern Language Association of America. *PMLA, 10* (Appendix I and II. Proceedings), pp. lvii–lxiii.

Thurber, C. H. (1895). The N. E. A. at Denver. *The School Review, 3*(7), pp. 422–433.

Thurber, C. H. (1896). College entrance requirements in French and German. *PMLA, 11*(Appendix I and II. Proceedings), pp. xxi–xxiv.

Chapter 2
The National *Standards* at the Postsecondary Level: A Blueprint and Framework for Change

Robert M. Terry, University of Richmond (Emeritus)

> *Stability in language teaching is synonymous with rigor mortis.*
> —Ernest Weekley, *The English Language* (1929)

Introduction

For many decades of foreign language education teachers have been engaged in numerous searches for "the one true way" to teach. We have experimented with the Direct Method, ALM, Total Physical Response (TPR), Suggestopedia, proficiency, and various other methods, approaches, trends, fads, and movements.[1] None of these have offered us *the* way. In 1996, we found ourselves in the midst of another phenomenon occasioned by the appearance of the *Standards for Foreign Language Learning in the 21*st *Century* (SFLL). These national standards have had an enormous impact on state frameworks, K-12 curricula, textbooks, and teaching methods. Yet, the haunting question remains: Why have they not had an effect—any noticeable effect—at the postsecondary level?

The national standards offer an exciting new way to look at learning a language. The old four-skills approach, or reading, writing, listening, and speaking, has given way to the three communicative modes.[2] Yet, phrases such as "a refreshing *new way*" imply change. Change, in turn, means abandoning what has worked so well for so many years (in some minds) and doing something new, untested, unproven, not yet validated through quantitative and qualitative studies.

Change, especially at the postsecondary level, is often an anathema. What is wrong with what we have been doing? Why change? The call for change is not from administration in response to the newest buzzword, the newest effort at effective marketing, or a new focus for accreditation. The impetus for change is from outside the university setting—and that is particularly bothersome to some. The impetus for change has been planted in the minds of certain faculty members—predominantly that body of people who exhibit an unhealthy interest in foreign language pedagogy and methodology and those who teach the foundation courses: those first- and second-year language courses that fulfill the so-called general education "proficiency requirement."

Why change? Why even consider change? Curiosity, if nothing more, should make us want to know why high school students are coming to us prepared differently in foreign languages, why our textbooks look and are different, why our language laboratories are being transformed into media centers or global studios. What we have been doing needs to be reconsidered in light of new thinking—revitalizing new thinking, in the shape of the national standards, that has already caused noticeable changes at the K-12 level. This new thinking energizes me with the possibilities for change, and those possibilities as well as a clear road map are laid out in the national standards. The national standards can offer us at the postsecondary level a new, different, better, and effective plan.

The National Standards

The national standards, a product of a collaborative effort among 10 different foreign language associations,[3] first appeared in 1996 as a response to the mandate by the U.S. Department of Education that all core subjects in American schools should have a set of national standards. The basic philosophical tenet of the standards is the following:

> Language and communication are at the heart of human experience. The United States must educate students who are equipped linguistically and culturally to communicate successfully in a pluralistic society and abroad. This imperative envisions a future in which ALL students will develop and maintain proficiency in English and at least one other language, modern or classical (Standards for Foreign Language Learning in the 21st Century [SFLL], 2006, p. 7).

To this end, the national standards offer 5 basic goals and 11 standards. These standards are content standards: They define what students should know and be able to do.[4] The implications of the national standards are timely and important.

> The development of standards has galvanized the field of foreign language education. The degree of involvement, and of consensus, among educators at all levels has been unprecedented. [...] Clearly, the foreign language standards provide the broader, more complete rationale for foreign language education that we have sought for decades but never managed to capture in words or in concept until now." (SFLL, 2006, p. 15)

> The bottom line is that "standards have defined the agenda for the next decade—and beyond" (p. 15).

The Modern Language Association and Foreign Languages

In May 2007, the Modern Language Association (MLA) published the report of its Ad Hoc Committee on Foreign Languages, *Foreign Languages and Higher Education: New Structures for a Changed World.* For many of us, this report is truly eye-opening; the MLA is supporting "a broad, intellectually driven approach to teaching language and culture in higher education" (p. 1). Yet, the *Standards for Foreign Language Learning in the 21st Century* are mentioned nowhere in the 2007 MLA report. This does not mean, however, that the essence of the report cannot be and is not grounded in the spirit and basic tenets of the standards.

The report gives a concise statement of the current situation: "… the usefulness of studying languages other than English is no longer contested. The goals and means of language study, however, continue to be hotly debated" (MLA, 2007, p. 2). There is a continuum of the various approaches to foreign language (FL) study, with one end anchored in an instrumental view—language consists of skills to use in communicating thought and information—and the other anchored in a constitutive view[5]—language represents what we are, think, and reveal about ourselves. Depending on institutional missions and teaching approaches espoused, we can find ourselves located at any point on this continuum. Most often at the university level, foreign language departments tend to emphasize the constitutive aspect of language, whereas freestanding language schools and some campus language resource centers have an instrumentalist focus.

The MLA report points out the narrow focus of goals of language study that exist in the standard configuration of university FL curricula: A 2- or 3-year language sequence feeds into a set of core courses that focus on canonical literature. "This configuration defines both the curriculum and the governance structure of language departments and creates a division between the language curriculum and the literature curriculum and between tenure-track literature professors and language instructors in non-tenure-track positions" (MLA, 2007, p. 2).

We are aware of the rifts that such a dichotomy can cause in language departments—"humanists do research while language specialists provide technical support and basic training" (MLA, 2007, p. 3). With the MLA report, the organization hopes to convince the humanists, the literature faculty, "that it is in our common interest to devise new models" (p. 3), and that means to change.

The MLA Report and the National Standards

The MLA report calls for getting rid of the two-tiered configuration that "has outlived its usefulness and needs to evolve" (MLA, 2007, p. 3). The report recommends replacing the two-tiered language/literature structure with

> … a broader and more coherent curriculum in which language, culture, and literature are taught as a continuous whole, supported by alliances with other departments and expressed through interdisciplinary courses…. […] [F]oreign language departments, if they are to be meaningful players in higher education—or indeed, if they are to thrive as autonomous units—must transform their programs and structure. (MLA, 2007, p. 3)

The report further recommends that the language major be structured to produce educated users of another language who have deep translingual and transcultural competence, and not users whose goal is to rival or equal the abilities of the native speaker[6] (MLA, 2007, p. 3).

With its 5 goals and 11 standards, the national standards reflect each of the elements in the MLA report's recommendations:

- language, literature, and culture taught as a coherent whole (the Cultures goal);
- interdisciplinary collaborative courses (the Connections goal);
- language learners functioning as informed and capable interlocutors with educated native speakers in the target language (the Cultures and Communities goals);
- understanding other cultures and languages (the Cultures and Comparisons goals);
- training language learners to reflect on the world and themselves through the lens of another language and culture (the Communication, Cultures, Connections, Comparisons, and Communities goals);
- comprehending speakers of the target language as members of foreign societies (the Communication, Cultures, Comparisons, and Communities goals);
- learners understanding themselves as Americans—as members of a society that is foreign to others (the Comparisons goal);
- relating to fellow members of their own society who speak languages other than English (the Communities goal). (MLA, 2007, p. 4)

The goals advocated by the MLA report evoke all of the SFLL goals: Communication, Cultures, Connections, Comparisons, and Communities. There are indeed common threads and goals between these two documents.

So, What Is the Problem?

As noted earlier, the MLA report is quite explicit in its recommendations that foreign language departments must change their programs and structure if they want to play a meaningful role in higher education. We as faculty bloc at the postsecondary level can no longer resemble the proverbial ostrich with its head in the sand, ignoring its surroundings. We must speak with a unified voice and not as opposing factions. We can no longer dig our heels in and resist change and ignore what is going on in foreign language education, all the more so when the products of a revamped, remodeled K-12 curriculum are arriving in our classrooms with a preparation that is quite different from what students presented a decade ago.

How and Why Did This Revamping and Remodeling Occur?

In the mid-1990s, most states began discussions about greater accountability in K-12 education. At a minimum, accountability revolves around content standards, curriculum development, teaching and learning, assessments, and professional development. During this period, many professional organizations for various content areas began a push for "national" standards in their respective subject areas. These so-called national standards were generally developed with input from a broad group of stakeholders, including K-12 educators, higher education faculty, and business leaders. Because the U.S. Constitution delegates the responsibility for education to the states, there was never any movement to encourage all states to adopt the national standards. Instead, most states revised their own standards after those established at the national level, with modifications to suit each state's circumstances.

The *Standards for Foreign Language Learning in the 21st Century* (SFLL, 2006), which first appeared in 1996, had a significant impact on the standards/ frameworks for many states by providing a blueprint for change. Specifically in foreign languages, the standards place much greater emphasis on communication than was the case in the past—both oral and written communication. In the past, a student entering college might have had a stronger background in reading works of literature rather than being able to talk about it. With the new standards, K-12 educators would be spending more time on oral skills (L. M. Wallinger, personal communication, November 18, 2008).

Here Is the Problem

I have pointed out that the newest K-12 curricula are different. I have mentioned that current materials are different. It appears, however, that postsecondary curricula are not keeping abreast of those at the K-12 levels. Why?

A large part of the problem lies in the fact that many teachers at the postsecondary level ignore the focus of foreign language programs and pedagogical instructions/guidelines that appear in current textbooks. Again, why? There is no apparent fit between the new focus and a curriculum and teaching mold that are outmoded and ineffective. Shrum and Glisan (2005) state, "... more attention to context is evident in some textbook series published in the last several years, since many of them have begun to integrate connections to other disciplines, exploration of cultural perspectives, and interaction with target-language communities" (p. 55). Although research in second language learning supports the notion that learners must engage in meaningful communication, we still find a heavy dependence on drill and form-focused activities that lack meaning. Nonetheless, K-12 teachers who are eager to include the national standards in their curriculum, yet who must use one textbook series for 7 to 10 years or even longer, can adapt these textbooks to bring them more up to date (pp. 55–56). Along with the changes and adaptations in textbooks, the atmosphere of the classroom has changed: communicative activities, the emphasis on culture, the integration of technology and media. There is a new look and a new enthusiasm for foreign language teaching and learning.

Change has indeed occurred at the K-12 level. Change is occurring much more slowly at the postsecondary level. Why? What is the obstacle? In 1989 in her article on reshaping the college-level curriculum, Dorothy James points out why there is such ignorance—both a lack of knowledge and unawareness—and avoidance of what can potentially help us reshape the curriculum of foreign language departments at the postsecondary level across the United States. Although James's comment that follows is an observation from 20 years ago, it astutely illustrates the continued slowness of change and reticence to change at the postsecondary level:

> In writing this chapter, I am very much aware that not many of my colleagues in the senior professoriat of foreign language departments are likely to read it. Nor indeed are many of those who aspire to the senior professoriat. They do not go to conferences like the Northeast Conference, and they do not read volumes like the Northeast Conference *Reports*. Why should they? They are no more professionally interested in the teaching of foreign languages than are nuclear physicists. It is not their field. (James, 1989, p. 79)

James goes on to say that "a new 'college-level' curriculum needs to play an integrated part in a new continuum from elementary to high school to college to graduate school" (James, 1989, p. 85). She laments the then present "ferment" in which the two-tiered college teaching profession (also referred to in the 2007 MLA report) regarded themselves as two distinct groups: the foreign language teachers and the literary scholars. A willingness to listen to and consider viable rationales for change must exist for there to be the remotest possibility and opportunity for a totally reformed college foreign language curriculum.

In her 1998 article, "Major Changes: The Standards Project and the New Foreign Language Curriculum," Swaffar suggests "some of the ways American institutions of higher education are changing and how those changes affect the way we, as a profession, need to think about the third and fourth year of language instruction in our colleges and universities" (Swaffar, 1998). While focusing on the "post-requirement" level of language study, Swaffar nonetheless gives a strong rationale for change at the postsecondary level, recognizing that some academics deplore the dual demands of accountability: "the mastery of our fields and the application of language skills in the workplace after graduation as extensions of cultural and literacy learning from the FL curriculum" (Swaffar, 1998).

In a similar vein to James's appeal for revision from the 1980s, Corral and Patai (2008), in their commentary that appeared in the *Chronicle of Higher Education*, sound the alarm—maybe the death knell—of foreign languages with their reports of the closure of the German department at the University of Southern California and the proposal to end German at Humboldt State University. They tell of the forcible merger of five separate language and literature departments at the University of Massachusetts–Amherst into one megadepartment renamed "languages, literatures, and cultures." Though such mergers or the demise of various language departments at smaller colleges and universities are particularly true of less commonly taught languages, including French, German, and Russian, Spanish seems to be apart and not undergoing such a fate. Nonetheless, the same phenomenon is occurring at much larger schools such as the University of Massachusetts–Amherst and Virginia Commonwealth University. This alarm should be heeded by all language departments and should be a prod to push foreign language faculty at the postsecondary level to action: reconsider, restructure, retool, or simply die out.

The MLA report takes a more positive approach:

> We expect that more students will continue language study if courses incorporate cultural inquiry at all levels and if advanced courses address more subject areas. [...] [F]aculty members will have the opportunity to bring into the classroom the full breadth of their knowledge of the society about which they teach, including that society's languages and language variants, literatures, and cultures." (MLA, 2007, p. 4)

The report points out that many colleges and universities have already made a successful transition toward this broad understanding of language study and urges others to follow. College/university foreign language faculty cannot afford to be ignorant or recalcitrant. To survive, they *must* consider this moment as an opportunity for a totally reformed college curriculum.

Conclusion

Let me repeat a statement by Weekley (1929): "Stability in language teaching is synonymous with *rigor mortis."*

Change is essential and inevitable, and most often good and slow to happen. The MLA report cautions that unless the kind and degree of change that it calls for "happens over the next ten years, college and university departments of foreign languages will not be in a position to provide leadership in advanced language education" (MLA, 2007, p. 7). In fact, the continued existence of autonomous/independent departments of foreign languages might be in jeopardy.

Corral and Patai (2008, p. A30) express their concern over an end to foreign languages and an end to the liberal arts. They say, "If foreign languages, whether under enrolled or not, are to survive today, they need to stake a claim for their intrinsic value and their relationship to the study of foreign cultures" (p. A30).

Foreign language educators know that there is indeed an intrinsic value to the study of foreign languages. We cannot sit idly and passively and watch our enrollments in so many language courses, especially involving less commonly taught languages, continue to decline, our departments be abolished, downsized, or merged. One thing is certain: We are not preparing and cannot prepare students to function in a 21st-century multilingual, multicultural world as long as we remain entrenched in the language/literature mode and mentality. The consequences will likely be that despite the need for greater global understanding, our programs at the postsecondary level will suffer. One effect will be a decrease in the number of majors. "Skills to succeed in today's world increasingly call for language and culture skills for both political and economic gain. The concentration of foreign language study based in the study of past and present literatures will not withstand the need for true communication" (L. M. Wallinger, personal communication, July 16, 2008).

Corral and Patai lament the current, apparently unimportant role that literature plays in the study of foreign languages. In the national standards, literature is considered a primary cultural artifact. Not only should students have experience with the language system, they will need to have access to "the richness of the cultures of the languages being studied. They will need to learn about everyday life and social institutions, about contemporary and historical issues that are important in those cultures, about significant works of literature and art, and about cultural attitudes and priorities" (SFLL, 2006, p. 34). All of these elements exist in literature. No one is advocating abandoning the study of literature. We need a new perspective, a restructuring of our goals, of what we are doing. How can we offer language for communicative purposes that can be blended with other fields such as medicine, journalism, law, business, rather than dwell on the old paradigm of a foreign language literature major?

We can look to the national standards to offer us the new perspective. Do not misunderstand me—they are not a panacea. They do, however, offer us a functional blueprint and framework that can help move our curricula and our goals into the 21st century. A change in perspective and practice will indeed make what we actually do reflect what we claim that we do.

The two-tiered college teaching profession will doubtlessly continue to exist, but one faction must realize that there is a new focus that does not forsake the teaching of literature for "culture-based courses, not to mention the ever-proliferating film courses that so many of us teach nowadays" (Corral & Patai, 2008, p. A30). Literature will continue to be important. Corral and Patai may have a fatalistic viewpoint tempered with a modicum of reality when they claim that

> deans typically speak the same language as faculty members: the language of multiculturalism and diversity, which tends to take a dim view of discrete literary fields, each with its own long history, while somehow imagining that we can teach all aspects of culture at once in a combined course. (2008, p. A30)

It might be too late to be proactive, but we can react by changing, by demonstrating our relevance in giving our students what they need to be equipped linguistically and culturally to *function* successfully in a pluralistic society both here and abroad.[7]

There is so much misunderstanding—or a lack of understanding or interest—of what is going on in the world of foreign language education. Many college/university foreign language faculty members do not attend language conferences or read publications that smack of or focus on pedagogy. Why? As James remarked 20 years ago, those faculty members are simply not interested in teaching *language* [my emphasis]; it is not their field.

Indeed, some colleges and universities have re-created their curricula using the national standards as a framework, especially for lower-level courses. Goals and objectives for lower-level courses are based on the national standards. New textbooks that are modeled on the *Standards* are being written and adopted. Assessment of learning is changing and is based on actual, realistic student performance and not simply on mastery of a given corpus of grammar. Even in some upper-level courses, especially conversation and composition, classroom activities and assessment are shaped by the three communicative modes.[8]

We simply cannot ignore what is going on in foreign language education. Do not misunderstand what I am saying: I am not claiming that the national standards are a cure-all. As I have said: they are not a panacea. They do not point the way to foreign language paradise. They are not *the* answer, just as the Audio-Lingual Method (ALM), the Natural Approach, and the ACTFL Proficiency Guidelines were not *the* answer either.

The national standards document (SFLL, 2006) is designed to "provide a gauge against which to measure improvement in foreign language education in the years to come" (p. 28). As is cautioned in the document, the standards do not describe the current state of FL education in the the United States. The *Standards* is not a curriculum guide nor a stand-alone document. This document must be used in conjunction with specific curricula, goals, and objectives of individual programs to determine the best approaches and reasonable expectations for students in that particular environment (SFLL, 2006, p. 28).[9]

We do need to examine the standards and learn just what they do have to offer as a blueprint and framework for our curricula. Just as a blueprint is drawn but can be modified according to needs, so it is with a curriculum based on the national standards. Curricula and goals do not have to be identical. At the K-12 level, the national standards serve as a core around which various state frameworks are built.[10] Different interpretations of the standards will lead to differences in programs, and this is fine. We simply need to consider quite seriously just what the national standards are advocating. We know the impact that the national standards have had on state frameworks and local curricula at the K-12 level; now it is up to foreign language educators at the postsecondary level to see what the blueprint might look like from their perspective. Though not *the* answer, the *Standards* can give us a refreshing new perspective on foreign language study in the most inclusive sense of the discipline: language, literature, culture and the knowledge, skills, and abilities that come with such study.

Ellen Glasgow said: "The only difference between a rut and a grave is their dimensions" (Glasgow, 2008). We must avoid staying in our rut if we want to be relevant, necessary, and important, and also if we want to survive.

Notes

1. For a brief summary of the chronological development of language teaching, see Shrum and Glisan's *Teacher's Handbook*, 3rd ed. (2005), pp. 444–447.

2. The three communicative modes are the Interpersonal, Interpretive, and Presentational. See the national standards (SFLL, 2006, pp. 36–38) for a full discussion of these three modes.

3. The American Council on the Teaching of Foreign Languages, American Association of Teachers of Arabic, American Association of Teachers of French, American Association of Teachers of German, American Association of Teachers of Italian, American Association of Teachers of Spanish and Portuguese, American Classical League, American Council of Teachers of Russian, Chinese Language Association of Secondary-Elementary Schools/Chinese Language Teachers Association, and the National Council of Japanese Language Teachers/Association of Teachers of Japanese.

4. The Proficiency Guidelines of the American Council on the Teaching of Foreign Languages (ACTFL) lay the groundwork for performance standards—standards that indicate how well a language user performs. ACTFL has already published the *Performance Guidelines for K-12 Learners* (1998), in which levels of performance are indicated for three different levels of proficiency.

5. "... language is understood as an essential element of a human being's thought processes, perceptions, and self-expressions; and as such it is considered to be at the core of translingual and transcultural competence" (MLA, 2007, p. 2).

6. In the MLA report we find the statement "Four-year language majors often graduate with disappointingly low levels of linguistic ability" (MLA, 2007, p. 7).

7. Much of the K-12 discussion with the business world and with higher education is now centered around preparing students for the 21st century—which is here and now—and for jobs that have not yet even been created. We at the postsecondary level must be aware of what skills K-12 educators are being asked to promote. (See http://www.21stcenturyskills.org/index.php?option= com_content &task=view&id =254&Itemid=120.)

8. At the University of Richmond, our general education, i.e., required course syllabi for both beginning- and intermediate-level French are firmly grounded on both the national standards and the ACTFL Proficiency Guidelines. A few years ago, we created a new capstone experience for our foreign language majors—a portfolio. A portfolio "documents the growth and development of students *over a period of time*; it is a rich description of a learner's work and offers perspectives that tests do not provide. [...] In a portfolio, learners have an opportunity to select evidence of their learning, reflect on, and make it part of the assessment of their learning. In this way, they become empowered to participate in their own assessment" (Shrum & Glisan, 2005, p. 383).

  While portfolios are not new, our framework was built on the national standards; students were to include artifacts from each of the five goals: Communication, Cultures, Connections, Comparisons, and Communities. Our faculty understood the national standards. Our graduating seniors were given an introductory session on the national standards, and we made all of that information and more available to them on the department's Web page.

9. The following figure points out the interrelationships among national, state, and local standards documents (SFLL, 2006, p. 28). While specifically illustrating K-12 documents, the figure clearly shows that individual mission statements,

goals, objectives, along with expectations of student performance can indeed fit well in any program at any level that is based on or structured around the national standards and maintain the integrity of that program.

Figure
The relationships among national, state, and local standards.

The Relationships Among National, State, and Local Standards Documents

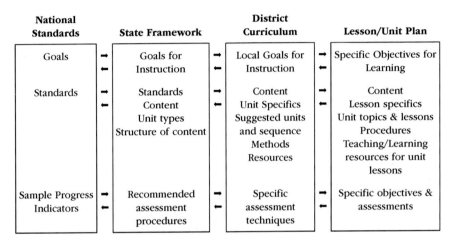

National Standards	State Framework	District Curriculum	Lesson/Unit Plan
Goals	Goals for Instruction	Local Goals for Instruction	Specific Objectives for Learning
Standards	Standards Content Unit types Structure of content	Content Unit Specifics Suggested units and sequence Methods Resources	Content Lesson specifics Unit topics & lessons Procedures Teaching/Learning resources for unit lessons
Sample Progress Indicators	Recommended assessment procedures	Specific assessment techniques	Specific objectives & assessments

Adapted with permission from the
Visual Arts Education Reform Handbook: Suggested Policy Perspectives on Art Content and Student Learning in Art Education National Art Education Association, 1995.

10. See for example Virginia's *Foreign Language Standards of Learning* (http://www.doe.virginia.gov/VDOE/Instruction/Language/#flsol. The following site on the Web offers links to state and local foreign language standards nationwide: http://www.utm.edu/staff/globeg/flstand.shtml. A simple perusal of any of these standards will show the widespread impact that the national standards have made throughout the United States.

References

American Council on the Teaching of Foreign Languages. (1998). *Performance guidelines for K-12 learners*. Alexandria, VA: author.

Corral, W. H., & Patai, D. (2008). An end to foreign languages, an end to the liberal arts. *The Chronicle of Higher Education, 54*(39), A30. Retrieved from http://chronicle.com/weekly/v54/i39/39a03001.htm

Foreign language standards of learning for Virginia public schools. Retrieved from http://www.doe.virginia.gov/VDOE/Instruction/Language/#flsol

Glasgow, E. Retrieved from http://www.quoteworld.org/quotes/5476

James, D. (1989). Re-shaping the 'college-level' curriculum: Problems and possibilities. In H. S. Lepke (Ed.), *Shaping the future challenges and opportunities* (pp. 79–110). Middlebury, VT: The Northeast Conference on the Teaching of Foreign Languages.

Modern Language Association. (2007). *Foreign languages and higher education: New structures for a changed world*. New York: The Modern Language Association of America. Retrieved from http://www.mla.org/flreport

National Standards in Foreign Language Learning Project. (2006). *Standards for foreign language learning in the 21*st *century* (3rd ed.). Alexandria, VA: author.

Shrum, J., & Glisan, E. (2005). *Teacher's handbook* (3rd ed.). Boston: Thomson Heinle.

Swaffar, J. (1998). Major changes: The standards project and the new foreign language curriculum. *ADFL Bulletin, 30*(1), 1–4. Retrieved from http://web2.adfl.org/adfl/bulletin/v30n1/301034.htm

Weekley, E. (1929). *The English language*. Retrieved November 17, 2008, from http://www.wordspy.com/waw/19980528070754.as

Chapter 3
Strengthening the Connection Between Content and Communication

June K. Phillips, Weber State University (Emerita)

The *Standards for Foreign Language Learning in the 21st Century*, now at age 13, are entering their middle-school years. They have survived the elementary grades and are in the throes of early adolescence, not fully formed in terms of acceptance or practice but on the path to maturity. The initial charge to the task force on foreign language standards in 1993 was to develop content standards for K-12 education; content in the enabling legislation (*Goals 2000: Education America Act*) was defined as describing what students should know and are able to do. A major challenge for the foreign language profession was that, unlike English or Mathematics or Social Studies, this discipline was neither a required nor a sequential discipline in schools or in colleges and universities. A beginning foreign language student might start (or restart) that study in elementary school, in middle school, in 9th grade (the most common first endeavor), or in a college/university setting. Though all beginners, regardless of age, face similar linguistic development, older learners, especially those in high school, colleges, and universities, are more intellectually capable. For these students, language study should offer more cognitively rich experiences. The *Standards,* for the first time in foreign language instruction, define goals in terms that incorporate content as a substantial outcome rather than leaving content as incidental to linguistic ones.

Foreign Language Standards: Intents and Events

At the outset, influencing curriculum in higher education was not a major consideration of the standards project. The discussion of the standards over the 3-year course of development did elicit opinions that saw a potential role for them in colleges and universities. The first edition in 1996 of *Standards for Foreign Language Learning: Preparing for the 21st Century* (SFLL), frequently referred to now as the generic volume, addressed only K-12 education. Subsequent to the appearance of that publication, and arising from discussions in many forums, language-specific organizations took two dramatic steps: Firstly, they wanted an expanded volume with applications and examples to specific languages, and secondly, most groups decided they wanted to extend coverage to higher education programs. This determination produced the second and third editions, *Standards for Foreign Language Learning in the 21st Century* [SFLL] (1999/2006), with 10 specific languages and inclusion of the undergraduate years for most groups.

This bit of history has relevance for the growing (albeit slowly) interest from college and university faculty in learning about the standards and experimenting with them in curriculum and instruction. Initially, faculty dedicated to teaching language in the lower division (first or second year) courses discerned implications in the standards for their work. The differentiations between first- and second-year language study in higher education and the high schools are not so great. The AAUSC audience was a natural one because many program coordinators had responsibility for language students at those levels and for preparing graduate students, adjuncts, and instructors to teach multiple sections with common goals, purposes, and sometimes assessments. With the passage of time, however, it seems that the *Standards* have instigated further reflection in terms of the content areas (e.g., cultures, interdisciplinary connections) and the attention to a more humanities rich curriculum integrated with communicative goals. A recent report of the Modern Language Association (2007) recognizes that the study of world languages must shift dramatically to engage a wider student body with distinct goals for continuing language study. Though that report does not cite the *Standards,* it does investigate the very principles and goals set forth in the *Standards* several years earlier.

The vision set forth in the *Standards* lends itself to multiple interpretations in terms of practice. The five goal areas (Communication, Cultures, Connections, Comparisons, Communities) describe outcomes but do not prescribe approaches, instructional strategies, or methods with capitalized names. At the same time, one must acknowledge not all practices will be conducive to reaching these goals. The logo for the Five Cs consisting of interlocking circles is intended to emphasize the linkages among them so that communication without culture or content from a variety of disciplines provides a limited experience for students. For many years, foreign language faculty have perceived language and humanities as fairly discrete areas; the lower division taught language as four skills and the upper division emphasized advanced language, culture, literature, film studies, and so on. When culture or literature was taught at the lower division, it was frequently incidental or done in English. Advanced language courses focused on composition, conversation or grammar but were often quite apart from the culture/civilization or literature courses. The standards development task force hoped that an understanding of the standards would result in a richer language program at all levels. To accomplish this goal, programs must pay attention to building language proficiency in all the modalities throughout the students' sequence of study. Upper division content courses must also assure that students continue to improve language skills. If these courses include practices of interaction in English or if students are limited to short sentence responses, their proficiency will plateau and not grow. Likewise, faculty teaching toward the standards must integrate content from the humanities into language practice even at beginning levels.

The logo of the *Standards,* the Five Cs, illustrates how all the goals, whether communicative or content-based, are linked together for learners. This is a shift from a hierarchical vision in which learning the language was the goal for several years and those who survived went on to study culture and other content.

The integration of communicative outcomes and meaningful content is now explored in the professional literature and especially in conference presentations. Some of the focus has been influenced by the standards and the attention given to goals other than communication; however, some of the emphasis is generated by parallel issues, such as research on multiple literacies, enrollments in language courses (or lack thereof), and student preferences and objectives for their own language learning whether it be limited to a few years of study or to achieve more advanced levels in conjunction with other disciplines. Byrnes (1998, p. 282) describes the need for change in higher education as follows:

> Among the students who will demand totally different curricula are those who are now graduating from secondary schools with curricula that follow a communicative approach, according to national standards that are communicatively oriented. With its focus on communication, cultures, connections, comparisons, and communities, the experiential (as opposed to analytic) learning these students have had cannot be readily fitted into or reduced to the form-focused language teaching that dominates in colleges. Totally different curricula will need to be conceptualized if foreign language departments wish to serve this very important student group.

The AAUSC volume, *SLA and the Literature Classroom: Fostering Dialogues* (Scott & Tucker, 2002), contains articles that address the curricular issues and faculty challenges of breaking down the traditional divisions. On the individual instructor level, integration occurs when the standards and their underlying constructs have been studied and probed for their application to teaching and when a mind-set is established that enables the teacher to incorporate these goals areas even when working with a common syllabus that is not explicitly standards oriented. Not everyone can change or create a curriculum, but every instructor can make certain decisions for a given class. We will explore this model here.

Underlying Concepts of Standards for Instruction

One of the major constructs of the standards was to expand traditional definitions of the four skills (listening, speaking, reading, writing) by framing them in a context that addresses both how the skills play out in real communicative acts and how learners acquire them. The Framework of Communicative Modes (SFLL, 1996) illustrates how listening in an interaction differs from listening to a recorded broadcast. Phillips (2008, p. 96) summarizes these modes as follows:

Interpersonal communication
This mode refers to the learner as a speaker/listener or reader/writer. It requires two-way interactive communication where negotiation of meaning may be observed. The exchange will provide evidence of awareness of the socio-cultural aspects of communication as language proficiency develops.

Interpretive communication

This mode views the learner as a reader or listener/viewer working with "text" whose author or deliverer is not present or accessible. It presumes that the interaction is with authentic written and oral documents where the language input is meaningful and content-laden. The learner brings background knowledge, experience, and appropriate interpretive strategies to the task to promote understanding of language and content in order to develop a personal reaction.

Presentational communication

This mode places the learner as speaker or writer for a "distant" audience, one with whom interaction is either not possible or limited. The communication is set for a specified audience, has purpose and generally abides by the rules of genre or style. It is a planned or formalized speech act or written document, and the learner has the opportunity to draft, get feedback, and revise before publication or broadcast.

As one analyzes, plans, and chooses instructional approaches with these modes in mind, it becomes possible to blend them with authentic materials and create lessons where students acquire new knowledge about target cultures, from a spectrum of disciplines, as they gain competencies in the various modalities. The authors of the *Standards* made an effort to promote communication on a content base, and when instructors keep this merger in the forefront, their students are challenged to acquire new knowledge with new language forms.

A second construct in the *Standards* that provides teachers and students with a means of organizing an infinite mass of information is the Cultural Framework (SFLL, 1996) which presents a model that looks at products, practices, and perspectives as a means of gaining knowledge about culture. Many other cultural models use different terms and are more expansive and complex, yet the framework in the *Standards* has an appeal in its simplicity as a template for lesson planning. For students, it serves as a graphic organizer to encourage them to seek information in each area and to hypothesize about perspectives when these are not explicit.

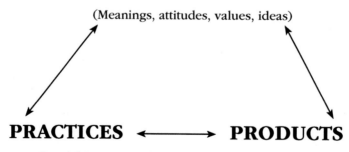

PERSPECTIVES
(Meanings, attitudes, values, ideas)

PRACTICES ⟷ **PRODUCTS**

(Patterns of social interactions)   (Books, tools, foods, laws, music, games)

Given that culture is a dynamic concept that may change dramatically from year to year, students benefit from learning a process for gathering information, analyzing it, hypothesizing, testing hypotheses, and keeping judgments open. Of course, there are traditional and stable aspects of culture as well. Nevertheless, it is not generally useful to codify a given set of cultural facts that may be random and disconnected and that add very little to understanding culture. Attempts to define culture from these stand-alone facts generally fail to help students become life-long learners who are able to engage intellectually in making cultural observations.

Books and articles in the professional literature in the past few years have applied findings from research in second language acquisition (SLA) to classrooms. Many of these researchers have suggested ways of working with texts (written and oral) that have a rich content base. These authors take into consideration genre, matrices based on text structure, and the like so that students can access meaning from authentic texts even though they provide a challenge because they contain material not already studied or familiar (see, for example, Byrnes, 1998; Swaffar & Arens, 2005). Most (but not all) curriculum development with a strong content base has been aimed at upper-division courses and advanced learners. However, the larger numbers of students who are in lower-division courses may be taught by graduate students, adjuncts, instructors, or those supervised by coordinators; they may also be part of the teaching load of tenure-track faculty with specialties other than SLA. When courses have a common syllabus created by a coordinator, there may be minimal room for the instructor to deviate from a syllabus; when courses are taught by a faculty member minimally versed in pedagogy, there may not be a syllabus other than the textbook or personal preference. Regardless of the teacher, the syllabus, or the program, opportunities should be provided to assure that all faculty acquire an understanding of the communicative modes and how the inclusion of a stronger content base can enhance curriculum and individual courses. Achieving that agreed-upon direction makes for a better articulated program without impinging upon academic freedom or expertise.

Planning and Teaching by Design

I have found that templates can enable teachers to plan lessons that maximize rich content while simultaneously thinking about approaches that advance interpersonal communication, interpretive communication, and presentational communication. The documents that are the source of content can be selected well in advance of the course, or they can be chosen a day or so ahead when time constraints are a factor. They may fit with a theme being taught, or they may reflect clusters of interest found in a class. For example, several years ago, I found myself in a class with a number of students majoring in science but with farm backgrounds, neither of which was in my realm of teaching or real-world experiences. But as students were helping me select video clips of news from French Web sites, they saw images of cows being burned in great numbers when an outbreak of hoof and mouth disease devastated the farming communities in

France and Britain. Certainly *fièvre aphteuse* was not in my vocabulary nor did I understand its biological causes or the epidemic that ensued. By tracking the trajectory of the outbreak in France, this group of interested students was motivated to watch and read the daily news, report back to the class, propose government interventions, and create posters for the community. None of this content was in my syllabus, but I was able to accomplish the communicative outcomes set forth basing them on an unexpected content theme, one for which they had background knowledge and motivation, with the documents providing key vocabulary. They listened to educated speakers from medical and governmental fields as well as to the dialects of farmers being interviewed. My job, as their teacher, was to adjust the communicative tasks so I could lead them to interpret, have them discuss interpersonally, and finally present a product appropriate to their level of formal writing.

The following templates have been designed, used, and presented by Phillips (2007). The first column represents tasks that the instructor needs to think about in the planning stage. There are specific questions that are appropriate to the content base; in these cases they are drawn from documents—written texts or video—that have cultural content, literary or film value, or that deal with current events. Once the teacher examines the documents, the general proficiency level of the students must be considered. In many instances, similar documents can be used with a range of students, but the response tasks change as do the communicative goals. Though the oral or written documents will be exploited to develop the interpretive mode, some of the concomitant work—brainstorming, identifying, restating at intermediate levels, and narrating, describing, explaining at more advanced levels—will be interpersonal. Presentational communication will be reserved for subjects that warrant the time necessary for drafting and revising.

Template for Cultural Documents

Tasks (For Planning and Teaching)	Intermediate Levels	Advanced Levels
What practices are described in the document?	Identify practices and actions.	Narrate how one performs practices described in the text or observed in visuals.
What products are shown or described?	List products you see or learn about.	Describe products to someone who has not seen them.
What perspectives are expressed in the document? If perspectives are not discussed, what is a reasonable hypothesis as to cultural attitudes, values, importance in the culture?	State a religious, historical, environmental, societal tie, or other connection of the topic to the culture.	Summarize evidence from the document and other sources about the value, attitudes, importance of the topic in the culture. Hypothesize and check for further evidence.

Example:
Students see a photo of a crowd carrying banners and demonstrating. They brainstorm what they think is happening. Then, they are shown the headline and subtitle from the Web site of *Le Monde* (French newspaper) *"La grève" RATP prévoit un métro sur dix pour la journée de mercredi.* (Strike. RATP envisions one metro out of ten for Wednesday.)

Drawing upon the interpersonal mode, the teacher and students discuss strikes in our country—who strikes, over what, and so on. Students then work with the Cultural Framework to identify products and practices they understand (e.g., announcing a strike in advance to be legal). Finally, as a group, students and teacher talk about the role of labor unions in modern French culture, the right to strike, and so on.

Template for Content from Literature and Film

Tasks (For Planning and Teaching)	Intermediate Levels	Advanced Levels
Who are the characters and what are their relationships?	Outline characteristics of main characters.	Describe characters' physical and personality traits; anticipate actions and behaviors.
What actions occur in a scene or clip?	List the actions of various characters in a scene. Compile them into a short summary.	Narrate a sequence of actions that occur; do so from the viewpoints of different characters.
What is/are the setting, time period, and/or historical background?	List information regarding setting of the film or literary piece.	Describe scenes or relate background knowledge of time/ place. Provide evidence from the document that expands upon your prior knowledge.
What cultural products, practices, or perspectives can be observed in the film or text or excerpt?	Identify or chart cultural products, practices, or perspectives.	Share, narrate, and/ or describe cultural observations from the document.

Example
Students view several clips from the film *Indochine* that shows the colonial presence of France in Vietnam. They describe time, place, dress, occupations. They react to several characters in terms of personality, attitude, relationships across cultures. Based on students' historical knowledge, discussion of influences of colonialism might ensue.

Template for Contemporary Issues and Events

Tasks (For Planning and Teaching)	Intermediate Levels	Advanced Levels
Why choose this document? Timeliness? Link to theme? Particular student interest?		
What is the genre, and how can that be exploited?	Report on the who, where, what, when, how, or why of a news article. List essentials of question/answer in interviews. Find categorical information in biographical documents.	Summarize essentials of a news article. Discuss unexpected responses from an interview; create extended questions. Describe the person and his or her contributions for another; identify information you wish you knew but do not yet.
What background knowledge should be elicited?	Brainstorm prior to interpreting document to assure adequate background as well as key language elements.	Create a list or establish the knowledge base from the student group. Create a list of new information to be sought.
What cultural information might the topic or document contain? What expansion may be necessary?	Identify products, practices, perspectives from the documents. Compare cultural information to one's own.	Describe the cultural concepts in the document and hypothesize about related issues. Discuss cultural similarities and differences.
What connections to other disciplines/subject matter are in the document?	Talk about known information in interactions that provide language support. List what we know going into the document/what we learned afterwards.	Describe new information, relate back to what was known. Prepare follow-up questions for further research. Summarize or retell for someone with less knowledge of the discipline.

Example

Students read of the death of Marcel Marceau (9/23/07). They share what they know about him and his work. They brainstorm what kind of information they expect to find in a news obituary. They then read the article and fill in a chart that gives information about his death, his life, his art, and the reactions of the public to his death. Finally, students choose an area in their realm of knowledge to explore in more detail (e.g., theater students about role of mime in acting development, students of history about WWII and Marceau's role in the Resistance).

Note that almost of all these documents can be classified in different ways. For example, an instructor could choose to address Marceau's death as a current a current event, a cultural topic, or as topic or as an art form through a film clip of a performance. The advantages of the template lie in its relatively quick lesson design feature and the fact that it gradually introduces students to a process of accessing and interpreting authentic texts. The ultimate test occurs when students can take better control of their own learning in further courses or after formal instruction.

In essence, the *Standards* can be part of a mind-set as teachers plan, design, and teach; they can also guide students to think about which communicative modes or combinations are the focus for the lesson. Those modes are not goals in and of themselves but rather a means to learning content; herein lies the challenge intellectually and the challenge of the humanities. Content learned in the foreign language class enriches and expands other knowledge and literacies in the college/university curriculum. Whether students are in a first or a last class, their knowledge of culture, literature, film, and society is enhanced through a new language. Students bring to a language class, even a beginning one, a vast repertoire of general and specialized knowledge; they are not *tabula rasa*. Our challenge as teachers is to build upon and stimulate their intellectual curiosity even as we develop their linguistic proficiency.

References

Byrnes, H. (1998). *Learning foreign and second languages. Perspectives in research and scholarship*. New York: Modern Language Association.

MLA Ad Hoc Committee on Foreign Languages. (2007) *Foreign languages and higher education: News structures for a changed world.*

National Standards in Foreign Language Education Project. (1996). *The standards for foreign language learning: Preparing for the 21st century (SFLL)*. Lawrence, KS: Allen Press.

National Standards in Foreign Language Education Project. (1999, 2006). *The standards for foreign language learning in the 21st century (SFLL)* (2nd & 3rd eds.). Lawrence, KS: Allen Press.

Phillips, J. K. (2007). *Content for communication*. Presentation at the ACTFL Annual Meeting. San Antonio.

Phillips, J. K. (2008). Foreign language standards and the contexts of communication. *Language Teaching, 41* (1), 93–102. Published online by Cambridge University Press.

Scott, V. M., & Tucker, H. (2002). *SLA and the literature classroom: Fostering dialogues*. AAUSC Issues in Language Program Direction. Boston: Heinle & Heinle.

Swaffar, J., & Arens, K. (2005). *Remapping the foreign language curriculum: An approach through multiple literacies*. New York: Modern Language Association.

Chapter 4

In Search of Relevance: The *Standards* and the Undergraduate Foreign Language Curriculum

Heather Willis Allen, University of Miami

Upon their initial development and publication, the *Standards for Foreign Language Learning in the 21st Century* (SFLL [1996, 1999, 2006]) began influencing foreign language (FL) education in the United States in significant ways. The pedagogical vision of what students "should know and be able to do with another language" represented in the *Standards'* 5 major goal areas (Communication, Cultures, Connections, Comparisons, and Communities) and 11 related content standards offered educators a broadened conception of FL teaching and learning that explicitly rejected a four-skills-plus-culture orientation (Klee, 1998; Scott & Huntington, 2007).

Among the most notable impacts of the *Standards* was their incorporation at the K-12 level into many states' and local school districts' curricular guidelines as well as into instructional materials (Allen, 2002; Bragger & Rice, 1999; James, 1998; Phillips, 2003; Wood, 1999). In the years following their first revision in 1999 to include program models for articulated sequences of FL study extending into postsecondary contexts, the *Standards* have continued to be seen as highly relevant to today's FL profession and have been described as "arguably the document that has dominated pedagogical thinking in US foreign language education for the past decade or so" (Byrnes, 2008, p. 103) and as "catalysts for bringing about new ways of envisioning classroom instruction" (Adair-Hauck, Glisan, Koda, Swender, & Sandrock, 2006). These observations are confirmed by ongoing dialogue on the *Standards* in published essays and research studies, professional development workshops, and conference presentations. As a case in point, the 2008 ACTFL conference lists no less than 15 presentations, workshops, and panel discussions on standards-based instruction and assessment with a wide variety of FLs represented. In addition, a 2011 special issue of *Foreign Language Annals* will be dedicated to discussing "Language Learning and the *Standards.*"

Yet despite the *Standards'* influence on K-12 language education policy and continued discussions of their relevance and application to FL instruction and assessment, in university-level FL departments, tangible impact of the *Standards* in shaping curriculum and classroom instruction has not been wide-ranging. Whereas an ACTFL White Paper (1998) predicted that the *Standards'* publication "signals the end of business as usual in departments of national languages and literature in our colleges and universities ... it will rock the boat" (James, p. 11); in the following years, numerous publications discussing the *Standards'* impact on higher education suggest they have been negligible (Beyer, 2000; Kadish, 2000; Knight, 2000; McAlpine, 2000; Steinhart, 2006; Swaffar, 2006; Tucker, 2000).

Among these, Swaffar (p. 248) described the *Standards* as "almost completely ignored" in postsecondary contexts, and Steinhart explained they have "failed to capture the imagination of college faculty" (p. 258). Taking a concrete example, consider the 2007 MLA report, *Foreign Language and Higher Education: New structures for a Changing World:* Among its forthright recommendations, it advocates that FL departments "set clear standards for achievement for undergraduate majors" (p. 7), yet nowhere in the nine-page summary of recommendations regarding "the challenges and opportunities facing language study in higher education" (p. 1) in the United States are the *Standards* mentioned.

In light of this situation, this chapter identifies and discusses three factors that have contributed to the reception of the *Standards* in higher education in general terms and, more specifically, in terms of the advanced undergraduate FL curriculum: the view that postsecondary contexts were not (in its original instantiation) and are not the *Standards'* intended audience; the sense that an articulated continuum of K-16 FL study as posited by the *Standards* may be either impossible or inappropriate; and the perception that the *Standards* are more relevant to language courses than to content-based courses and that they marginalize the role of literature. In addition, and based on the discussion of these three factors, I will respond to the question of whether the *Standards* provide a framework adequate for addressing the critical challenge facing university-level FL programs today, namely, the meaningful integration of language and content across the curriculum.

The *Standards* as a Reflection of Consensus at All Levels

The introductory section of the *Standards* (1999) contains the following statement: "The development of standards has galvanized the field of foreign language education. The degree of involvement, and of consensus, among educators at all levels has been unprecedented" (p. 15). But standing in contrast to this touted consensus was James' (1998) very different interpretation of events leading to the creation of the *Standards*:

> While large numbers of university professors of language and literature were paying little if any attention to what was going on, a relative consensus was emerging among the leaders in the pre-college sphere ... There is indignation in the colleges at the thought that pre-college standards might drive the college curriculum. (p. 11)

James' (1998) vision of what happened harkens more to a scenario wherein higher education was blindsided by standards more or less foisted on them by the K-12 sector. So which is the case—the *Standards* document (1999) claiming it was founded on a consensus among educators at all levels or James' assertion that many in higher education were, at the least, ignorant of the *Standards* movement or, worse, opposed to it?

Although little empirical research exists documenting university FL professors' opinions and understandings of the *Standards*, Knight (2000) conducted a small-scale survey of 34 professors' familiarity with the *Standards*, from which three interesting results can be summarized as follows: First, 75% of the respondents were unfamiliar with the *Standards*. Second, of the 25% familiar with the *Standards*, the majority did not think that "college classes and curricula would need to change to accommodate the various skills of incoming freshmen" (p. 69) who, presumably, had received previous FL instruction based on *Standards*-oriented curricula. Further, Knight explained that many respondents did not see how the *Standards* applied to their subject or the university curriculum. Third, many respondents did not think that incoming students with prior *Standards*-based FL instruction were better prepared for university-level courses, particularly in grammar, or that their communication skills were stronger in comparison to students from the past.

These results, albeit based on the responses of a very small group of professors from three universities, point to several concerns. First and foremost, most respondents (75%) were ignorant of the *Standards* altogether. Second, for those who were aware of the *Standards*, they did not see them as significantly influencing their instructional practices or curricular decision-making. Finally, many rejected the notion that university FL curricula need to be consistent or tailored to fit with students' previous language-learning experiences, an idea to be further developed in the following section of this chapter.

One could argue that the results of Knight's survey could be due to professors' unfamiliarity with the *Standards* or strategies for incorporating them into FL teaching. Although research has not investigated factors impacting the reception of the *Standards* at the postsecondary level, for K-12 teachers, a large-scale study showed that factors influencing teachers' beliefs about the *Standards* included gender, urban versus rural location, membership in professional organization, highest educational degree, and private versus public school (Allen, 2002). A 1998 essay by Welles suggested that FL professors' reluctance to embrace the standards stemmed from the format of the *Standards* document, the language used within it, and professors' unfamiliarity with theories of language acquisition undergirding the *Standards*' content.

McAlpine (2000) described the difficulty involved in implementing the standards in a postsecondary context in spite of coordinated efforts on the part of a FL department to implement professional development for faculty members. Although university-level FL faculty worked together with high school faculty to develop learning scenarios in a workshop led by the former director of the *Standards* project and received a copy of the *Standards* document, McAlpine concluded:

> While the above approaches are a good beginning in bringing the *Standards* into the postsecondary world, the *Standards* still have not changed the way the university language faculty delivers its courses. At several faculty meetings the suggestion of using the *Standards* to redesign the university language program has been met with a lukewarm response.... Why wouldn't faculty members want to embrace standards that focus on communication strategies, cultural content, learning strategies, connections with other subjects within the curriculum, critical thinking skills, and technology? Do we believe that these arenas are beyond our scope as university professors? (p. 75)

A possible explanation for why those professors and respondents to Knight's (2000) survey did not see the applicability of the standards to their teaching context is the view that the they were not originally designed for higher education and that the chief participants in their design were not FL faculty at the university level (Davis, 1997; Kadish, 2000; Siskin, 1999). Siskin, while identifying the standards as "signifiers of innovation" also called the discourse of consensus surrounding their creation "rhetoric" that "expose[d] a power struggle between K-12 and university pedagogical practice" (p. 86). In addition, Kadish claimed that the most important developers of the *Standards* did not include "professors who teach upper-division college courses" of FLs and added that "[i]t is perhaps not surprising, then that today many professors know nothing about the Standards and have little interest in learning about them" (p. 49). Davis's own reflection on historical and political dimensions of the *Standards'* implementation was consistent with Kadish's claim yet provided an important nuance, insomuch as he explained that university FL faculty in various specializations were, in fact, actively involved in the *Standards* project, yet the 11-member task force, what they called "the most visible ... element in the development phase," did not include literature professors (p. 153).

To provide some brief background, the *Standards* were developed under Goals 2000, a federal grant supporting the development of K-12 content standards in art, civics and government, English language arts, FLs, geography, history, and science (Davis, 1997; Phillips, 2008). The fact that the *Standards* were funded by the federal government has been cited as a factor causing skepticism on the part of academics who may distrust any form of government intervention in light of strongly held feelings about academic freedom and classroom autonomy (Klein, 2000; McGinnis, 1999; Swaffar, 2006). However, note that FLs were not originally designated as a content area for which standards would be created; it was instead the "intense and well-organized efforts" of ACTFL and the Joint National Committee on Languages to participate in standards-setting that led to FL being included in Goals 2000 (Davis, p. 153). Phillips explained that this choice arose from the sentiment by language educators that "if the profession opted out, efforts to place greater emphasis on language study in schools could not succeed" (p. 94).

A second point concerning the development of the *Standards* and their reception in higher education relates to the task force that worked for 3 years prior to the *Standards'* publication in 1996 to draft, revise, and present the document to the FL profession (Phillips, 2008). This task force was composed of 11 "classroom teachers (elementary and secondary), administrators ... and university faculty (in such fields as teacher preparation, bilingual education, and cross-cultural training)" rather than FL faculty specializing in literature (Davis, p. 153). Though the development and publication of the *Standards* entailed the collaboration of ACTFL and the American Associations of Teachers of French, German, and Spanish and Portuguese, it did not include the MLA, considered by most university-level FL professors as the dominant professional organization, although in 1996 the MLA Executive Council endorsed the document (Bragger & Rice, 1999), specifically citing their agreement with the *Standards'* call for extended sequences of FL learning (Welles, 1998).

In addition, the 1996 *Standards* contained no sample progress indicators or learning scenarios (to describe how particular standards might be met) beyond K-12; in 1999, the Standards document was revised to include progress indicators and learning scenarios for some (but not all) languages—French, German, Italian, Japanese, Portuguese, and Spanish. However, those indicators are part of the language-specific *standards* and therefore no "generic" standards across languages were created. Tucker (2000), who compared the various languages' progress indicators, explained that "important inconsistencies" are found among them, particularly in regard to "how sophisticated the study of literary interpretation should be" (p. 55).

Finally, my own perusal of the 1999 *Standards* document resulted in a surprising observation related to their applicability in higher education. Immediately following the introductory subsection explaining the rationale for K-16 program models, the reader of the document next encounters a chapter entitled "About *Standards for Foreign Language Learning*" (p. 27). In its first paragraph, the various audiences for the *Standards* document are listed as "K-12 foreign language teachers and teacher educators, curriculum writers, administrators, policy makers at all levels of government, parents, and business and community leaders." However, the mention of university-level FL professors is found nowhere in the document. Perhaps a simple oversight, the unintended message to postsecondary educators might be the one that has, seemingly and unfortunately, been received: The *Standards* were not written for you and do not apply to you.

The Possibility of a Secondary and Postsecondary Continuum

Although the *Standards* (1999) clearly state that "[n]o single continuum of language learning exists for all students" (p. 14) insisting "multiple entry points into the curriculum" are critical to ensure maximal learning opportunities, an ideal K-16 model is posited:

> The standards set forth here presume that sequential study for an extended period of time is the ideal for achieving the highest levels of performance in the five goal areas, and the progress indicators also assume that instruction has begun in the early grades and continues throughout the secondary years (most of the language-specific documents attached to this edition extend the sequence into college and university programs). (p. 22)

Further, the document makes the following statements regarding the entry of students into postsecondary FL study:

> Students entering colleges and universities of the 21st century will be competent in second languages and cultures.... Students will desire an array of options beyond that of today's curriculum. Colleges and universities have an exciting challenge to redesign programs in new and innovative ways.... The inclusion of post-secondary

programs in the language-specific documents insures a seamless continuity, student-centered articulation and high levels of performance among graduates. (pp. 21–22)

The preceding citations are informed by at least two assumptions: First, that articulated, coherent instruction would be available to students at the K-12 level; second, that creating a curricular continuum between high school- and university-level FL study is necessary to achieve the ideals set forth by the *Standards*.

However, in terms of the first assumption, little evidence exists that articulated sequences of K-12 FL study are widely available to today's students. Citing research by the Center for Applied Linguistics (CAL) conducted for K-12 FL enrollments from 1987 to 1997, Met (2003) concluded that "significant gaps of equity and access" exist, particularly in public elementary and middle schools (p. 590). A closer examination of CAL data from 1987 to 2007 shows after increases in the number of schools offering FLs as well as total FL enrollments from 1987 to 1997, a statistically significant decline occurred in the number of elementary (31% in 1997, 25% in 2007) and middle schools (75% in 1997, 58% in 2007) offering FLs (CAL, 2008). Only at the high school level did FL offerings remain steady. These figures suggest that the majority of elementary and middle school students are not engaging in FL learning. As Schulz (2006) summarized the situation, "The sad fact is that on the precollegiate level, 2-year FL programs are the norm, 5-year programs are the exception, and U.S. school districts with well-articulated K-12 foreign language instruction are exceedingly rare" (p. 253).

Similarly troubling is the lack of agreement in higher education surrounding the second assumption, namely, that the continuum stipulated in the *Standards* between high school and university-level FL curricula is necessary or desirable. Consider the viewpoints represented in the ADFL "Forum on *Standards for Foreign Language Learning*" (2000) by Beyer and Davis, two FL professors (italics to indicate contrasts between the two opinions are my own). The first reads as follows:

While the Standards indicate common ground for articulation, this topic has been around for the past twenty-five years and seems to defy solutions. Quite frankly, the needs and expectations of the college environment are *dramatically different* from high school realities.... It is *unrealistic* to think that the aims of secondary or postsecondary education need to or even should coincide. (Beyer, p. 59)

Standing in opposition to Beyer's statement is Davis' equally strong assertion:

There are still among us college instructors who *worship religiously the false divide* between secondary-school and college-level language study and teaching.... I dismiss the notion that the goals and objectives of college and university programs are significantly different from those of secondary education programs.... Our role is to continue to build on all the language skills when students enter our college programs. (p. 61)

Once again, we witness the incompatibility of these opinions as well as the fervor evoked as to the question of whether postsecondary FL study should be shaped by what precedes it at the secondary level. Several other publications (Bragger & Rice, 1999; James, 1998; Knight, 2000; Peters, 1999; Siskin, 1999; Steinhart, 2006) have discussed whether curriculum should bubble up, that is, come from elementary and secondary schools, or should be built from the top down, that is, by getting professors to agree on outcomes of university-level FL study. Predictably, opinions vary, with the only consensus being that the lack of articulation between high school- and university-level FL study and the lack of communication between high school- and university-level educators are serious obstacles to improving student learning outcomes, leaving the ideal of an articulated K-16 sequence as envisioned by the *Standards* "yet to be realized" (Steinhart, 2006, p. 258).

But if, in fact, the primary problem responsible for the lack of progress in bridging the gap between FL teaching in high schools and colleges lies in the "clash of cultures between the two levels" as Peters (1999, p. 82) suggested, we are led to ask the following question: How do we define the culture of FL learning and teaching at the postsecondary level and what in this culture renders it incompatible with K-12 *Standards*-oriented instruction?

The Challenge of Integrating Language and Content at the University Level

In responding to the question of if the *Standards* are relevant to the undergraduate FL curriculum and if they could function as a means of meaningfully integrating language and content within the undergraduate FL curriculum, I will first examine the content of the *Standards* and highlight three key elements that are critical to understanding the *Standards'* reception in university FL departments. For each, I will suggest how it relates (or fails to relate) to current challenges and priorities in FL education at the university level.

Framework

The *Standards* are grounded in five interconnected goal areas—Communication, Cultures, Connections, Comparisons, and Communities. Phillips (2008) explained, "The five goal areas do not suggest a curriculum that builds communicative skills in early years and then layers on culture or literature or specialized content in more advanced courses"; rather, they envision that students will "engage in all these goals at all levels" (p. 94). Each goal contains two to three related content standards, and under each content standard are sample progress indicators that define progress in meeting standards for grades 4, 8, and 12 in the generic *Standards* document. As mentioned in a preceding section, some languages have articulated progress indicators for the "postsecondary" or "grade 16" level.

For most university-level FL educators, the envisioned integration of the different goal areas at all curricular levels posited in the *Standards* is not a curricular reality. A well-documented divide, both pedagogical and structural, exists in most FL departments between lower-division language and upper-division content (e.g., literature) courses (Byrnes, 2001; Kramsch, 1993). The critical issue of the bifurcated undergraduate curriculum was addressed in the recent MLA report *"Foreign Languages and Higher Education: New Structures for a Changed World,"* which stated that the "two-tiered language-literature structure"needs to be replaced by "a broader and more coherent curriculum in which language, literature, and culture are taught as a coherent whole" (p. 3).

For students, the classroom culture, materials and activities, and assessment in lower-division courses vary significantly from those of upper-division ones. For teachers, there is often little communication between lower-division instructors, typically teaching assistants and non tenure-stream faculty, and those teaching the upper-division courses, usually tenured and tenure-stream faculty (Maxwell, 2003; Modern Language Association, 2007; Swaffar, 2006). Rifkin (2006) called this lack of communication "the principal obstacle to curricular success." Certainly the notion of barriers to curricular coherence applies implementing the *Standards* in the undergraduate curriculum as it is only in lower-division FL courses where the *Standards* have made some impact in shaping instructional materials such as textbooks and syllabi (Barnes-Karol, 2000; Knight, 2000; Schulz, 2006). Given the factors listed earlier, there is little chance that the *Standards* will bubble up from lower-level to higher-level courses.

Overarching Goal

The *Standards* (1999) center on "[w]hat students should know and be able to do with another language," (p. 32) a definition that is almost synonymous with communicative competence (Hymes, 1971) the concept explicitly foregrounded in the introduction to the Communication standard (p. 40). Although this important goal would seem to apply to the entire undergraduate FL curriculum, it is more readily identified with lower-level language courses. Kramsch (2006) explained that because communicative competence emerged as an important framing construct for language learning in the 1970s, its implications have evolved:

> Not only has communicative competence become reduced to its spoken modality, but it has often been taken as an excuse largely to do away with grammar and to remove much of the instructional responsibility from the teacher who becomes a mere facilitator of group and pair work in conversational activities. In public life, the notion of communication has changed its meaning ... communication has been slowly resignified to mean the ability to exchange information speedily and effectively and to solve problems, complete assigned tasks, and produce measurable results. (p. 250)

Any university-level FL professor engaged in teaching upper-level content courses recognizes little in these limited notions of communicative competence and communication that are consistent with the goals of advanced FL learning and teaching in the university context. Although the continued development of communication in various modalities is of critical importance, the more obvious goal (stated or otherwise) typically present in the advanced undergraduate curriculum and the one missing in this notion of communicative competence is analysis and interpretation of FL texts, a point to be developed further in the following section.

Instructional Approach

The *Standards* do not stipulate a favored approach or approaches conducive to bringing about desired learning outcomes ("a variety of approaches can successfully lead learners to the standards") but claim the best approach depends on factors such as the learner's age, learning preferences, and goals (1999, p. 24). However, because the *Standards* foreground communicative competence and focus on developing communicative FL abilities in three modes (Interpersonal, Interpretive, and Presentational), they have been closely associated with communicative language teaching (CLT) (Byrnes, 2006, 2008; Magnan, 2008; Schulz, 2006). Although CLT might be called the most dominant approach to FL teaching employed in the United States since the 1990s, in recent years, its adequacy for university-level FL teaching and learning has come into question (Kern, 2000; Kramsch, 2006; Schulz, 2006; Steinhart, 2006; Swaffar, 2006). These criticisms, centering on perceived limitations of communicatively oriented lower-division FL courses, have included the following:

1. CLT's overemphasis on orality in normative contexts rather than the development of a "broad range of communicative acts"(Kramsch, 2006; Swaffar, 2006, p. 246);

2. CLT's relative lack of success in developing students' extended discourse competence and written communicative abilities, capabilities that are extremely important in academic contexts (Kern, 2000; Steinhart, 2006);

3. CLT's association (fairly or not) with deemphasizing accurate language use, that is, focus on grammar (Kramsch, 2006; Schulz, 2006).

Perhaps, the perceived failures of CLT and its implicit relationship to the *Standards* may inform many university-level FL faculty's view of the relevance of the *Standards* to their context of teaching and their goals for their students. Several scholars (Magnan, 2008; Schulz, 2006; Steinhart, 2006) have pointed to this observation and to the differences between the ideals of the *Standards*, representing a vision articulated more than a decade ago of what it means to know and use a FL, and the somewhat different understandings of FL learning and the real-life challenges faced by university FL departments that inform professional dialogue today. In the following section, I will discuss one such challenge facing FL programs today, namely, the meaningful integration of language and content across the curriculum and whether the *Standards* provide a framework to address this ongoing dilemma.

Toward a Meaningful Role for the Standards in Higher Education?

Although the *Standards* envision coherent, integrated sequences of FL study wherein students engage in each of the five goal areas at every curricular level (Phillips, 2008), in undergraduate FL education, this ideal is not a reality. Lower-division FL courses typically focus on interactive oral communication in normative contexts, whereas upper-division courses emphasize analysis and discussion of literary texts. For various reasons outlined earlier, the *Standards* are seen to "fit" more readily with the goals of lower-level language courses than with advanced-level content courses. Indeed, the *Standards'* expanded vision of what it means to know and use a FL challenges practices and norms of the advanced undergraduate FL courses in at least two ways.

First, the *Standards* explicitly prioritize the goal of developing FL learners' communicative competence, whereas advanced undergraduate courses often de-emphasize explicit attention to language development, operating under the assumption that students already possess adequate linguistic skills to discuss and analyze literary texts (Steinhart, 2006). Upon reflection, this is a rather ironic assumption, as it is often faculty teaching advanced-level literature or cultural studies courses who criticize deficiencies related to reading, writing, and grammar they perceive in their students, who have learned language with a CLT paradigm, yet they persist in ignoring the need to incorporate linguistic objectives into their own courses.

In recent years, research on classroom communication in advanced undergraduate FL courses has revealed problems associated with the "completely unrealistic" expectation that content should be the sole focus of instruction (Steinhart, 2006, p. 260) and that advanced language use emerges naturally during literary discussions. For example, several qualitative studies of upper-level literature courses showed that students did not engage in sustained interactions with peers or their teachers nor did they use the FL in advanced ways (such as defending opinions, elaborating, hypothesizing, or initiating dialogue with others); moreover, lecturing, controlling the topic of discussion, and asking questions for which they already knew the answers was common on the part of teachers (Donato & Brooks, 2004; Mantero, 2002; Zyzick & Polio, 2008). In addition, Maxwell (2003) suggested that a disconnect exists between students' goals for engaging in advanced-level FL study, typically to use the language in a professional setting, and departments' own goals at that level of the curriculum for preparing students to engage in graduate-level FL study. This observation was also supported by Donato and Brooks, who found significant differences between teachers' and students' goals related to literature study.

Issues highlighted in these studies of advanced FL learning within literature courses lead us to consider the second way that the *Standards* challenge practices in the undergraduate FL curriculum—by decentralizing literature's role. In fact, the *Standards* posit literature as one possibility in a list of "cultural content" that students "will need to have access to," a list that also includes everyday life situations, social institutions, contemporary and historical issues, art, and cultural attitudes and priorities (*Standards*, 1999, p. 34). Tucker (2000) criticized the near-total absence of literature in K-12 learning scenarios in the first version of the *Standards*—with just 2 of 34 learning scenarios incorporating literary texts—and the same trend is found in the 1999 *Standards*, which contain only 2 of 33 learning scenarios involving literature. On the other hand, a great number of the scenarios include informational texts with a few indicating the use of film. This perceived marginalization of literature in the *Standards* is troubling for university FL professors as it calls into question literature's place in advanced FL learning and the pedagogies that inform the upper-level FL curriculum (Scott & Huntington, 2007; Tucker, 2000).

Could it be that the *Standards'* most notable impact on FL study in higher education is not in the form of concrete curricular or instructional changes but, instead, in the ways in which it provoked, from its inception, and continues to motivate a reexamination of how and what teachers teach and what they prioritize as pedagogical goals in FL departments (Beyer, 2000; Scott & Huntington, 2007)? After all, the *Standards* must be credited, at least in part, with leading postsecondary FL educators to grapple with the notions of spiraling content and language in meaningful ways, of thinking beyond a four-skills-plus-culture approach, and considering the role of context in various forms of communication.

Although these rather nebulous outcomes do not match initial expectations of those involved in the *Standards* project, the 1996 document and its revisions (1999, 2006) have provoked a tremendous amount of dialogue in the form of published essays and opinion pieces. Among these, the *ADFL Bulletin's* two-part "Forum on the Standards for Foreign Language Learning" (1999, 2000) included 18 published responses including 17 by university FL professors ("Forum," 1999, p. 70). In addition, since the inception of *The Modern Language Journal* "Perspectives" column (a position paper on an issue related to second or FL teaching and learning followed by several commentaries) in 2002, the role of the *Standards* has been discussed in several issues including columns on language education policy in the United States (*The Modern Language Journal,* 87, vol. 4), the relation between the goals of FL study and the metaphors dominating FL pedagogy (*The Modern Language Journal,* 90, vol. 2), and the assessment and evaluation of university-level FL programs (*The Modern Language Journal,* 90, vol. 4). That the *Standards* continue to figure in these discussions indicates their relevance to real-world issues facing the FL profession as well as, more specifically, to concerns of university FL departments. On the other hand, in comparison to the numerous publications discussing and debating the merits of the *Standards* and the viability of their implementation at the postsecondary level, the number of published reports documenting their actual implementation by FL departments or individual professors is much shorter (Barnes-Karol, 2000; Gifford & Mullaney, 1998; Mathews & Hansen, 2004; Morris, 2006; Tucker, 2000; Yamada & Moeller, 2000).

It also bears mention when situating the *Standards* in their historical context and discussing their reception in higher education that they did not initiate a professional dialogue seeking change in the goals, means, and assessment of FL study when published in 1996; such dialogue was already in motion. Coinciding with the publication of the *Standards* in the mid-1990s, momentum for change was building, partially in response to the perceived limitations of CLT as a framework for postsecondary FL study (as previously discussed in this chapter). This momentum was evidenced in the appearance of several volumes dedicated to rethinking the undergraduate FL curriculum over the next decade (Byrnes & Maxim, 2004; Kramsch, 1995; Scott & Tucker, 2001; Swaffar & Arens, 2005). So, although the *Standards* may not be credited for sparking this dialogue for change, as Beyer (2000) noted, they certainly "provide[d] a new context for the latest series of self-studies and reappraisals, at the college level, of what and how we have been teaching in the past decade" (p. 59). In fact, several scholars have framed their own reflections on the *Standards* within a larger professional climate seeking change: Siskin (1999) described them, for university-level FL educators, as "signifiers of innovation, within a larger discourse of change that drives the profession" (p. 86) and Long (2000) called them "one of the megatrends in foreign language study ... [that] are steering us to the common ground of culturally based foreign language education" (p. 74).

During the years following the *Standards'* publication in 1996, however, the doomsday prediction of James (1998) that failing to implement the *Standards* at the university level would result in significant declines in FL enrollments was not fulfilled. That said, continued healthy post-secondary FL enrollments might be credited more realistically to external forces (e.g., heightened interest in FL education in light of post 9/11 national security needs, the economic pressures of globalization, steadily increasing heritage language populations) rather than efforts of university-level FL educators to put into place coherent, articulated sequences of language study or agree on common goals for FL learning (Modern Language Association, 2007). Current enrollment trends confirm the impact of these forces—since 2002, overall FL enrollments have increased by 13%, helped by a proliferation in the diversity of FL studied and significant growth in the study of languages such as Arabic, Chinese, and Korean (Furman, Goldberg, & Lusin, 2007).

In many ways, the same challenges that existed in 1996 when the *Standards* were first published still inform professional dialogue about FL study at the university level today. Ultimately, the *Standards* do not provide us an adequate blueprint for designing integrated university FL curricula. As James described them, the *Standards* provide "a destination rather than a road-map" (1998, p. 14). In other words, they are more outcome- than process-oriented; they point us to goals but do not show us the pathways (or approaches) to reach those goals. And though this flexibility may be, in many ways, desirable and necessary, given their design to be applied in various educational contexts, university-level FL departments struggle most with the very things (i.e., approach and curricular articulation) not addressed in the *Standards*. As Byrnes (2008) pointed out:

> The *Standards* document remains largely silent on precisely how those learning goals are to be attained. In a curious two-step it presents itself as a "framework for the reflective teacher to use in weaving [these] curricular experiences into the fabric of language learning" while restricting itself to pedagogical guidance and offering little explicit treatment of curricular issues. (p. 104)

Where does this leave university FL departments? In short, we are still searching for guiding frameworks, overarching goals, and instructional approaches to inform how and what we teach. Moreover, it remains an open question whether any one approach, framework, or set of goals could possibly "fit" for what, in reality, is a varied landscape of institutions of higher education and populations of FL learners who continue language study for varied reasons. This reservation aside, a number of promising approaches and pedagogical frameworks, many informed by research from linguistics, education, and psychology, have gained visibility and attention from members of the higher education FL community over the past decade as viable starting points for rethinking the undergraduate FL curriculum. These include a multiple literacies approach (Kern, 2000; The New London Group, 1996; Swaffar & Arens, 2005), genre-based approaches (Byrnes, 2008), and symbolic competence (Kramsch, 2006). In addition, there is some evidence that these concepts are serving as useful means for moving toward more integrated curricula wherein it is not necessary to privilege textual analysis over oral communication or vice versa; a number of publications provide concrete examples of how these approaches have been successfully implemented at various levels of the curriculum (e.g., Allen, in-press; Byrnes & Sprang, 2004; Paesani, 2006; Swaffar, 2004).

In conclusion, as Tesser (2002) suggested in her discussion of the role of the *Standards* in higher education, it is ultimately less important whether one embraces or rejects the *Standards* than whether one takes advantage of engaging in a dialogue about what they represent—finding meaningful and coherent ways to teach FL. Considered in this way, the *Standards* can be seen as an important document within a professional dialogue that has, since their publication in the mid-1990s, both continued to pursue certain ideals embodied in it and evolved as new directions have emerged in FL-learning pedagogy and research.

References

Adair-Hauck, B., Glisan, E. W., Koda, K., Swender, E. B., & Sandrock, P. (2006). The integrated performance assessment (IPA): Connecting assessment to instruction and learning. *Foreign Language Annals, 39*, 359–382.

Allen, H. W. (in press). A multiple literacies approach to the advanced French writing course. *The French Review, 83.*

Allen, L. Q. (2002). Teachers pedagogical beliefs and the Standards for Foreign Language Learning. *Foreign Language Annals, 35*, 518–529.

Barnes-Karol, G. (2000). Revising a Spanish novel class in the light of *Standards for Foreign Language Learning. ADFL Bulletin, 31*(2), 44–48.

Beyer, T. R. (2000). What standards? Standards—So what? *ADFL Bulletin, 31*(2), 59–60.

Bragger, J. D., & Rice, D. B. (1999). The implications of the standards in higher education. *ADFL Bulletin, 31*(1), 70–72.

Byrnes, H. (2001). Reconsidering graduate students' education as teachers: "It takes a department!" *The Modern Language Journal, 85*, 512–530.

Byrnes, H. (2006). Perspectives. *The Modern Language Journal, 90*, 244–246.

Byrnes, H. (2008). Articulating a foreign language sequence through content: A look at the culture standards. *Language Teaching, 41*, 103–118.

Byrnes, H., & Maxim, H. H. (Eds.). (2004). *Advanced foreign language learning: A challenge to college programs.* Boston: Heinle.

Byrnes, H., & Sprang, K. A. (2004). Fostering advancing L2 literacy: A genre-based cognitive approach. In H. Brynes & H. H. Maxim (Eds.), *Advanced foreign language learning: A challenge to college programs* (pp. 47–86). Boston: Heinle.

Center for Applied Linguistics. (2008). *Fingertip facts: National K-12 foreign language survey. Trends over a decade: 2008 vs. 1997.* Retrieved from http://www.cal.org/flsurvey/fingertip_facts.pdf

Davis, J. J. (2000). From where I sit: The standards and university instruction. *ADFL Bulletin, 31*(2), 61–63.

Davis, J. N. (1997). Educational reform and the Babel (babble) of culture: Prospects for the *Standards for Foreign Language Learning. The Modern Language Journal, 81,* 151–163.

Donato, R., & Brooks, F. B. (2004). Literary discussions and advanced speaking functions: Researching the (dis)connection. *Foreign Language Annals, 37,* 183–199.

Furman, N., Goldberg, D., & Lusin, N. (2007). *Enrollments in languages other than English in United States institutions of higher education, Fall 2006.* Retrieved May 28, 2008, from http://www.mla.org/pdf/06enrollmentsurvey_final.pdf

Gifford, C., & Mullaney, J. (1998). From rhetoric to reality: Applying the communication standards to the classroom. *Northeast Conference Review, 46,* 12–18.

Hymes, D. (1971). *On communicative competence.* Philadelphia: University of Pennsylvania Press.

James, D. (1998). The impact on higher education of *Standards for Foreign Language Learning: Preparing for the Twenty-First Century.* ACTFL White Paper. *ACTFL Newsletter, 11*(1), 11–14.

Kadish, D. Y. (2000). The challenge we face: Applying National Standards to the college foreign language curriculum. *ADFL Bulletin, 31*(2), 49–52.

Kern, R. (2000). *Literacy and language teaching.* Oxford: Oxford UP.

Klee, C. A. (1998). Communication as an organizing principle in the National Standards: Sociolinguistic aspects of Spanish language teaching. *Hispania, 81,* 339–351.

Klein, B. E. (2000). The standards: Market appeal and implementation. *ADFL Bulletin, 31*(2), 66–69.

Knight, S. (2000). Standards-specific speculation: K-12 or K-16? *ADFL Bulletin, 31*(2), 69–71.

Kramsch, C. (1993). *Context and culture in language teaching.* Oxford: Oxford UP.

Kramsch, C. (Ed.). (1995). *Redefining the boundaries of language study.* AAUSC Issues in Language Program Direction, Boston: Heinle.

Kramsch, C. (2006). From communicative competence to symbolic competence. *The Modern Language Journal, 90,* 249–252.

Long, S. S. (2000). Common ground: K-12 standards and higher education. *ADFL Bulletin, 31*(2), 72–74.

Magnan, S. S. (2008). Reexamining the priorities of the National Standards for Foreign Language Education. *Language Teaching, 41,* 349–366.

Mantero, M. (2002). Bridging the gap: Discourse in text-based foreign language classrooms. *Foreign Language Annals, 35,* 437–456.

Mathews, T. J., & Hansen, C. M. (2004). Ongoing assessment of a university foreign language program. *Foreign Language Annals, 37,* 630–640.

Maxwell, D. (2003). The leadership vacuum. *The Modern Language Journal, 87,* 595–597.

McAlpine, D. (2000). Is there a place for the National Foreign Language Standards in higher education? *ADFL Bulletin, 31*(2), 75–78.

McGinnis, S. (1999). RE: Standards. *ADFL Bulletin, 31*(1), 80–81.

Met, M. (2003). Developing language education policies for our schools. *The Modern Language Journal, 87,* 589–592.

Modern Language Association Ad Hoc Committee on Foreign Languages. (2007). *Foreign language and higher education: New structures for a changed world.* Retrieved May 28, 2008, from http://www.mla.org/pdf/forlang_news_pdf.pdf

Morris, M. (2006). Addressing the challenges of program evaluation: One department's experience after two years. *The Modern Language Journal, 90,* 585–588.

The New London Group. (1996). A pedagogy of multiliteracies: Designing social futures. *Harvard Educational Review, 66,* 60–92.

Paesani, K. (2006). *Exercices de style*: Developing multiple competencies through a writing portfolio. *Foreign Language Annals, 39*, 618–639.

Peters, G. F. (1999). A modest proposal. *ADFL Bulletin, 31*(1), 81–84.

Phillips, J. K. (2003). Implications of language education policies for language study in schools and universities. *The Modern Language Journal, 87*, 579–586.

Phillips, J. K. (2008). Foreign language standards and the context of communication. *Language Teaching, 41*, 93–102.

Rifkin, B. (2006). A ceiling effect for communicative language teaching? *The Modern Language Journal, 90*, 262–264.

Schulz, R. A. (2006). Reevaluating communicative competence as a major goal in postsecondary language requirement courses. *The Modern Language Journal, 90*, 252–255.

Scott, V. M., & Huntington, J. A. (2007). Literature, the interpretive mode, and novice learners. *The Modern Language Journal, 91*, 3–14.

Scott, V. M., & Tucker, H. (Eds.). (2001). *SLA and the literature classroom: Fostering dialogues*. AAUSC Issues in Language Program Direction, Boston: Heinle.

Siskin, H. J. (1999). The National Standards and the discourse of innovation. *ADFL Bulletin, 31*(1), 85–87.

Standards for Foreign Language Learning in the 21st Century. (1996/1999/2006). New York: ACTFL and the National Standards in Foreign Language Education Project.

Steinhart, M. M. (2006). Breaching the artificial barrier between communicative competence and content. *The Modern Language Journal, 90*, 258–261.

Swaffar, J. (2004). A template for advanced learner tasks: Staging genre reading and cultural reading through the précis. In H. Brynes & H. H. Maxim (Eds.), *Advanced foreign language learning: A challenge to college programs* (pp. 19–46). AAUSC Issues in Language Program Direction, Boston: Heinle.

Swaffar, J. (2006). Terminology and its discontents: Some caveats about communicative competence. *The Modern Language Journal, 90*, 246–249.

Swaffar, J. K., & Arens, K. M. (2005). *Remapping the foreign language curriculum: An approach through multiple literacies*. New York: Modern Language Association.

Tesser, C. C. (2002). Moving from debate to dialogue: The standards and articulation. *ADFL Bulletin, 31*, 2, 78–79.

Tucker, H. (2000). The place of the personal: The changing face of foreign language literature in a Standards-based curriculum. *ADFL Bulletin, 31*(2), 53–58.

Welles, E. (1998) Standards for foreign language learning: Implications and perceptions. *ACTFL Newsletter*, 7–9.

Wood, P. (1999). Who is using the National Foreign Language Standards? *Foreign Language Annals, 32*, 435–440.

Yamada, Y., & Moeller, A. J. (2000). Weaving curricular standards into the language classroom: An action research study. *Foreign Language Annals, 34*, 26–34.

Zyzick, E., & Polio, C. Incidental focus on form in university Spanish literature courses. *The Modern Language Journal, 92*, 53–70.

Part Two

Curricular Reform:
Shifting Paradigms

Chapter 5

A Chronicle of *Standards*-Based Curricular Reform in a Research University

Elizabeth Bernhardt
Guadalupe Valdés
Alice Miano[1], Stanford University

In 1995, Stanford University embarked upon curricular renewal in all of the major foreign languages. This curricular renewal was motivated by the university senate's concern that campuswide internationalization could not come about without a serious commitment to language teaching and learning. *Serious commitment* meant language programs that accomplished rigorous learning goals based in research, that employed teachers with the highest level of professional credentials, and that infused significant technology into the curriculum to assist in meeting the goals. This commitment was institutionalized in the Stanford Language Center, which was charged with encouraging excellence in language teaching, establishing and maintaining performance standards, providing professional development opportunities for the teaching staff, and developing a research program about language teaching and learning. Since 1995, the teaching staff has increased from 20 to 64; the budget is six times its original size; and enrollment beyond the required first-year has increased by 24%. By many yardsticks, although surely not by all, the original conception of the Stanford Language Center successfully met the objectives as laid forth by the university senate.[2]

Educational success is always multivariate and multidimensional, rooted in hard work, research-based knowledge, and serendipity. Only naiveté would assume a firm cause-and-effect conclusion. Indeed, since 1995, there has been some staff change and an increased availability of technology. The public has also become more urgently focused on language learning. Arguably, some of the success of the language programs may have come about merely as a consequence of natural developments within higher education. Yet, there were also two interrelated constants at play throughout this period at Stanford that bear significant responsibility for the success of the Stanford language programs. The first element, a professional development program principally focused on Oral Proficiency Interview (OPI) certification, was implemented and financed for all language teachers (including graduate students). This constant helped the teaching staff to acquire a common framework and professional language within which to engage and interact. The second constant element, the primary focus of the following narrative, focused on the *Standards for Foreign Language Learning in the 21st Century* as blueprints for program development.

The Professional Development Focus

Teachers teach in a manner consistent with their beliefs. If teachers believe that language is an act of communication, they can be given a telephone book or a warehouse catalogue and teach communicatively from them. If teachers believe that language fluency can only progress from a firm and complete knowledge of the grammatical syllabus, then programs full of colorful ancillaries, films, Web sites, and suggestions for group projects will be analyzed and deconstructed for their grammatical content. The list of beliefs can expand in almost any direction: from convictions about age and intelligence through attitudes about drill and practice to ideas about the use of the mother tongue in a classroom or to orthodoxies about the value of literature learning; the impact of standardized assessments; or the whole concept of whether assessment or learning standards are useful or important. These beliefs come into play in individual classrooms and they confront each other with full force in staff development workshops and meetings. Research on effective and successful teaching staffs indicates that strong leadership must set a direction and that teachers must understand and support the direction (Joyce & Showers, 1988). Those who cannot or do not support the direction tend to leave that particular staff.

The initial course set for all programs under the leadership of the Stanford Language Center was for each program to determine its objectives and to decide on a method for measuring those objectives. Setting objectives and determining or measuring these objectives are key activities in "exemplary professional development programs" (Peredo, 2000, p. 1). This exercise of goal setting and articulating was met with some resistance—resistance in the form of "we already know what we're doing and don't need to articulate objectives" to "there is no outside standard that we should subscribe to" to the invoking of the elite nature of the institution in that "we are not teaching at some State school" (Bernhardt, 2000). Much of this resistance was really a form of insecurity articulated by individuals who had never had opportunities for professional development or professional education in educational and applied linguistics. Staff members who had had some professional education (i.e., those with degrees in education-related fields) welcomed the exercise. In general, these teachers with some knowledge of applied linguistics had a concept of setting program objectives, but they were equally wary of measuring those objectives. Importantly, however, they were willing.

These teachers were interested in attending the OPI training. Both professional interest and eagerness to attend a 4-day workshop off-site at the expense of the university inspired the first group of language teachers who participated in OPI training.[3] This first group of attendees (only one of whom ultimately became certified) provided the tipping point. They returned with enthusiasm for the experience and a sense of a larger professional community. They urged others to attend. This attitude then led to the sponsoring of OPI workshops on campus, ultimately enabling by 2008 almost 100% of the teaching staff (including graduate students) to participate in the training and to begin the certification process.

Considering that by the late 1990s there was already much criticism of the approach, the question of *why the OPI?* is often raised. The answer is relatively straightforward and deeply rooted in the effective staff development literature.[4] The OPI was the only language assessment mechanism available that had a long and studied history. It encompassed a concept of the development of function, content, and accuracy in language—a discursive subtext that was absolutely critical at the time with a staff that had tremendous diversity in the professional education that it possessed; there were strict grammarians and social constructivists among them. Though not perfect, the OPI procedure was recognized nationally for what it could and could not do (Liskin-Gasparro, 2003). Further, the training and certification processes attached to the interview procedure were normed and were clearly articulated by a professional organization, ACTFL. The external nature of the training was critical. Rather than having staff trained by either their peers or their supervisors that would cause significant affective disruption, the process established by ACTFL enabled distinguished outside professionals to train the staff. In addition, a focus on the learning of oral skills had been behind many of the university's reforms. Faculties were seeking students prepared to go abroad and to become involved in various activities and research projects. Enabling students to function at the intermediate level of oral proficiency met the wider and immediate university-level goal. Finally, using the OPI as a benchmark for student learning and professional development reflected the remaining characteristics of exemplary professional development. By providing a common topic for conversation, the OPI training workshops encouraged "collaborative partnerships" across languages as well as enabled the "utilization and sharing of expertise among teachers, programs directors, and administrators" (Peredo, 2000, p.1).

The final piece of the puzzle, though, was the acknowledgment by the core group that objective-setting and a focus on oral assessment fell short of capturing deeper dimensions of oral language (such as formal presentational speech); the broader language functions (such as persuasion in a professional setting); and the expansive critical abilities regarding other languages and cultures that all students needed to acquire (not just the ability to interact at a sentence level). This was, in fact, part of the impetus behind the development of research-based nationwide standards. Indeed, by 1997, the foreign language profession was well underway with its project, *National Standards in Foreign Language Education* (NSFLE [1996]). Not unlike other professional organizations that were driven by a spirit of accountability, the foreign language profession, too, produced a lengthy position statement with accompanying materials. These policy documents provided the blueprints for effective language programs intent on offering students opportunities to learn an array of language functions across all communication modes as well as opportunities to see how language builds communities, connects across all academic fields, and enables students to compare and contrast cultural products from the micro- to the macro-levels. The push toward standards began a massive curricular reform project in the Spanish language program at Stanford—a project that continues to the present.

The Standards Focus

As the summer of 1997 began, the campus formed a group of language teachers in Spanish and Portuguese to hammer out common objectives for their respective language programs. As the largest language program on campus, larger, in fact, than all other language programs combined, it was important for the group to emphasize program objectives in Spanish; other languages could then follow suit. Given that more than 50% of Stanford students would take at least one class in the Spanish language program, Spanish had significant visibility in all sectors of the campus. This situation put a particular kind of pressure on developments within the Spanish language program. At the same time, we were very fortunate to have among us professor Guadalupe Valdés of the School of Education and the Department of Spanish & Portuguese, who had served on the task force that had recently created the *National Standards*. Valdés led our on-site committee to create the objectives in Spanish and Portuguese. Other team members included Elizabeth Bernhardt, the director of the Language Center; Alice Miano, the coordinator of the Spanish language program; Lyris Wiedemann, the coordinator of the Portuguese language program; and Ana Sierra and Claudi Angelleli, two additional Spanish lecturers who had formal knowledge of applied linguistics.

From the beginning, we were clear about two things. First, we wanted to equip our students, within 2 years, to participate in an overseas program in Puebla, Mexico, in which Stanford students would study alongside Mexican university students rather than separately in courses designed solely for foreigners. Second, we needed to expand our notions of communication in the creation of our objectives to meet the needs of our students. Professional development activities, most especially the OPI workshops, underlined the inadequate nature of the popular four skills approach that was governing much of the language instructors' teaching and assessment. The *Standards'* tripartite view of communication (Interpersonal, Interpretive, and Presentational) enabled us to think of language in terms of production (speaking and writing) and reception (listening and reading). It also motivated us to examine varying thematic content illustrating diverse sociolinguistic, stylistic, and structural features that would meet the Cs beyond communication. A mere focus on the four skills did not permit such a multidimensional view and appreciation of linguistic divergence nor did the OPI training.

For 2 weeks, the group met in a classroom for several hours, brainstorming ideas and jotting notes on the chalkboard. Miano acted as note taker for the group and, using a template that Valdés suggested, she compiled the ideas in chart form each evening, e-mailed them to Valdés, and then continued the day's discussion with Valdés by phone to editing the evolving document based on the conversations with her. The resultant work was brought back to the committee the following day for further discussion. The objectives were thus hammered out recursively and continuously for 2 weeks, leading to the finished product (Appendix A). In addition, Valdés worked with Miano to create accompanying syllabi, course calendars, and progress cards for the Spanish program to highlight and showcase the newly minted objectives. The curricular document includes objectives for interpersonal, presentational, and interpretive language based on a quarter system calendar for 2 years of Spanish language instruction.

At first glance, the document in Appendix A is heavily focused on the Communication standard. It lists particular forms to be developed and learned across time as well as particular language functions. Yet, a closer reading brings the standards of Comparisons, Cultures, Connections, and Communities into clearer view. Comparisons between English and Spanish as languages as well as between English-speaking and Spanish-speaking cultures are encouraged. The good fortune of being present in a heavily dominant Spanish-speaking culture also made objectives regarding interacting with and developing communities possible. Students in Spanish 2, for instance, compare cultural practices and artistic products surrounding the Virgin of Guadalupe from the perspectives of different communities. Spanish 13 students, meanwhile, participate in discussions of a contemporary Spanish language novel not only in the classroom but also alongside native speakers in a local community book club. Connections were fostered linguistically by requiring students to make presentations in the semantic space of their academic interests as well as by using these objectives within an array of themed courses such as "Spanish for International Relations" "Spanish, a Cultural Emphasis" "Spanish for the Biological Sciences." Assignments within these themed courses most often reflect the Connections standard because students are asked to draw relationships between and among their majors courses with their Spanish language courses.

Standards at the Programmatic Level

Such curricular innovations and assignments did not become immediately apparent, however, in initially establishing the objectives. Indeed, following the creation of the objectives, the real challenge was implementing them. Once classes were underway, meetings among Spanish lecturers were held two to three times per quarter to discuss the objectives, brainstorm ideas, and produce materials and activities that would ease the implementation process. Still, the process was an arduous one. Other than the aforementioned lecturers included in initial discussions and development, not all instructors embraced the objectives. Some felt the objectives were simply too demanding. Others, traditionally schooled in university literature departments with mostly on-the-job training in language instruction, found the objectives' language to be too technical if not wholly inaccessible. Indeed, in order to make the objectives transparent to students, Miano had created progress cards—easy-to-understand checklists of linguistic functions that corresponded to the formal objectives. An example is provided in Appendix B. For some instructors, it seemed the progress cards similarly acted as a bridge to the actual, formal document; that is, some instructors were able to conceive of activities but were not able to conceptualize particular language forms and functions in the abstract. As part of the implementation process, in fact, the progress cards served a dual function: first, to make clear to students the goals and expectations of the course; and second, to make teachers accountable. If students knew what was expected of them, they would likewise anticipate that teachers would address those expectations. Yet, with some instructors who remained skeptical and dubious, it was unclear whether they were actually communicating with the students in terms of the program-established objectives. The publication of the objectives on the Spanish language Web site ensured that all students received the information even while their instructors remained dubious.

To better publicize the Spanish Language Program, we gave it a Web presence that touted the program's ambitious nature, posted syllabi and course calendars, and most importantly, explained the philosophy of the program's objectives and posted its progress cards. We later made the progress cards interactive, so that instructors and students looking for materials to help them put the objectives into practice could merely click on a link and find assistance in reaching particular objectives.[5] We likewise began to publicize the Web site at student orientation placement testing, at information tables set up at the beginning of each quarter, and at regular meetings among instructors. Continuously reinforcing the message that all programmatic expectations—from prerequisites to objectives to assignments—were available in plain view on the Internet helped program participants at all levels begin to internalize a *Standards*-based philosophy. The Web site gave us a vehicle for accountability. At the same time, through attrition, instructors who did not or could not cope with this level of accountability eventually left the program, paving the way for even more enthusiastic instructors. These instructors were often energized by the ambitious nature of the program and its increasing efforts to make the objectives even more doable through materials creation and instructor collaboration. In fact, all prospective instructors, whether job applicants or future teaching assistants, continue to be provided with copies of the objectives. This process helps to socialize them from the very beginning of their tenure into our programmatic practices as a *Standards*-based language program and not a program that merely follows a textbook. In addition, with a grant from the university's Center for Teaching and Learning, an online instructors' manual was added to the Spanish language program's Web site. The manual provided further support materials as well as easy access to electronic copies of the Spanish program objectives, and ACTFL oral and writing proficiency guidelines.

The efforts of the Spanish language staff were extremely influential with staff across all of the language programs as well as in those curricula. As professional development programs continued, all of the language teaching staff members got to know and respect colleagues in all other language programs, from Arabic to Zulu. OPI training continued both in special language sections and in mixed language sections for staff and graduate students alike. Further, other professional programs such as training in crossing major borders on the ACTFL/FSI scale; developments in writing and reading; and perhaps most importantly for the context of this chapter, workshops on the *Standards* encouraged all staff to become involved with and knowledgeable about the Spanish language program—the pioneer program. Presently, most language programs have used the template developed by the Spanish language staff as the model for their curricula. They have also emulated the progress cards and the Spanish language Web site to communicate similarly with their instructors and students.

Continuing Standards-Based Programmatic Development

As the initial process to create the objectives evolved recursively, so has their ongoing implementation process. Ten years after the creation of the objectives, during the 2007–2008 academic year, Spanish lecturers continued to meet to compare the objectives with the *Standards* themselves to see how they could be improved further. Instructors worked in small discussion groups and created written comments and suggestions, which Miano then summarized in blog format, providing an online diary to allow continued access to and review of all comments. Successive meetings likewise focused on improved implementation of the presentational objectives, which are especially emphasized in the second year of instruction. A common outcome for both sets of meetings was teachers' continuous clamor for authentic materials, indeed corpora, of various oral and written genres that could help illuminate for students the precision that language use entails at all levels. To address these needs, two Spanish lecturers were given release time to seek out electronically available materials exemplifying various genres, from written exposés, to formal panel discussions, to political speeches, and more. If publicly available, links to these materials were incorporated into the interactive progress cards on the Spanish language program's Web site.[6] Items not publicly available were made accessible, within fair use guidelines, posted on a site available only to instructors within the program. Future projects include continued discussion and action along these lines, that is, recursive examination of the objectives vis-à-vis the *Standards*; retooled and improved activities, materials, and techniques to aid implementation of the objectives; and use of a common Web site that helps to continuously put curricular innovation into practice and establish accountability within the program.

Confronting Presentational Language

In spite of decade-long significant work in developing, using, and refining the *Standards*-based Spanish curriculum, instructors were never quite comfortable with the notion of presentational language. We had to confront the view that classroom instruction, particularly at second year, necessitated a broader vision of formal language use, well beyond the interpersonal. Learners had to learn and practice how to structure presentations per se. They also had to know how to answer questions in a one-to-many format using extended and structured formal discourse. At some level, the OPI helped with the latter because a portion of instructors, fully certified OPI testers, knew how to approach and assess the advanced and superior levels of language that characterize some dimensions of presentational speech. Another portion did not have that experience or insight. In fact, the OPI experience may have exacerbated the problem of understanding the complexities of presentational language by reinforcing notions of interpersonal language use. Frankly, even though the curriculum as it appears in Appendix A had always acknowledged and accounted for presentational language, noting that students needed to learn to use language in formal, one-to-many settings, holding the floor and structuring their extemporaneous language in response to questions and commentaries, those kinds of performances were never normed in the same way as interpersonal language performance. Because there was no framework that could match up with presentational language in the real and intuitive way that the OPI matches with interpersonal language, the OPI remained the default assessment scheme. Complicating these concerns was the appearance of the Writing Proficiency Test (American Council on the Teaching of Foreign Languages [ACTFL], 2008) and its concomitant rater certification process that provided a framework for assessing the written portion of presentational language. Instructors who were fully certified in the OPI began to pursue writing certification. Again, the recursive nature of professional development and standards reappeared: With further professional development with writing, instructors began to perceive an even greater hole in the curriculum on the basis of oral presentational language.

To address this gap in the assessment of oral presentational language, we first videotaped the final oral presentations of second-year Spanish students in the spring of 2006. Then, as a summer project, we asked Spanish lecturers to rate 10 student samples each as "good," "better," or "best," without providing instructors with any particular criteria. Each sample was rated by two instructors to test inter-rater reliability. The results of the project were disconcerting, to say the least: There was near universal disagreement among 20 lecturers as to which student performances merited a rating of "good," "better," or "best." So, we went back to the drawing board, having demonstrated, if nothing else, an urgent need for clear assessment criteria for oral presentational language.

We then followed an earlier successful strategy and formed a brainstorming committee with the Language Center director; associate director; and the respective coordinators of the French, Italian, and Spanish programs to discuss the development of an assessment tool. The committee devised five principal criteria that apply to oral presentational language: (a) organization and structure; (b) critical thinking: content analysis and use of evidence; (c) delivery, presentational manner; (d) vocabulary: use of academic, presentational language; and (e) linguistic accuracy (Bernhardt, Gelmetti, Miano, Molitoris, & Tsethlikai, 2007; Miano & Molitoris, 2008). With these criteria in mind, Miano created a graded assessment rubric for the second year of instruction, in keeping with program objectives that placed increasing emphasis on pre-sentational language in the second year. We then tested the rubric, first in staff meetings within the Spanish program, in which we gathered and independently rated several of the aforementioned videotaped presentations. Two results became immediately apparent. First, inter-rater reliability increased dramatically: The tendency was for half of the group to agree on students' scores exactly, with the rest of the group giving a contiguous rating, with only one outlier. Second, through viewing various student performances and discussing them (after ratings were independently recorded and collected), instructors realized how variable student performances could be regardless of a student's level of instruction (first, second, or third quarter of the second year). This underlined the need to define and apply explicit programmatic assessment criteria, and to explain the criteria clearly to students. Instructors then tested the rubric in their classrooms. In further staff meetings, instructors suggested modifications and improvements to the rubric. At instructors' request, Miano then formulated a version of the rubric using simpler, more student-friendly language, as had been done with the progress cards. This version was given to students and tested in second-year classes in the fall of 2008. Instructors continue to use a refined draft of the rubric designed for actual grading of student performances.

Reflections on Using the Standards for Curriculum and Staff Development

The ACTFL Standards Document (1996) made a unique contribution to the language teaching profession in that it defined what students should know and be able to do as a result of foreign language study. The *Standards* movement, moreover, created a national consensus as to the overall objectives of language instruction and to a more precise conceptualization of the focus of five principal goal areas: Communication, Cultures, Connections, Comparisons, and Communities. From a *Standards*-based perspective, language instruction was seen, not as a traditional academic subject for which students could study and cram isolated facts, but as a unique area of endeavor centered on acquiring real-life competencies and proficiencies. Communication, therefore, was seen as the heart of foreign language, whether that communication took place in oral or written language, in a face-to-face mode with real speakers, or in writing over centuries through the reading of literature. Through foreign language study, students would come to develop an awareness of culture, of other people's world views, of the different patterns of language systems and cultures, of how languages are used in various disciplines, and of their actual use by communities of speakers.

Although the *Standards* did offer examples of progress indicators for each of its goals, it did not present a set of ordered developmental stages or progress indicators that could be used to guide instruction. For instructors accustomed to grammatical syllabi and to a view of language growth measured by an ordered list of grammatical topics (present tense, stem-changing verbs, the subjunctive mood), the *Standards* examples did not clearly specify how teachers might shift their instruction to ensure the development of what the *Standards* document referred to as Interpersonal, Interpretive, and Presentational communicative modes. For most instructors (and this was the case at Stanford) a communicative approach meant, for example, simply using the present tense in communicative exercises in class. It did not mean guiding students to develop increasingly more complex functional abilities for participating in interpersonal communicative exchanges, to interpret written and oral texts, and to use language for one-to-many interactions (e.g., formal oral presentations and written reports).

For our program, however, the *Standards* documents provided a framework that allowed us to develop a set of ordered objectives that could be used by both instructors and students to gauge their growth over time in carrying out particular communicative tasks. In this context we use *their* deliberately, for the *Standards* not only focused us on student performance in important ways, but also directed instructors' attention to what they needed to know about language and language learning and also what they needed to be able to do. As we noted earlier, and as predicted by the 1996 *Standards* document (p. 13), the difference in the skill-based organizational framework of the ACTFL Proficiency Guidelines undergirding the OPI and the communication modes used by the *Standards* did create a number of problems and tensions to which we were obliged to respond. Our response resulted in a heightened level of professional discussion and an even more intense focus on how to enable students to perform in a sophisticated, culturally authentic manner with the languages they are learning.

Our chronicle of curricular reform continues as we are pushed by the *Standards* to constantly reevaluate the challenges related to assessment and to confront them with confidence and professionalism. Reforming the language curriculum in a diverse, research-based university is not an easy task. The *Standards* complicated our endeavor in part because they are conceptually rich and sophisticated, and demanded vigilance, attention, time, and commitment from many stakeholders. In fact, we are often asked by colleagues whether what is chronicled in these pages is replicable and/or applicable in other university contexts. Though we cannot address other contexts, we believe that if there is a commitment to reform accompanied by expertise and diligence, and if there is an authority that respects the views of others but also sets and evaluates programmatic direction, our process can be implemented in any context. Finally, in spite of the rigors of our decade-long journey, we are relatively content, though we will never be fully satisfied, with our labors.

Notes

1. We acknowledge the importance of the critical contribution of Lyris Wiedemann, Ana Sierra, and Claudia Angelleli to the work discussed in this chapter.

2. Several detailed descriptions of the development of the Stanford Language Center exist in the literature. For more extensive information, see Bernhardt, 1997, 2000, 2006, 2009.

3. The OPI certification process is rigorous, taking between six months and a year to complete. It involves several stages that train candidates to rate speech samples and conduct oral proficiency interviews at various levels. Candidates first attend an intensive 2- or 4-day spell out numbers workshop to learn and practice procedures for rating and interviewing. They then prepare and submit practice and final rounds of interviews and have their own proficiency assessed. Certification is granted based on rating reliability and interviewing technique. In the 2-day workshop (called "Modified") candidates practice the scale through advanced-level speech) and a successful certification is "Limited"; in the 4-day workshop they practice the entire scale and successful completion of all phases results in "Full Certification."

4. Page space does not permit us to provide a full discussion of this literature. In brief, the literature indicates that effective professional development deepens teachers' knowledge of content and how to teach it; helps teachers understand how students learn; provides opportunities for active, hands-on learning; enables teachers to acquire new knowledge, apply it in practice, and reflect on the results with colleagues; is part of a school reform effort that links curriculum, assessment, and standards to professional learning; is collaborative and collegial; and is intensive over time. (Darling-Hammond & Richardson, 2009, p. 49)

5. Many thanks to Joseph Kautz for his assistance with developing interactive progress cards.

6. The Spanish language program Web site: http://spanlang.stanford.edu.

References

American Council on the Teaching of Foreign Languages. *Writing Proficiency Guidelines and Writing Proficiency Test*. Retrieved from www.actfl.org

Bernhardt, E. (1997). Victim narratives or victimizing narratives? Discussions of the reinvention of language departments and language programs. *ADFL Bulletin, 29*, 13–19.

Bernhardt, E. B. (2000). The professional development of highly experienced and less experienced teachers: Meeting diverse needs. In B. Rifkin (Ed.), *Mentoring foreign language teaching assistants, lecturers and adjunct faculty* (pp. 41–54). AAUSC Issues in Language Program Direction. Boston: Heinle.

Bernhardt, E. B. (2006). Student learning outcomes as professional development and public relations. *The Modern Language Journal, 90*, 588–590.

Bernhardt, E. B. (2009). Systemic and systematic assessment as a keystone for language and literature programs. *ADFL Bulletin, 40*(1), 14–19.

Bernhardt, E., Gelmetti, S., Miano, A., Molitoris, J., & Tsethlikai, K. (2007, November 16). *From placement testing to exit testing and assessments in between*. ACTFL Annual meeting, San Antonio, TX.

Darling-Hammond, L., & Richardson, N. (2009). Teacher learning: What matters? *Educational Leadership, 66,* 46–53.

Joyce, B., & Showers, B. (1988). *Student achievement through staff development.* New York: Longman.

Liskin-Gasparro, J. (2003). The ACTFL proficiency guidelines and the oral proficiency interview: A brief history and analysis of their survival. *Foreign Language Annals, 36,* 483–490.

Miano, A., & Molitoris, J. (2008, June 6). *Oral presentational language: Process, collaboration, results.* Presentation at *ADFL West,* Stanford University.

National Standards in Foreign Language Education Project. (1996). *Standards for foreign language learning: Preparing for the 21st century.* Yonkers, NY: Author.

Peredo, M. W. (2000, September 1999). Directions in professional development. In David R. Schwandt, Ph.D. & Timothy J. Tobin (Eds.), *Adapted from Report on Title VII, Subpart 1 Professional development activities.* Washington, DC: National Clearinghouse for Bilingual Education.

Appendix A
Descriptions of Target Student Abilities: First-Year Spanish

Interpersonal Abilities	Spanish 1	Spanish 2	Spanish 3
Students will be able to: engage in interactions with speakers of Spanish for a variety of purposes and in a variety of contexts using socially and culturally appropriate forms for participating in conversations, establishing relationships with others, providing and obtaining information, expressing feelings and emotions, and expressing opinions.	During the first quarter of language study, students will be able to interact with members of their class and to talk about themselves. At the end of the quarter, students will be able to: • meet, greet and introduce themselves • name their immediate world: family, place of origin, activities, personal interests, major, health and well-being, the body, possessions, foods, weather, likes and dislikes • express politeness within the cultural framework of their native culture	During the second quarter, students base their communicative repertoire on tasks from the previous quarter and expand their repertoire to include new and more complex tasks. Communication becomes more other-oriented and students engage in interactions with Spanish speakers at Stanford, in the Bay Area, and in California. At the end of the quarter, students will be able to: • carry out all communicative tasks carried out in the previous quarter with greater sophistication and complexity of expression • occasionally express politeness within the framework of the target culture	During the third quarter, students expand their interests and interactions to the broader Spanish-speaking world. They base their communicative repertoire on tasks from the previous quarter and expand their repertoire to include new and more complex tasks. They become more aware of sociolinguistic appropriateness. At the end of the quarter, students will be able to: • carry out all communicative tasks carried out in the previous quarter with greater sophistication and complexity of expression, and growing sociolinguistic appropriateness • express politeness within the framework of the target culture with increasing frequency

- participate effectively in simulated service encounters such as: ordering a meal and asking for the check in a restaurant
- in service encounters, begin to use linguistic strategies to interact and obtain information

- simulate telephone conversations
- describe people, places, daily activities
- give, request information
- ask and answer simple questions
- express gratitude
- apologize
- give instructions, directions

- become acquainted with other speakers (native or non-native) of the language (in person and through electronic means)
- begin to become aware of sociolinguistically appropriate ways to address and interact with Spanish speakers.

- participate in more elaborate simulated service encounters and in service encounters in the surrounding community
- in service encounters, use linguistic strategies to interact and obtain information with greater frequency

- converse on the telephone with acquaintances (e.g., make a date, refuse an invitation, ask for information)
- communicate wishes and preferences
- make comparisons
- give an opinion
- talk about future plans for themselves and the world

- initiate conversations with strangers and acquaintances and nominate topics of conversation in order to sustain a conversation with Spanish speakers in sociolinguistically appropriate ways

- participate in more elaborate simulated service encounters in the surrounding community that more accurately reflect conditions in a Spanish-speaking country
- in service encounters, use linguistic strategies to interact and obtain information

- interact with strangers and acquaintances on the telephone
- ask for favors
- express emotions such as sympathy, admiration anger or surprise
- accept apologies
- offer assistance
- complain
- suggest/give advice

(Continued)

Appendix A
Descriptions of Target Student Abilities: First-Year Spanish (continued)

Interpretive Abilities	Spanish 1	Spanish 2	Spanish 3
	• communicate lack of understanding and ask for help in managing language	• express intentions • give reports on Spanish-speaking acquaintances • talk about their own interests and also those of the community	• express opinions • express (lack of) agreement • share doubts • clarify and restate information
	• begin to become aware of the role of self-monitoring in language development	• become increasingly aware of the role of self-monitoring in language development	• become increasingly aware of the role of self-monitoring in language development

Interpretive Abilities	Spanish 1	Spanish 2	Spanish 3
Students will be able to understand and interpret written and spoken language on a variety of topics and manifest growing awareness of the social and cultural influences shaping the production of oral and written texts in the Spanish- and English-speaking worlds.	During the first quarter, students will listen to and read a variety of oral and written texts relating primarily to their own lives and the classroom as community. Students will manifest their understanding of both oral and written texts, using English as necessary to demonstrate that understanding. At the end of the quarter, students will be able to:	During the second quarter, students will listen to and read a variety of oral and written texts and expand their interests to include the surrounding community. Students will manifest their understanding of both oral and written texts, using English less frequently to demonstrate that understanding. At the end of the quarter, students will be able to:	During the third quarter, students will listen to and read a variety of oral and written texts and expand their interests to include the broader Spanish-speaking world. Students will manifest their understanding of both oral and written texts, using primarily Spanish to demonstrate that understanding. At the end of the quarter, students will be able to:

- identify topic, focus, or purpose of interaction between members of their class when they:
- participate in simulated service encounters such as: ordering a meal and asking for the check in a restaurant
- describe people, places, daily activities
- give, request information
- ask and answer simple questions
- express gratitude
- apologize
- give instructions, directions
- communicate lack of understanding and ask for help in managing language

- identify, restate, and explain topic, focus, or purpose of interaction between members of their class and individuals in the surrounding community when they carry out the communicative tasks focused on during the first quarter, as well as when they:
- participate in more elaborate simulated service encounters
- converse on the telephone with acquaintances (e.g., make a date, refuse an invitation, ask for information)
- communicate wishes and preferences
- make comparisons
- give an opinion
- talk about future plans for themselves and the world
- express intentions
- give reports on Spanish-speaking acquaintances
- talk about their own interests and also those of the community
- describe experiences and events

- identify restate, and explain topic, focus, or purpose of interaction between members of their class and individuals in the surrounding community when they carry out the communicative tasks focused on during the first two quarters, as well as when they:
- initiate conversations with strangers and acquaintances and nominate topics of conversation
- interact with strangers and acquaintances on the telephone
- ask for favors
- express emotions such as sympathy, admiration anger or surprise
- accept apologies
- offer assistance
- complain
- suggest/give advice
- express opinions
- express (lack of) agreement
- share doubts
- clarify and restate information

(Continued)

Appendix A
Descriptions of Target Student Abilities: First-Year Spanish (continued)

Interpretive Abilities	Spanish 1	Spanish 2	Spanish 3
	• list ideas expressed in brief (5–10 minute) oral presentations on factual topics about which they have some knowledge • identify topics in a set of television news program excerpts • identify genre of oral and written texts (movies, announcements, news broadcasts, etc.)	• restate key details expressed in longer (10–20 minute) oral presentations on factual topics about which they have some knowledge • list topics in a set of TV news excerpts • take notes on ideas expressed in brief (5–10 minute) oral presentations on factual topics about which they have little or no knowledge	• summarize key points and main ideas expressed in longer (20–40 minute) oral presentations on factual topics about which they have some knowledge • using connected discourse, list topics and some details in a set of TV news excerpts • take notes on ideas expressed in longer (10–20 minute) oral presentations on factual topics about which they have little or no knowledge
	• begin to become acquainted with the sociogeography of the Spanish-speaking world • understand connected discourse in straight forward expository texts (of approximately 250 words) on known topics involving familiar vocabulary • glean biographical information from written materials	• become better acquainted with the sociogeography of the Spanish-speaking world • understand connected discourse in straight forward expository texts (from 250 to 500 words) about the immediate Spanish-speaking world, such as short articles from local Spanish-speaking newspapers	• draw comparisons among sociogeographic features of the Spanish-speaking world • understand connected discourse and identify point of view in less straightforward, editorial expository texts (from 500 to 750 words) dealing with student interests or with contemporary issues in

	Spanish 1	Spanish 2	Spanish 3
	understand information in the types of materials found in service encounters (menus, bus and train schedules, movie and theatre listings, signs in public places, weather reports)		• which the students have some background • using the Internet and newspapers, seek and read articles that correspond to their interests • compare the treatment of current events in the target language with the treatment of the same events (in English)
Presentational Abilities Students will be able to present information, concepts, and ideas to an audience of listeners or readers on a variety of academic topics.	During the first quarter, students will present information about themselves and their classroom community orally and in writing. At the end of the quarter, students will be able to: • present rehearsed reports (5–10 minutes) on such topics as: own autobiography, family, interests, sports, recipes, recent trips • answer questions about the prepared presentation topic	During the second quarter, students will increase in sophistication in presenting information about themselves and their classroom community orally and in writing. At the end of the quarter, students will be able to: • present rehearsed reports (10–20 minutes) on topics of broader interest reflecting knowledge of the sociogeography of the Spanish-speaking world • ask and answer questions about the prepared presentation topic using language appropriate for academic presentations	During the third quarter, students will continue to increase in sophistication in presenting information about themselves and their classroom community orally and in writing. At the end of the quarter, students will be able to: • present rehearsed reports (20–30 minutes) on topics of broader interest reflecting knowledge of the sociogeography of the Spanish-speaking world as well as reflecting knowledge of academic topics of particular interest to students such as: their major, current events, international relations, the sciences

(Continued)

Appendix A
Descriptions of Target Student Abilities: First-Year Spanish (continued)

Presentational Abilities	Spanish 1	Spanish 2	Spanish 3
	• write what they can say, for example: • describe people, places, daily activities • give, request information • ask and answer simple questions • express gratitude • apologize • give instructions, directions • write 1-page reports on such topics as: own autobiography, family, interests, sports, recipes, recent trips • edit their work for high frequency errors	• write what they can say displaying a wider array of language functions than the previous quarter including: • communicate wishes and preferences • make comparisons • give an opinion • talk about future plans for themselves and the world • express intentions • give reports on Spanish-speaking acquaintances • talk about their own interests and also those of the community	• present information on research carried out • place greater emphasis on socioculturally appropriate presentational language • ask and answer questions about the prepared presentation topic using language appropriate for academic presentations • write what they can say displaying a wider array of language functions than the previous quarter including: • express emotions such as sympathy, admiration anger or surprise • suggest/give advice • express opinions • support opinions • explain • give examples • express (lack of) agreement • share doubts • clarify and restate information

- describe experiences and situations
- summarize readings
- write 2-page reports on topics of broader interest reflecting knowledge of the sociogeography of the Spanish-speaking world
- edit for errors based on the material taught

- write 3-page reports on topics reflecting knowledge of the sociogeography of the Spanish-speaking world as well as reflecting knowledge of academic topics of particular interest to them such as: major, current events, international relations, the sciences
- quote others in reports
- prepare topics using authentic material
- edit for errors based on the material taught

Appendix A
Descriptions of Target Student Abilities: Second-Year Spanish

During the 2nd year of language study, students will build on the interpersonal, interpretive, and presentational abilities developed during the 1st year:

	Spanish 11	Spanish 12	Spanish 13
Interpersonal Abilities	In the 2nd year of language study, students will continue to interact with speakers of Spanish for a variety of purposes and in a variety of contexts, using socially and culturally appropriate forms. Additionally, students will interact with increasing sociocultural appropriateness in academic and professional settings.	During the first quarter of 2nd-year language study, students will be able to access information about their content area of focus and to discuss this information with peers, in written reports, and formal academic presentations. Students will exhibit growing confidence in carrying out face-to-face interactions and academic discussions with same age, younger and older people in culturally appropriate ways. At the end of the quarter, students will be able to:	During the second quarter of 2nd-year language study, students will be able to access information about their content area of focus and to discuss this information with peers, in written reports, and formal academic presentations. Students will exhibit growing confidence in carrying out face-to-face interactions and academic discussions with same age, younger and older people in culturally appropriate ways. At the end of the quarter, students will be able to:	During the third quarter of 2nd-year language study, students will be able to access information about their content area of focus and to discuss this information with peers, in written reports, and formal academic and professional presentations. Students will exhibit growing confidence in carrying out face-to-face interactions, and academic and professional discussions, with same age, younger and older people in culturally appropriate ways. At the end of the quarter, students will be able to:
oral/written language	• carry out all communicative tasks of the previous quarter with greater sophistication, confidence and ease	• carry out all communicative tasks of the previous quarter with greater sophistication, confidence and ease	• carry out all communicative tasks of the previous quarter with greater sophistication, confidence and ease

oral language			
• discuss their opinions (outlooks, views of events, hopes, fears, doubts) and exchange information about their content area of focus (culture, international relations, etc.) • use *tú* and *usted* with growing appropriateness • vary language according to the relative formality or informality of their interlocutor with growing appropriateness • address other speakers with growing appropriateness according to their age, social rules, position, title • communicate respect, politeness, gratitude, friendliness, distance with growing appropriateness • clarify and restate information • invite and interact with classroom speakers	• continue to discuss their opinions with growing complexity • begin to engage in interactive argumentation of an academic nature • use *tú* and *usted* with growing appropriateness and greater confidence • vary language according to the relative formality or informality of their interlocutor with growing appropriateness and greater confidence • address others speakers with growing appropriateness and greater confidence according to their age, social rules, position, title • communicate respect, gratitude, friendliness, distance with growing appropriateness and greater confidence • clarify and restate information • invite and interact with classroom speakers	• support their opinions • discuss academic and professional topics and fully engage in interactive argumentation • anticipate an argument • contrast arguments • use *tú* and *usted* appropriately • vary language according to the relative formality or informality of their interlocutor • address other speakers according to their age, social rules, position, title • communicate respect, gratitude, politeness, friendliness, distance appropriately • clarify and restate information • invite and interact with classroom speakers	

Appendix A
Descriptions of Target Student Abilities: Second-Year Spanish

Interpersonal Abilities	Spanish 11	Spanish 12	Spanish 13
	• listen to and imitate how others speak	• listen for tone (humor, sarcasm)	• listen for tone and react appropriately
	• seek support and feedback from others	• seek support and feedback from others	• seek support and feedback from others
	• self monitor and evaluate language development	• self monitor and evaluate language development	• self monitor and evaluate language development
	• correspond with friends and family	• correspond with same-age pen pals	• write invitations and thank you letters
			• write simple cover letters and a simple résumé to Spanish-speaking businesses
written languge	• correspond with an individual or agency to request information	• begin professional correspondence with a known receiver	• continue professional correspondence with a known receiver
	• use a dictionary to validate their choice of language	• use a dictionary to validate their choice of language	• use a dictionary to validate their choice of language
	• share information with peers about their content area of focus via the Internet	• share information with peers about their content area of focus via the Internet	• share information with peers about their content area of focus via the Internet
	• self-edit with increasing frequency	• self-edit with increasing frequency	• self-edit with increasing frequency
	• respond to work of peers	• respond to work of peers	• respond to work of peers

Interpretive Abilities	Spanish 11	Spanish 12	Spanish 13
Students will understand and interpret written and oral texts on a variety of complex topics, including texts related to the individual student's academic and professional fields, demonstrating a continually growing awareness of the social and cultural influences shaping the production of oral and written texts in the Spanish- and English-speaking worlds.	Students will grow in ability to interpret a variety of written and oral texts and will use Spanish with greater frequency to manifest their understanding of both oral and written texts. At the end of the quarter, students will be able to:	Students will grow in ability to interpret a variety of written and oral texts and will be able to use Spanish to manifest their understanding of both oral and written texts. At the end of the quarter, students will be able to:	Students will grow in ability to interpret a variety of written and oral texts and will be able to use Spanish to manifest their understanding of both oral and written texts. At the end of the quarter, students will be able to:
oral/written texts	• carry out all interpretive tasks of the previous quarter with greater sophistication, depth and complexity	• carry out all interpretive tasks of the previous quarter with greater sophistication, depth and complexity	• carry out all interpretive tasks of the previous quarter with greater sophistication, depth and complexity
	• begin to develop a more culturally authentic frame of reference	• continue to develop a more culturally authentic frame of reference	• continue to develop a more culturally authentic frame of reference
	• identify and begin to draw comparisons	• draw comparisons	• analyze and make predictions
	• summarize an argument	• analyze an argument	• anticipate an argument
			• take detailed notes on content
	• take limited notes on content	• take more detailed notes on content	• take detailed notes on content

Appendix A
Descriptions of Target Student Abilities: Second-Year Spanish (continued)

Interpretive Abilities	Spanish 11	Spanish 12	Spanish 13
oral/written texts	• get meaning from context	• get meaning from context	• get meaning from context
	• begin to keep individual notes on language	• keep individual notes on language	• keep detailed individual notes on language
	• follow and document shifting topics in a conversation	• follow and restate shifting topics in a conversation	• follow and summarize shifting topics in a conversation
	• list important ideas and supporting data in oral interactions between speakers (of the type that they themselves can carry out)	• identify ideas and details in more extensive and complex oral interactions between speakers (of the type that they themselves can carry out)	• connect and synthesize information obtained when listening to extensive and complex oral interactions between speakers (of the type that they themselves can carry out)
	• understand the main ideas and significant details of extended texts such as news and radio broadcasts	• analyze and reflect upon the meaning of extended texts such as academic lectures, and documentary and feature films	• evaluate and take notes on language (register, tone, syntax) and content of extended texts such as academic lectures, professional presentations, and feature films
	• understand the main ideas and significant details of live oral presentations	• comprehend academic presentations on a variety of topics by speakers from a variety of regions	• comprehend academic and professional presentations on unknown topics by speakers from a variety of regions

• begin to recognize different regional varieties and social registers of Spanish	• recognize different regional varieties and social registers of Spanish • identify phrases and collocations typical of formal academic language use	• compare different regional varieties and social registers of Spanish • become increasingly aware of phrases and collocations typical of formal academic language use
written texts		
• with respect to authentic written texts (of at least 4 pages) of a variety of genres and styles, on known and unknown topics: • summarize the main ideas and supporting data • answer most fact-based and some analytical reading comprehension questions • scan to locate information • skim to gain a sense of organization and content • exhibit an unreflected understanding of what was read • synthesize information in charts or outline form • begin to identify the tone and stance typical of formal, academic writing	• with respect to authentic written texts (of at least 5 pages) of a variety of genres and styles, on known and unknown topics: • analyze the main ideas and supporting data • answer all fact-based and most analytical reading comprehension questions • connect knowledge from texts with their academic field and content area of focus when appropriate • read to gain information • develop a more complete understanding, beyond initial impressions • represent the sequence of events in narratives • identify the tone and stance typical of formal, academic writing	• with respect to authentic written texts (of at least 7 pages as well as 1 book-length reading) of a variety of genres and styles, on known and unknown topics: • analyze and synthesize the main ideas and supporting data • answer all fact-based and all analytical reading comprehension questions • connect knowledge from texts with knowledge in a variety of areas • make observations, extrapolations and hypotheses • demonstrate increased understanding of the cultural nuances of meaning in written language

Appendix A
Descriptions of Target Student Abilities: Second-Year Spanish (continued)

Presentational Abilities	Spanish 11	Spanish 12	Spanish 13
written texts (cont.)	• research information (using the Internet, library materials, newspapers, etc.) on academic topics, including their field of interest or content area of focus	• recognize the tone of socio-cultural, political or professional orientations • research information on various academic topics, including their field of interest or content area of focus	• identify more subtle nuances of tone and stance typical of formal, professional or academic writing • research topics related to their academic and professional fields of interest

Presentational Abilities	Spanish 11	Spanish 12	Spanish 13
Students will be able to present information, concepts, and ideas to an audience of listeners or readers on a variety of academic and professional topics.	During the first quarter, students will exhibit growing confidence in presenting information to an audience, mainly on topics relating to the Spanish-speaking world, their academic interests and content area of focus. At the end of the quarter, students will be able to:	During the second quarter, students will increase in sophistication in presenting information about topics relating to the Spanish-speaking world as well as to their academic interests and content area of focus. At the end of the quarter, students will be able to:	During the third quarter, students will continue to increase in sophistication in presenting information about topics relating to the Spanish-speaking world, their academic and professional interests, and their content area of focus. At the end of the quarter, students will be able to

oral/written presentations	• carry out all presentational tasks of the previous quarter with greater sophistication, confidence and ease • become aware of and begin to employ appropriate (oral and written) presentational language • prepare oral and written presentations using authentic materials	• carry out all presentational tasks of the previous quarter with greater sophistication, confidence and ease • place increasing emphasis on appropriate (oral and written) presentational language • prepare oral and written presentations using authentic materials	• carry out all presentational tasks of the previous quarter with greater sophistication, confidence and ease • place increasing emphasis on appropriate (oral and written) presentational language • prepare oral and written presentations using authentic materials
oral presentations	• give rehearsed presentations, using some notes, of 10–15 minutes in length • answer questions about the presentation topic • orally summarize main points of authentic texts (both oral and written) and of class discussions • begin to summarize extemporaneously	• give less rehearsed presentations, using less extensive notes, of 15–20 minutes in length • begin to answer questions about the presentation topic extemporaneously • present oral analyses of authentic texts (both oral and written) and of class discussions • summarize extemporaneously • begin to compare and analyze extemporaneously	• give less rehearsed, more extemporaneous presentations of 20–30 minutes in length • give an audiovisual presentation using computer software (such as PowerPoint) • answer questions about the presentation topic extemporaneously • present oral analyses of authentic texts (both oral and written) and of class discussions • compare and analyze extemporaneously • begin to hypothesize and conjecture extemporaneously

Presentational Abilities	Spanish 11	Spanish 12	Spanish 13
oral presentations	• begin to monitor their speech for features not characteristic of formal academic language	• increasingly monitor their speech for features not characteristic of formal academic language	• increasingly monitor their speech for features not characteristic of formal academic language
written presentations	• write short reports in response to oral texts	• write reports in response to oral texts	• write more extensive reports in response to oral texts
	• write 3-page papers in expository prose	• write 5-page papers in expository prose	• complete a research paper of at least 10 pages and cite sources
	• begin to write persuasive papers stating and supporting an opinion	• write persuasive papers stating and supporting an opinion in supporting an opinion, begin to use logical reasoning (e.g., cause and effect), comparison and contrast	• write persuasive papers stating and supporting an opinion in supporting an opinion, use logical reasoning (e.g., cause and effect), comparison and contrast, and appropriate rhetorical devices
	• self-edit with increasing frequency	• self-edit with increasing frequency	• self-edit with increasing frequency
	• edit their work for high frequency errors	• edit their work for high frequency errors	• edit their work for high frequency errors
		• begin to edit their work for style, register and syntax appropriate to academic language	• edit their work for style, register and syntax appropriate to academic language
		• begin to employ appropriate rhetorical devices	• employ appropriate rhetorical devices

Appendix B
Student Progress Card • Spanish 11

Name: _____

How your progress card works: The attached checklist is designed to help you track your development in Spanish. As you learn to do each item, check the ( ) the "Yes" column. Your instructor or native conversation partner may concur with your assessment by placing his/her initials in the "Yes" column, or they may suggest areas for you to continue to work on.

Alternatively, you may instead wish to indicate your level of confidence in your ability to carry out each objective: do this by using a scale of 1 to 5, 5 being best, when you check off items in the "Yes" column.

Presentational Abilities

I have...	Yes (1-5)
become aware of and begun to employ appropriate (oral and written) presentational language	
I can...	
prepare oral and written presentations using authentic materials	
give rehearsed presentations, using some notes, of 10-15 minutes in length	
answer questions about the presentation topic	
orally summarize main points of authentic texts (both oral and written) and of class discussions	
often summarize extemporaneously	
write short reports in response to oral texts	
write 3-page papers in expository prose	
write a persuasive paper stating and supporting an opinion	
correct my writing much more often than I used to be able to	
use a dictionary to check my choice of words or phrases	
edit my papers for common mistakes	

Interpretive Abilities

I have...	Yes (1-5)
list important ideas and supporting data in oral interactions between speakers (of the type that I myself can carry out)	
follow shifting topics in a conversation	
understand the main ideas and significant details of extended texts such as news and radio broadcasts	
understand the main ideas and significant details of live oral presentations	
take notes on oral and written texts (e.g., articles, presentations, news reports)	
summarize arguments conveyed in oral presentations	
read authentic texts (texts designed for Spanish-speakers and not necessarily for language learners) and:	
scan the reading to locate information	
skim to gain a sense of the organization and content	
exhibit an unreflected ("off the top of my head") understanding of what I read	
synthesize information about the reading by using charts or outlines	
answer most fact-based and some analytical reading comprehension questions	
begin to recognize different regional varieties and social registers (e.g., slang versus formal speech) of Spanish	
begin to identify the tone and stance that is typical of formal, academic writing	
research information (using the Internet, library materials, newspapers, etc.) on academic topics, including my field of interest or content area of focus	

Interpersonal Communication

I can...	Yes (1-5)
discuss my...	
opinions	
views of events	
hopes	
fears	
doubts	
exchange information about my content area of focus (culture, international relations, etc.)	
use tú and usted appropriately	
address other Spanish-speakers appropriately according to their age, position or title, or according to other social rules	
use formal or informal language with other Spanish-speakers according to their age and how well I know them	
communicate...	
respect	
politeness	
gratitude	
friendliness	
clarify and restate information	
listen to and imitate how others speak	
seek support and feedback from others	
self-monitor and evaluate my language development	
correspond with friends (and family members)	
correspond with an individual or agency to request information, for instance:	
write to a local consulate to request tourist information	
write to a news service, Web site or news group to request	
information an a social or political event	
exchange information about my content area of focus (culture,	
international relations, etc.) using the Internet	
often correct myself when speaking	
respond to the work of my peers	

Chapter 6

Reconceptualizing the Goals for Foreign Language Learning: The Role of Pragmatics Instruction

Lisa DeWaard Dykstra, Clemson University

> *You are as many people as the number of languages you speak.*
> —Arabic saying

Introduction

In 1996, when the *Standards* were first introduced, they represented an unprecedented collaborative effort on the part of language educators from various language backgrounds. They were groundbreaking not only for the extensive cross-language collaboration that went into them, but also because for the first time a set of well-articulated goals were produced that validated the common-sense notions that language educators had about what was important to include in classroom teaching. Culture was moved to the forefront, not as a diversionary activity from the rigors of teaching linguistic form, but as an object of study in its own right. The *Standards* were an essential move toward the recognition that language learning is more than grammar learning, and they validated a focus on communication. In addition to the academic collaboration that took place, the *Standards* encouraged new thinking about the connections between theory and practice, with major foreign language textbook companies structuring their content to reflect the Five Cs, or goal areas, of foreign language learning. This had a filter-down effect: Given that many instructors plan their syllabi according to the textbook they use, the *Standards* were included in syllabi even by those who may not have understood their importance.

Many language educators hoped this new focus on a more holistic approach to language learning would move the discipline forward in a significant way. Five years later, the events of 9/11 demonstrated the depth of need for competent foreign language speakers in the United States and likewise revealed the dearth of truly competent multicultural individuals in American society. Though it is true that 5 years is a short time in which to hope for discipline-wide change, 11 years after the advent of the *Standards*, in 2007, the Modern Language Association (MLA) released a report on the state of foreign language teaching in higher education in which the lack of competent foreign language speakers was lamented—an indication that the profession still had not reached the goals set out in the *Standards*. The MLA report, *Foreign Languages and Higher Education: New Structures for a Changed World*, cites academic departmental structures and their internal fractures as potential culprits. Included in the report is a set of recommendations designed for application at the university level. However, in this chapter, I argue that neither set of goals—those of the *Standards* or the MLA report—is sufficient to address the needs of college-level instructors to develop truly proficient language professionals. Both documents lack a crucial element, namely learning goals that include transforming the self into another multilingual self. In the following pages I present an analysis of where and how both documents fall short. I also review the literature of an area of investigation—interlanguage pragmatics—that provides a point of departure for instruction that has the potential to lead to this important personal transformation in students.

The *Standards* are a framework for teaching and learning based around five goal areas: Communication, Cultures, Connections, Comparisons, and Communities. Briefly, the *Standards* propose that students be able to speak and understand language, to understand the practices and products of other cultures, to draw connections across disciplines, to make comparisons between the native and second language, and to have opportunities to connect with members of other speech communities. The area of focus in this chapter will be the confluence of Communication and Culture.

In their approaches to culture, both the *Standards* and the MLA report identify what they feel are essential issues in culture learning. The *Standards* advocate learning the "patterns of social interactions" (p. 47) of other cultures, by which they mean "rites of passage, the use of forms of discourse, the social 'pecking order' and the use of space" (p. 50). At first glance, they come close to advocating for individual transformation by stating that students "must be able to participate appropriately in face-to-face interaction with members of other societies" and "must develop… an awareness of how language and culture interact in societies. Students must apply this knowledge as they express and interpret events and ideas in a second language and reflect upon observations from other cultures" (p. 39). Although they do advocate for the development of sociocultural knowledge, unfortunately the primary emphasis in the *Standards* is learning to identify, examine, discuss, and analyze the patterns of practice described above. In addition, even though they state "[s]ome would argue that equivalent knowledge of language and cultural systems can be acquired in other types of courses (e.g., linguistics, anthropology). However, when students study another language and participate in communicative interactions, the actual experiential dimension makes such an understanding more real" (p.57), their indicators of performance include only minimal engagement in interaction or experiential dimension of any kind.

The MLA report also falls short in this area. The report states that it is imperative for language students to be trained to "reflect on the world and themselves through the lens of another language and culture … and grasp themselves as Americans—that is, as members of a society that is foreign to others" (pp. 4–5). The authors call for students to achieve "translingual and transcultural competence" (p. 3). In addition, the report defines what it calls "transcultural understanding" (p. 4) as "the ability to comprehend and analyze the cultural narratives that appear in every kind of expressive form—from essays, fiction, poetry, drama, journalism, humor, advertising, political rhetoric, and legal documents to performance, visual forms, and music" (p. 4). Even more important, the authors lament the fissures that exist in foreign language departments, yet they present an almost exclusively literature-based approach to understanding culture by focusing primarily on understanding narrative texts.

Neither set of recommendations puts sufficient emphasis on teaching students to interact with other cultures; both advocate learning about them and learning to understand them. This objective is simply not sufficient to produce competent multilinguals. In fact, it raises the argument that the *Standards* purport to address—can knowledge of another language and culture be learned without knowing the language? What, then, can bridge the gap? The transformation that results in a multilingual self necessitates a model that includes linguistic and cultural knowledge as well as interaction with the embedded elements of culture, namely the pragmatic elements. According to Chen (1996), "pragmatics takes the viewpoint of language users, especially of the choices they make, the sociocultural constraints they encounter in using the language, and the effects their language has on the interlocutor" (p. 3). The important feature here is the shift from viewing the student as a student *of* culture to a participant *in* intercultural interactions. Pragmatics instruction can provide a way to meet and exceed the goals of both the *Standards* and the MLA report. Much work has been done in the area of pragmatics over the last 20 years, and though the insights into how culture is enacted in language have been incorporated into models of communicative competence at the theoretical level (Bachman, 1990; Canale & Swain, 1980), the teaching of such elements has not made its way into mainstream pedagogy.

Although many foreign language texts include samples of pragmatically appropriate speech,[1] explicit discussions of pragmatics have not yet made their way into the most commonly used foreign language textbooks. Much emphasis in the pragmatics literature points to the need for the inclusion of pragmatic factors in language curricula, and many studies show that pragmatic features are teachable even at the beginning levels. Pragmatics study provides a path to the deconstruction of the original self by presenting to learners the idea that they operate within a culturally bound pragmatic system and by showing how their own system differs from the system in the target language.[2] In addition, pragmatics study presents a concept familiar to students—the idea that speakers use politeness strategies to frame discourse—along with the unfamiliar idea that the way to be polite in speech differs across cultures. What constitutes politeness can be seen as the basic building block of interaction for all interpersonal discourse, both oral and written. For example, in some cultures it is polite to use less direct speech when requesting, such as in American English, where modals are used to soften requests: "Would you mind handing me the salt?" The opposite is true in Russian, where the bare imperative is the polite form in a request: *"Daite mne, pozhaluista, sol'i"* (*Hand me, please, the salt*). Though both sentence structures communicate the same information, the use of a complicated American structure in Russian comes across as weak and overdone, whereas the use of a bare imperative such as "hand me" comes across as rude in the United States. When politeness is assumed to function identically across cultures, severe breakdowns in communication can occur. These breakdowns are more serious than grammatical lapses, because they often suggest a personality problem instead of a linguistic one (Takahashi & Beebe, 1987).

When politeness preferences are found to be distinct across cultures (and they almost always are), the sense of politeness as an anchor of communication gives way and the self as it has been understood is challenged. Instruction in pragmatics that illuminates cross-cultural politeness conventions can provide students with the tools they need to adapt their language—and themselves—to the second language culture. Pragmatics instruction can provide students with varying sets of workable frames for intercultural interaction and help them make informed choices about the self that they show in interaction. The result is not an assimilated self, but rather an amplified self with multiple functional schemata for communication. It is in this way that truly meaningful entrance into and interaction with the target culture can take place. The *Standards* and the MLA report both come up short because they either underemphasize or ignore this important aspect of language learning.

Analysis of the *Standards* and the MLA report

The National *Standards* for Foreign Language Learning

What the *Standards* did was revolutionary in the field of foreign language instruction. The authors set out to develop goals for foreign language education for the kindergarten through 12th (K-12) grade learning sequence. In addition, an articulation plan for how the *Standards* integrate with university-level instruction was added and, although not in the language-generic *Standards*, grade 16 progress indicators are included in many of the language-specific *Standards*. Along the way, they flesh out why language learning is important, what assumptions go into the idea of what makes for a fluent speaker of a second language, as well as provide foreign language instructors and program administrators a set of reasonable and attainable goals for their students. Each set of goals includes a list of indicators that the goal has been met. These indicators are broken down at three points along the K-12 learning sequence: 4th grade, 8th grade, and 12th grade. In the following paragraphs I will address specific points in the *Standards*, discussing what they propose, what they do, and where they fall short. I will focus exclusively on the language-generic *Standards* in this chapter.

As the *Standards* document itself declares, "the development of standards has galvanized the field of foreign language education" (p. 15). They set out a very clear goal that "ALL students will develop and maintain proficiency in English and at least one other language, modern or classical. Children who come to school from non-English-speaking backgrounds should also have opportunities to develop further proficiencies in their first language" (p. 7, emphasis in the original). Their theoretical position on what constitutes language learning is clearly based on models of communicative competence, although they do not state this explicitly. Such a position takes into account more than linguistic form and includes cultural knowledge, interdisciplinary study, comparisons with their own and the second language as well as engagement with the second language speech community. The goal is to raise language expectations in the United States to be equivalent to those in other countries (p. 14). In elaborating this point, they propose that language learning begin at the kindergarten or 1st-grade level and continue through the 12th-grade level. Along the way, they suggest multiple entry points into the curriculum that allow students to continue with one language while beginning another. These points correspond with the 5th- and 9th-grade levels, with the expectation that the 4th- and 8th-grade indicators are met for the first foreign language before a student studies a second foreign language.

The *Standards* address pragmatic competence both in their general statements on communicative competence and under their goal headings for Communication and Culture. They state that "[a]cquiring communicative competence... involves the acquisition of increasingly complex concepts centering around the relationship between culture and communication" (p. 26), and later, "[t]he language system is also much more than words and rules; it includes the sociolinguistic elements of gestures and other forms of nonverbal communication, of status and discourse style, and 'learning what to say to whom and when.' These elements form the bridge between language and culture and must be present if students are ever to learn to interact appropriately in the target language" (p. 33), and finally,

> [i]n essence, a communicatively competent individual combines knowledge of the language system with knowledge of cultural conventions, norms of politeness, discourse conventions, and the like, in order to transmit and receive meaningful messages successfully. In order to develop such competence, students must learn how interpersonal interactions are conducted in the cultures in which the language is spoken, how individuals use language effectively to achieve different purposes, how discourse conventions work, how oral and written texts are structured, and how the language system operates. They must weave this knowledge *together* in the process of transmitting and receiving meaningful messages . . . they must learn how to [transmit meanings effectively] by using a different language system and by following what may be very different rules of interpersonal interaction." (p. 40, emphasis in the original)

It is evident that the *Standards* argue for pragmatic competence in theory; however, their inclusion of pragmatics does not ensure that students will develop this competence. The *Standards* are successful in establishing a foreign language learning agenda for the 21st century and in creating a set of goals against which instructors can model their programs. They also provide a list of measureable indicators for determining whether the requisite learning has taken place. Where do they then fall short?

In their framework the authors of the *Standards* envision an academic environment in which students leaving high schools are thoroughly prepared in a foreign language and are ready to engage in content study in that language. The problem lies in the fact that there is a mismatch between the goals and the indicators. First of all, the authors do not describe how they arrived at the indicators. Although the indicators for achievement are not presented as a prescriptive and exhaustive list, nonetheless they reflect the relative weight placed on the various features of the curriculum. Of the 144 indicators listed with the Five Cs, only 4 of those relate to interactional abilities in pragmatics, with only one of the four aimed at the 12th-grade level. The most common approach to cultural difference found in the indicators is a focus on analyzing, knowing, and comparing—all skills that can be developed apart from interactional ability in the language.

The Modern Language Association 2007 Report

Whereas the *Standards* were aimed at student the K-12 level, with some articulation through the K-16 sequence, the MLA report addresses the dearth of competent foreign language speakers coming out of our college and university systems. The report begins with an examination of the state of the field following the post 9/11 tragedy and posits that one of the reasons the United States has had difficulty suppressing terrorism is our general lack of understanding of other languages and cultures. The imperative in both the *Standards* and the MLA report is the same; however, the events of 9/11 change the rosy idealism of the *Standards* to a stark national imperative in the MLA report. The report states that the "MLA is prepared to lead the way in the reorganization of language and cultural education around these objectives" (p. 2). To that end, it proposes language as a link between individuals and as a way for us to see ourselves more objectively. The stated goal is that American programs should prepare students who possess "translingual and transcultural competence" (p. 3) and who are able to "operate between languages" (p. 4).

The authors of the report describe how this competence can be taught, citing the use of literature, film, and other media as well as by directly teaching differences in meaning, mentality, and worldview. However, they stop short at advocating for proficiency in the language, which they define as the ability to "converse with educated native speakers on a level that allows both linguistic and metalinguistic exchanges" (p. 4) and knowledge of cultural subsystems, such as the mass media and social/historical narratives, among others (p. 5). Unlike in the *Standards*, where they address the criticism that these features could be learned in disciplines like history and anthropology, the MLA report does not respond to this potential argument, nor do they address pragmatic knowledge/ability in any way. The authors advocate for the personalization of language and culture (such as the recommendation that students learn to view themselves as possessors of a culture) but they do not advocate for personal transformation via the language studied.

What, then, are the conclusions of the MLA report? The report places blame for the lack of competent speakers firmly on the structuring of academic departments, stating that the divisions among the faculty who teach the language at the beginning levels (typically graduate student teaching assistants or instructors) and the faculty who teach content courses (typically the tenure-track cadre) are to blame. The fissures that exist along faculty and curricular lines (language versus literature) need to be repaired and, the authors warn, literature specialists need to be willing to share their decision-making power. In their model, linguists need to be included as well, since their research "enrich[es]" (p. 6) the overall curriculum.

Although a call for interdepartmental harmony is certainly commendable, the MLA report misses the mark in several ways. First of all, in presenting their ideas for how to implement change, the authors focus almost exclusively on literary goals in language study (e.g., understand the mass media, literary and social works) and not on interaction in the language, apart from citing the need for "enough linguistic proficiency in the language to converse with educated native speakers" (p. 4). Their approach implies an emphasis on linguistic and cultural competence, but not communicative competence. Moreover, their notion of cultural competence is based on literary texts as well; they state that students should "understand how a particular background reality is reestablished on a daily basis through cultural subsystems" (p. 4) such as media and political systems. In the following sections I describe pragmatics study and some of its theoretical underpinnings, and argue that inclusion of pragmatics instruction can help us bridge the gap between producing linguistically capable students and truly multicultural ones.

Pragmatics

An oft-cited definition of pragmatics is that of Crystal (1985): "Pragmatics is the study of language from the point of view of users, especially of the choices they make, the constraints they encounter in using language in social interaction and the effects their use has on other participants in the act of communication" (p. 240). In other words, communication involves interaction between interlocutors, and we cannot divorce interlocutors from their cultural backgrounds; both must be attended to in interaction. Kasper (1997) fleshes this idea out further by stating that "communicative action includes not only speech acts—such as requesting, greeting, and so on—but also participation in conversation, engaging in different types of discourse, and sustaining interaction in complex speech events" (para. 1). Any discussion of pragmatics takes engagement in conversation with another person as its point of departure. Learning about language and culture is different from experiencing the way the two come together in interaction. Successful communication is achieved only when each participant feels that the other is participating appropriately in the conversation.[3] When referring to appropriateness in language in pragmatics, it is understood that certain ways of speaking are, conversely, inappropriate. Appropriateness in speech refers to utterances that are delivered politely and without offense. Much of pragmatics theory draws on work in linguistic politeness. In the following paragraphs I discuss the concept of politeness as it relates to cross-cultural encounters, focusing primarily on the idea of universal politeness as postulated by Brown and Levinson (1987) as well as their theory of face and the controversy surrounding it.

"Face" in Brown and Levinson's work is defined as an "individual's self-esteem" (Brown & Levinson, 1987, p. 2) and is further divided into positive face and negative face. Positive face is defined as "the expression of solidarity" whereas negative politeness face is viewed as "the expression of restraint" (p. 2). Individuals are thought to have both kinds of face, and the preference for one over the other has been linked to cultural values; this linkage has caused the majority of the controversy surrounding the concept of face. For example, Bergelson (2003) has noted that Russians prefer positive face and that their desire for solidarity leads to greater directness of speech. In an interaction with an American interlocutor for whom negative politeness—or freedom from imposition—is valued, this kind of directness can be off-putting. Brown and Levinson suggest that certain types of speech threaten face, whereas others do not. A person's positive face is threatened when he or she faces disapproval or when treated with indifference. Conversely, a person's negative face is threatened when burdened by impositions, such as being asked to do something, or accept something, against one's wishes (Brown & Levinson, 1987, pp. 65–66). Brown and Levinson's view is that "[p]oliteness operates only when face interests are at risk, and actors are therefore required to make strategic choices about how to handle imminent face-threat" (Kasper, 2005, p. 60).

But is face, as Brown and Levinson conceptualize it, universal? A significant number of studies have been done since the original conceptualization of politeness in which face has been viewed through various cultural lenses. Much of the criticism leveled at this theory has come from those who feel that the concern for face that it espouses is based on Western models of human interaction (Fukada & Asato, 2004) which may not be adequate for explaining interaction in non-Western societies. Western societies here are contrasted with non-Western societies in that the former are viewed as individualistic whereas the many of the latter are considered to be communal in nature (Agyekum, 2004). Specifically, communal non-Western societies are likely to be more hierarchical which results in a different view of imposition, among other things. In addition, the idea that only some speech acts are face-threatening acts (FTAs) according to Brown and Levinson has been challenged by Scollon and Scollon (2001), who claim that the push-and-pull nature of face (which involves the simultaneous maintenance of the face of the speaker and that of the listener) results in the assertion that *"there is no faceless communication"* (p. 48, emphasis in the original). On one hand, criticism has been particularly heavy in research on Japanese, with critics of Brown and Levinson stating that their theory of face does not account for aspects of Japanese honorific usage and hierarchical culture (Ide, 1989), or that it does not allow sufficient room for cultural variability (Matsumoto, 2003). On the other hand, other examinations of Brown and Levinson's theory applied to the Japanese cultural context have found support for their theory, claiming that its universality can, in fact, account for the various levels of politeness in Japanese (Fukada & Asato, 2004; Pizziconi, 2003). The concept of face is, then, a framework for the examination of politeness preferences in interaction. Misunderstandings can arise when opposing frameworks clash in interaction.

The work by Brown and Levinson coincided with an upsurge in the related field of pragmatics. With the advent of a systematic theory of face,[4] pragmatics studies and politeness studies began to converge, at least in part. Pragmatics can be viewed as what people do in interaction as well the consequences of their choices in interaction, whereas linguistic politeness can be seen as one of the motivating factors regarding what undergirds specific choices and is useful in explaining why certain interactional consequences arise. In pragmatics, studies typically investigate one of 4 related areas: speech acts (studies are descriptive/comparative or acquisitional), other pragmatic features (formal versus informal forms of address, etc.), metapragmatics, and the issue of whether pragmatics routines are teachable.

I will briefly touch on speech act and feature studies before turning my attention to the issues of metapragmatics and teachability, both of which are linked to the transformational power of pragmatics.

Speech Act Studies

Speech act studies[5] (cf. for a sample of languages and approaches: Bacon, 1992; Barron, 2003; Billmyer, 1990; Bordería García, 2006; Boxer, 1996; Cohen & Olshtain, 1993; García, 1989; Hernández-Flores, 1999; Hinkel, 1997; Ide, 1998; Koike, 1989; Márquez Reiter, 2000; Mills, 1994; Owen, 2001; Rose, 2000; Shardakova, 2005) are by far the most common type of study in pragmatics research. These studies involve the investigation of a particular speech act (e.g., greetings, apologies, advice, leave-takings) in one or more cultures and use natural or elicited data to make determinations about preferences within a speech community.[6] Data reveal patterns that can be compared cross-culturally. In acquisitional studies learners may be asked to provide their second language responses to a prompt to determine whether their response is pragmatically native, pragmatically a transfer from the first language (L1), or somewhere in between. Results of these studies reveal the clash of approaches across languages and elucidate areas of potential difficulty for students.

Formality in Language

Another pragmatic variable of interest (and one that can cause trouble for study abroad students in particular) is the area of formal versus informal address. Many languages differ in their address term systems. For example, in Vietnamese, there are over 20 different kinship terms (Chiung, 1990), which is typical of the complexity of Asian languages. In most European languages, there is a pair of pronouns corresponding to the English *you*. French is often used as an example of this phenomenon because the pronoun *tu* (T) is used to address a single familiar person or friend, whereas *vous* (V) is used to address a group or a single person of greater age or higher status (Heilenman, Kaplan, & Tournier, 2006). In many western European countries, such as Spain, this distinction is losing prominence, but in Eastern European cultures, such as Russia, the feature still tends to hold great sociocultural importance.

Speakers who come from a language background that makes a T/V distinction have what Braun (1988) calls "address competence," (p. 31), which she defines as including "a repertory of forms of address for active use and a set of application rules, [and] also some knowledge of address variation within the community" (p. 31). Speakers, in addition to differing in their individual use, may also avoid the use of a direct pronoun, preferring instead to use passive or impersonal expressions, nominal reference, and the like (p. 55).

T/V use is always constrained by the politeness norms of the culture group in question. In her ethnographic monograph, Fitch (1999) examines the sociocultural importance of personal address as a function of the "communal understandings of the aspects of personhood" important in a given society. She states that the pronouns are used to refine relationships within a social structure by identifying where a relationship falls along the following continuums: "close/ distant, personal/professional, peers/rank-differentiated" (pp. 34–35). Furthermore, violations of expected usage can have important social repercussions. In her description of the address forms used in Colombia, Fitch cites three variables that affect address pronoun choice: gender, regional variation, and social class. Violations of address form usage allow conclusions to be drawn about the speaker, including a perceived deficiency of manhood, a "too-friendly" behavior, trying to identify with a social class of which they are not a member, or trying to curry favor (pp. 47–48).

Norris (2001) studied the sociocultural competence of learners of German by examining their ability to appropriately use the T/V pronouns *du* and *Sie* on the German Speaking Test. The German Speaking Test is a SOPI[7]-type test in which the "influence of contextual variables may be controlled" (p. 251). A microanalysis was conducted on 44 German Speaking Test tapes that involved a coding and quantification of address terms, taking into account contextual variables present in the task. He found that learners used the formal pronoun, *Sie* with more accuracy than its T counterpart, a finding he states may be attributed to its use as a "default" (p. 279) pronoun. In terms of the proficiency of the learners tested, there was a strict divide between learners below and above intermediate high on the ACTFL scale; the number of usages of an address pronoun per task more than doubled at that level. Corresponding data from beginners and advanced learners led to the conclusion that the lower the proficiency rating, the lower the level of sociopragmatic accuracy (p. 268). Finally, Norris notes that in other respects proficiency examinees did not necessarily show a corresponding knowledge of or control over address term behavior (p. 282). The data from this study showed how complex a sociopragmatic phenomenon the T/V feature is. His study points to a strong effect of proficiency on learner outcome on the task; however, Dykstra (2006) found no effect of proficiency on understanding of T/V.

Whereas the Norris study was a cross-sectional study of address term acquisition, Belz and Kinginger (2002) examined the development over time of proficiency with T/V by studying the acquisition of T/V in both French and German by learners participating in e-mail and online chat correspondence with native speakers of the respective languages over a time span of 60 days. Microgenetic analysis of the data, which was defined by the authors as "the observation of skill acquisition during a learning event" (Belz & Kinginger, 2003, p. 594), showed that the first learner showed increased consistency over the time of the experiment in her use of the French pronouns, as did the second learner (who studied German). The first learner received explicit feedback from her native speaker interlocutor, but showed no immediate uptake; the second learner experienced a "critical incident" (p. 205) regarding his pronoun use, which led to what the authors termed "social consequences" (p. 205). Overall the authors found that T/V is so inherently complex that learners do not acquire it per se, but rather that their awareness and sensitivity to the feature can be heightened. The importance of this feature of language cannot be understated because an error in usage can cause the speaker to be perceived as socially unacceptable—a consequence that can lead to breakdowns in the relationship that can be difficult, if not impossible, to repair.

Metapragmatics

Though the use of language requires knowledge and the ability to deploy a vast arsenal of linguistic forms, the term *appropriate use* includes an understanding of the impact of one's words and utterances beyond their literal comprehension within a given cultural context. Metapragmatics is the understanding a learner has about pragmatics; this area of study deals with the explicit knowledge a learner has of the pragmatic weight of language and the learner's ability to articulate what is acceptable and unacceptable in the target culture. Chen (1996) describes metapragmatics (from the standpoint of L2 metapragmatics) as "one level *above* pragmatics, [it] examines the implicit operational rules and the sociocultural patterns embedded in language use" (p. 5, emphasis in the original). Until learners understand on a metacognitive level the sociocultural function of their speech in interaction, they will not be able to enter fully into the target culture.

According to Mey (1993), metapragmatics represents another level of knowledge that is separate from pragmatics; pragmatics may represent the what, whereas metapragmatics can provide us with the motivation for why pragmatic principles operate the way that they do (p. 270). Metapragmatics is similar to metacognition, which has been defined as referring "to any knowledge or cognitive process that monitors or controls cognition" (Fernández-Duque, Baird, & Posner, 2000, p. 288). I would argue that this definition can be adapted to metapragmatics to describe any knowledge or cognitive process that monitors or controls pragmatic behavior or perception. In this way, metapragmatic knowledge serves to clarify the perception of pragmatic inference in the input as well as to guide learners in their use of pragmatic features of language. Wenden (1998) argues that metacognitive knowledge is statable or available to the learner in an explicit form that he or she can explain or describe.

Metapragmatics and metacognition part ways when we take into account the language learner as a language user—an important consideration in second language acquisition (Firth & Wagner, 1997). Although the field of metacognition is primarily concerned with cognitive processes and their application to tasks, metapragmatics is not a theoretical construct disconnected from the language user. In fact, metapragmatics takes into account both language users and the societal constraints facing them. Mey (1993) points out that "[t]he fact of the matter is that the whole of pragmatics ... is tightly bound up with what people do in their daily lives, and what they use language for. Nothing in our existence can be explained in isolation; neither can our language" (p. 271). In studying metapragmatics, teachers must take both levels of constraint into account—the metapragmatic knowledge possessed by the language learner and the societal preferences for how specific pragmatic routines are enacted; the tension between the two makes up part of the difficulty experienced in interacting in another language. In this way, learners can begin to achieve understanding of themselves as cultural actors working within culture-specific sets of politeness parameters.

How learners acquire this pragmatic competence is an area of debate. Textbooks typically include some guidelines for speech in interaction, but textbook presentations alone do not ensure acquisition. The literature suggests that teaching pragmatics routines may aid in understanding; however, few studies explore the degree to which students acquire appropriate metapragmatic knowledge in the classroom. To date, research on pragmatic perception has been scant; only a handful of studies that focus on listening for pragmatic information are available. In the following paragraphs I review four studies and discuss the important points of each.

First, in Cook's (2001) study, "Why can't learners of JFL (Japanese as a Foreign Language) distinguish polite from impolite speech?" JFL learners listened to three taped interviews in which three nonnative speakers of Japanese role-played a job interview. For the role plays, each applicant provided a Japanese speech sample for the prospective employer. Each applicant's sample was carefully constructed by the researchers to provide a continuum of appropriateness. The least desirable applicant spoke Japanese well, but displayed American interview strategies—strategies that are wholly inappropriate in the Japanese interview context (e.g., confidently stating one's abilities and how they can contribute to successful performance at the job in question). The students were asked to pick the best applicant according to the appropriateness of their speech. The second language learners consistently favored the worst applicant (the pragmatically American applicant), failing to recognize the serious inappropriateness of her speech style.

Second, Bardovi-Harlig and Dörnyei (1998) examined the grammatical and pragmatic awareness of English as a second language (ESL) and English as a foreign language (EFL) learners. One hundred seventy-three ESL learners and 370 EFL learners completed a language awareness listening task in which 20 video conversation scenes were shown. The final utterance of each conversation contained either (a) a pragmatic error, (b) a grammatical error, or (c) no error. Learners were asked to identify if an error occurred and to rate its severity along a scale of "not bad at all" to "very bad" (p. 260). Results indicated that the ESL learners identified more pragmatic errors than the EFL learners and rated them more severely. Conversely, the EFL learners recognized more grammatical errors and rated them more severely. Their results indicate a strong effect of the learning environment on pragmatic awareness.

In 2001 Niezgoda and Röver replicated Bardovi-Harlig and Dörnyei's study. They tested 48 ESL learners and 124 EFL learners with the same instrument, with somewhat different results. As in Bardovi-Harlig and Dörnyei's (1998) study, the ESL learners demonstrated a higher level of pragmatic awareness than the EFL group; however, the EFL learners in Niezgoda and Röver's study performed almost as well as the ESL learners in Bardovi-Harlig and Dörnyei's study, also outperforming their EFL population. Niezgoda and Röver attribute this finding to a combination of learner characteristics and learning environment; the EFL learners in their study were a select group from a highly specialized English language school. The authors suggest that a combination of capability and the desire to enter a career for which English would be a job requirement may have influenced the results of these learners. Also of interest is the high pragmatic awareness displayed by Niezgoda and Röver's low-proficiency EFL learners; possible explanations for this include that low-proficiency learners were free to choose English in the Czech Republic (high proficiency learners were required to take Russian) and thus had greater exposure to the language than might be expected of a low-proficiency learner. Also, these findings suggest that pragmatic awareness can be developed in an EFL setting.

Finally, Dykstra (2006) investigated pragmatic awareness in second language listening. In this study, learners of Russian completed two tasks to determine whether they were aware of (a) the sociocultural constraints inherent in the T/V contrast as well as (b) whether they could identify the use of pronouns in live speech as a key marker of a change in interpersonal dynamic between the speakers. To test the first question, a metapragmatic judgment task was administered to 32 learners of Russian at a domestic immersion program. On the task, learners were presented with a series of situations contextualized for their experience at that school and then were posed a question to answer in response to the situation. For each question four answer choices were presented: one that used the appropriate pronoun for the context, one that used the other pronoun, and the response choices "both are fine" and "I don't know." Results indicated that learner understanding of which pronoun was more appropriate was evident; however, there was no difference in performance across student levels, which was surprising because the range of experience with Russian was 4 weeks of study to 13 years. On the second task, which included learners from the domestic immersion program as well as a large Midwestern university, learners were shown a series of video clips from classic Soviet and Russian films and were asked to respond to questions such as, "When the dynamic between the speakers changed, what changed about their language as well?" Results on this task indicated that, in an active listening event, learners were not able to grasp the additional interpersonal information contained in the pronouns. Of note is that, again, there was no statistically significant difference across proficiency levels, nor did those students who spent time abroad in Russia score higher than others to a statistically significant degree. The only factor that provided a statistically significant result was the gender of the participant, with female learners outperforming male learners at both institutions. This unusual finding argues for the inclusion of the variable of gender in analyses of pragmatic results on a consistent basis.

The Teachability of Pragmatics

The review of the literature presented in this chapter indicates that learners can benefit from instruction in pragmatics routines. According to Bardovi-Harlig (1999), studies done in this area "are going to form the most significant body of acquisitional interlanguage pragmatics studies" (p. 702). Several empirical studies focusing on the teachability of pragmatics have found that instruction in pragmatics yields positive results; that is, students benefit from explicit classroom instruction in pragmatics. Kasper (1998) states that "it seems doubtful whether children or adults can acquire pragmatic competence without some direct teaching and assistance in noticing relevant information in the input" (p. 201), citing encouraging results in studies by Bouton (1994), House (1996), and Wildner-Bassett (1984) which bear out this claim. Furthermore, Tateyama et al. (1997) found that even beginning learners benefited from instruction in pragmatic routines.

Bardovi-Harlig (2001) reviewed the literature on the performance of speech acts (e.g., requests, refusals, apologies) to determine whether instruction of pragmatics is warranted. She concludes that (a) no instruction in pragmatics leads to a very different second language (in a pragmatic sense) from that of native speakers, and (b) that the job of instructors should be to help nonnative speakers find a happy medium between second language norms and their own first language comfort zone. Other studies (Billmyer, 1990; Kasper & Rose, 2002; Olshtain & Cohen, 1990) report a similar finding, namely that instruction in pragmatics aids in the development of pragmatic competence. Martínez-Flor (2006) concluded that instruction does make a difference, finding that both implicit and explicit instruction of pragmatic routines aided in the development of learner confidence in judging the appropriateness of native speaker utterances. Pearson (2006) investigated what learners think about being instructed in pragmatics and reported that students found instruction relevant and helpful in understanding Spanish speech act routines. Finally, Félix-Brasdefer (2006) investigated the use of a conversation-analytic framework as a vehicle for the instruction of Spanish pragmatic routines. He sets out a series of detailed recommendations for instruction, which he has also posted on a Web site[8] for interested instructors.

It is clear that research in pragmatics is complex; in addition to learner variables such as the learners' first language and individual desire to emulate (or not to emulate) second language pragmatics routines, other factors such as the style of instruction that learners are accustomed to bear on the effectiveness of instruction. However, it is also clear that knowledge of pragmatics routines and the ability to navigate both first and second language pragmatics are assets in successful communication in a second language. Moreover, the literature points consistently to success with teaching these routines in the classroom.

Discussion

In this chapter I have examined where the *Standards* and the MLA report fall short and have proposed pragmatics instruction as a potential solution to make up for this shortfall. I have defined pragmatics and provided an overview of the literature in the field. In the following section I will discuss how instruction in pragmatics can provide the catalyst for the personal transformation that I argue is lacking in the field.

As I stated previously, monolingual students are often unaware that they are members of a culture group, and that the politeness and pragmatic conventions of their group permeate their discourse in all interactions. The realization that they are cultural actors anchored in a specific politeness paradigm is a crucial first step in the process of personal transformation, because without this step it will be difficult for them to understand that other functional paradigms exist. Both the *Standards* and the MLA report highlight the need for this first step, but both recommend learning about the culture to overcome it; research on interlanguage pragmatics recommends participation in the culture to overcome it. The first step, therefore, is the development of awareness. Pragmatics researchers have been investigating various ways to raise awareness and to design appropriate classroom strategies to develop metapragmatic awareness, or the awareness that pragmatics systems exist and how they function differentially across the L1 and target speech cultures. Though the *Standards* do address this feature (and have six indicators that deal with the development of pragmatic awareness), the MLA report does not address metapragmatic awareness at all.

Raising metapragmatic awareness involves two phases: making students aware they have a system in the first place and often use pragmatic conventions without realizing it, and then presenting them with appropriate frames of interaction within the target culture. In the past, research on pragmatics has taken as its goal the attainment of native speaker ability with pragmatics. Recently, however, there has been a shift in the field that recognizes that (a) not all native speakers behave in the same way, but that certain general patterns within each speech culture group do exist, and (b) proficient bilinguals show somewhat different patterns than monolingual natives, resulting in the idea that a more appropriate standard to set for our students is that of the proficient bilingual. Using this standard, learners are more likely to understand and navigate both native and target-language pragmatic systems in interaction, while also retaining personal choice in interaction—a point of crucial importance to learners, since the development of an alternative way to communicate implies a shift in one's own identity.

The concept of identity can be described in a variety of ways. It can be defined in terms of gender, race, level of education, region of residence, cultural heritage, and so forth. We are just beginning to understand the effect that bilingualism and multilingualism have on the perceived self-image of the learner; a more complex self can emerge and may take the learner by surprise. The stark contrast between the former and new self is often most strongly felt upon return home from a study abroad experience when culture shock about being in one's own culture sets in.[9]

It is important to note that transformation does imply that a shift in identity results in a bi/multilingual person, distinctly different from a monolingual person. Pragmatic learning promotes flexibility for shifting language code as well as cultural code. Moreover, pragmatics instruction does not produce mindless cultural copiers but rather provides students with various workable frames from which they can choose the degree to which they assimilate into the target culture cultural system. In addition, instruction in pragmatics can reduce stereotyping, such as "Russians are rude" and "Japanese are deferential," by exposing learners to the fact that there are different systems within which speakers work but that are polite and appropriate within that culture. In this way the learner can find that all people are cultural actors—influenced, but not controlled by cultural values. Pragmatics instruction can provide students with the opportunity to work in another frame, exposing their cultural discomfort in a safe space where stakes are low so that they can adjust to the new system before, for example, going abroad, to ensure that they experience a smoother, more successful transition into the target culture.

The *Standards* in their current form address pragmatics but do not place enough emphasis on it. Likewise, the MLA report sets admirable goals but identifies only part of the problem: the fissures in academic departments. Ironically, after calling for greater intradepartmental unity, the report spells out a list of recommendations that come from an almost entirely literary perspective.

If pragmatics instruction has the potential to provide students with a vehicle for personal transformation that results in a multilingual self, and if instruction in pragmatics routines has been found to give positive results in this area, then it stands to reason that language program directors must begin to incorporate it into our curricula. The questions that remain are (a) at what level should we begin and (b) how should we do it. Though some researchers (Canale & Swain, 1980) advocate for saving pragmatics instruction for the more advanced levels, much research points to positive results in pragmatics with beginning college learners (Bordería García, 2006; Dykstra, 2006; Huth & Taleghani-Nikazin, 2006; Konovalova, 2007; Pearson, 2006). Studies on the teachability of pragmatics routines suggest that they can be taught explicitly, and more and more resources are being made available to practitioners to help bridge the gap. The idea proposed in this chapter builds on the positive work in the *Standards* and the MLA report by including pragmatics instruction thereby providing students with opportunities to develop the cultural flexibility necessary to be truly multilingual individuals.

Notes

1. See, among others, Spinelli, García, and Flood's (2009) Spanish text *Interacciones*, Gallego and Godev's (2004) Spanish text *Más allá de las palabras*, and Gor Davidson, Gor, and Lekic's (1996) Russian text *Live from Moscow: Stage One*.

2. This is not to suggest that there is a single pragmatic system operating in each foreign language.

3. It is not within the scope of this chapter to include a discussion on other aspects of communicative intent, for example, Grice's Maxims of Communication (1975) or Lakoff's rules of pragmatic competence (1973).

4. The conceptualization of politeness around the imagery of "face" is not Brown and Levinson's invention; many languages have expressions related to politeness phenomena that include reference to a metaphorical "face," such as the English expressions "to save face," "to lose face," and so on.

5. Of interest is a bibliography of studies on speech acts sponsored by the Center for Advanced Research on Language Acquisition at the University of Minnesota, http://www.carla.umn.edu/speechacts/bibliography/index.html.

6. I am using "speech community" loosely here, not in the specific way that it is used by authors working within the communities of practice framework. Here I simply mean a dialect group of a particular language.

7. Simulated Oral Proficiency Interview, a test developed by the Center for Applied Linguistics. For more information, see http://www.councilnet.org/papers/Winke.doc.

8. http://www.indiana.edu/~discprag

9. It is not within the scope of this chapter to investigate in detail the implications of bilingualism on identity, but see Mantero (2007) and Niño-Murcia and Rothman (2008) for excellent introductions to this topic.

References

ACTFL. (2006). *Standards for Foreign Language Learning: Preparing for the 21st Century.* (1996). Yonkers, NY: National Standards in Foreign Language Education Project.

Agyekum, K. (2004). *The socio-cultural concept of face in Akan communication.* Retrieved March 28, 2006, from http://www.benjamins.nl/jbp/series/P&C/12-1/art/0005a.pdf

Bachman, L. F. (1990). *Fundamental considerations in language testing.* Oxford: Oxford University Press.

Bacon, S. (1992). The relationship between gender, comprehension, processing strategies, and cognitive and affective response in second-language listening. *The Modern Language Journal, 76,* 160–178.

Bardovi-Harlig, K. (1999). Exploring the interlanguage of interlanguage pragmatics: A research agenda for acquisitional pragmatics. *Language Learning, 49,* 677–713.

Bardovi-Harlig, K. (2001). Empirical evidence of the need for instruction in pragmatics. In K. R. Rose & G. Kasper (Eds.), *Pragmatics in language teaching* (pp. 13–32). New York: Cambridge University Press.

Bardovi-Harlig, K., & Dornyei, Z. (1998). Do language learners recognize pragmatic violations? Pragmatic vs. grammatical awareness in instructed L2 learning. *TESOL Quarterly, 32,* 233–259.

Barron, A. (2003). *Acquisition in interlanguage pragmatics: Learning how to do things with words in a study abroad context.* Amsterdam: John Benjamins.

Belz, J. A., & Kinginger, C. (2002). The cross-linguistic development of address form use in telecollaborative language study: Two case studies. *The Canadian Modern Language Review/La revue canadienne des langues vivantes, 59,* 189–214.

Belz, J. A., & Kinginger, C. (2003). Discourse options and the development of pragmatic competence by classroom learners of German: The case of address forms. *Language Learning, 53,* 591–647.

Bergelson, M. (2003). Russian cultural values and workplace communication styles. In *Communication studies 2003: Modern anthology* (pp. 97–112). Volgograd: Peremena.

Billmyer, K. (1990). "I really like your lifestyle": ESL learners learning how to compliment. *Penn Working Papers in Educational Linguistics, 6,* 31–48.

Bordería-García, A. M. (2006). *The acquisition of pragmatics in Spanish as a foreign language: Interpreting and giving advice.* Unpublished Ph.D. dissertation, University of Iowa.

Bouton, L. F. (1994). Conversational implicature in the second language: Learned slowly when not deliberately taught. *Journal of Pragmatics, 22,* 157–167.

Boxer, D. (1996). Ethnographic interviewing as a research tool in speech act analysis: The case of complaints. In S. M. Gass & J. Neu (Eds.), *Speech acts across cultures: Challenges to communication in a second language* (pp. 217–239). Berlin: Mouton de Gruyter.

Braun, F. (1988). *Terms of address: Problems of patterns and usage in various languages and cultures.* Berlin: Mouton de Gruyter.

Brown, P., & Levinson, S. (1987). *Politeness: Some universals in language usage.* New York: Cambridge University Press.

Canale, M., & Swain, M. (1980). Theoretical bases of communicative approaches to second language teaching and testing. *Applied Lingusitics, 1,* 1–47.

Chen, H. J. (1996). *Cross-cultural comparison of English and Chinese metapragmatics in refusal.* Unpublished Ph.D. dissertation, Indiana University.

Chiung, Tan. (1990). Russkie formy obrashcheniia na ty/Vy v zerkale v'etnamskogo iazyka. [The Russian forms of address ty/Vy mirrored in Vietnamese]. *Russkii iazyk za rubezhom, 3*, 94–99.

Cohen, A. D., & Olshtain, E. (1993). The production of speech acts by EFL learners. *TESOL Quarterly, 27*(1), 33–56.

Cook, H. M. (2001). Why can't learners of JFL distinguish polite from impolite speech styles? In K. Rose & G. Kasper (Eds.), *Pragmatics in language teaching* (pp. 80–102). New York: Cambridge University Press.

Crystal, D. (1985). *A dictionary of linguistics and phonetics* (2nd ed.). Oxford: Blackwell.

Davidson, D. E., Gor, K. S., & Lekic, M. D. (1996). *Live from Moscow: Russian Stage One* (Vol. 1). Dubuque, IA: Kendall/Hunt Publishing Company.

Dykstra, L. (2006). *On pragmatic perception: Do learners of Russian perceive the sociocultural weight of the address pronouns?* Unpublished Ph.D. dissertation, University of Iowa.

Félix-Brasdefer, C. (2006). Teaching the negotiation of multi-turn speech acts: Using conversation-analytic tools to teach pragmatics in the FL classroom. In Bardovi-Harlig, K., C. Félix-Brasdefer & A. S. Omar (Eds.), *Pragmatics and language learning*, (Vol. 6 pp. 165–198). Manoa, Hawai'i: National Foreign Language Resource Center.

Fernández-Duque, D., Baird, J. A., & Posner, M. I. (2000). Executive attention and metacognitive regulation. *Consciousness and Cognition, 9*, 288–307.

Firth, A., & Wagner, J. (1997). On discourse, communication, and (some) fundamental concepts in SLA research. *The Modern Language Journal, 81*, 285–300.

Fitch, K. (1999). *Speaking relationally: Culture, communication, and interpersonal connection.* New York: Guilford Press.

Fukada, A., & Asato, N. (2004). Universal politeness theory: Application to the use of Japanese honorifics. *Journal of Pragmatics, 36*, 1991–2002.

Gallego, O., & Godev, C. (2004). *Más allá de las palabras: A complete program in intermediate Spanish.* Hoboken, NJ: John Wiley and Sons, Inc.

García, C. (1989). Apologizing in English: Politeness strategies used by native and non-native speakers. *Multilingua, 8*, 3–20.

Grice, H. P. (1975). Logic and conversation. In P. Cole & J. Morgan (Eds.), *Syntax and semantics, 3: Speech Acts* (pp. 41–58). New York: Academic Press.

Heilenman, L. K., Kaplan, I., & Tournier, C. (2006). *Voilà! An introduction to French* (5th ed.). Boston: Thomson Learning.

Hernández-Flores. (1999). Nieves Hernández-Flores, Politeness ideology in Spanish colloquial conversation: The case of advice. *Pragmatics, 91*, 37–49.

Hinkel, E. (1997). Appropriateness of advice: DCT and multiple choice data. *Applied Linguistics, 18*, 1–26.

House, J. (1996). Developing pragmatic fluency in English as a foreign language: Routines and metapragmatic awareness. *Studies in Second Language Acquisition, 18*, 225–252.

Huth, T., & Taleghani-Nikazm, C. (2006). How can insights from conversation analysis be directly applied to teaching L2 pragmatics? *Language Teaching Research, 10*, 53–79.

Ide, R. (1998). "Sorry for your kindness": Japanese interactional ritual in public discourse. *Journal of Pragmatics, 29*, 509–529.

Ide, S. (1989). Formal forms and discernment: Two neglected aspects of universals of linguistic politeness. *Multilingua, 2*, 223–248.

Kasper, G. (1997). *Can pragmatic competence be taught?* (NetWork #6) [HTML document]. Honolulu: University of Hawai'i, Second Language Teaching & Curriculum Center. Retrieved March 28, 2006, from http://www.nflrc.hawaii.edu/NetWorks/NW06

Kasper, G. (1998). Variation in interlanguage speech realization. In S. M. Gass, C. Madden, D. Preston & L. Selinker (Eds.), *Variation in second language acquisition* [Multilingual matters, 49, 50] (pp. 37–58). Clevedon: Multilingual Matters.

Kasper, G. (2005). Linguistic etiquette. In S. Kiesling & C. Paulston (Eds.), *Intercultural discourse and communication* (pp. 58–77). Malden, Mass.: Blackwell Publishing.

Kasper, G., & Rose, K. R. (2002). *Pragmatic development in a second language.* Oxford: Blackwell.

Koike, D. A. (1989). Pragmatic competence and adult L2 acquisition: Speech acts in interlanguage. *The Modern Language Journal, 73,* 279–289.

Konovalova, I. L. (2007). *Grammar and agency in L2 pragmatic proficiency: Toward an integrated view of L2 pragmatics.* Unpublished Ph.D. dissertation, University of Alabama.

Lakoff, R. (1973). *The logic of politeness; or, minding your p's and q's.* CLS 10: Chicago Linguistics Society.

Mantero, M. (2007). *Identity and second language learning: Culture, inquiry and dialogic activity in educational contexts.* Charlotte, NC: Information Age Publishing.

Márquez Reiter, R. (2000). *Linguistic politeness in Britain and Uruguay: A contrastive analysis of requests and apologies.* Amsterdam, Netherlands: John Benjamins.

Martínez-Flor, A. (2006). The effectiveness of explicit and implicit treatments on EFL learners' confidence in recognizing appropriate suggestions. In K. Bardovi-Harlig, C. Félix-Brasdefer & A. S. Omar (Eds.), *Pragmatics and language learning* (Vol. 6, pp. 199–226). Manoa, Hawai'i: National Foreign Language Resource Center.

Matsumoto, Y. (2003). Reply to Pizziconi. *Journal of Pragmatics, 35*(10–11), 1515–1521.

Mey, J. L. (1993). *Pragmatics: An introduction.* Malden, MA: Blackwell.

Mills, M. H. (1994). Context, culture and (non) transference of speech acts: Requesting a simple favor in Russian and English. *Collegium, 1,* 69–83.

Modern Language Association. (2007). Foreign languages and higher education: New structures for a changed world? Retrieved February 1, 2008 from the World Wide Web: http://www.mla.org/flreport

Niezgoda, K., & Röver, C. (2001). Pragmatic and grammatical awareness: A function of learning environment? In K. R. Rose & G. Kasper (Eds.), *Pragmatics in language teaching* (pp. 63–79). New York: Cambridge University Press.

Niño-Murcia, M., & Rothman, J. (2008). *Bilingualism and identity: Spanish at the crossroads with other languages.* Amsterdam, Netherlands: John Benjamins.

Norris, J. M. (2001). Use of address terms on the German Speaking Test. In K. Rose & G. Kasper (Eds.), *Pragmatics in language teaching* (pp. 248–282). New York: Cambridge University Press.

Olshtain, E., & Cohen, A. D. (1990). The learning of complex speech act behavior. *TESL Canada Journal, 7,* 45–65.

Owen, J. (2001). *The development of pragmatic competence in request speech acts by students of Russian.* Unpublished Ph.D. dissertation, Bryn Mawr College.

Pearson, L. (2006). Teaching pragmatics in Spanish L2 courses: What do learners think? In K. Bardovi-Harlig, C. Félix-Brasdefer & A. S. Omar (Eds.), *Pragmatics and language learning* (Vol. 6, pp. 109–134). Manoa, Hawai'i: National Foreign Language Resource Center.

Pizziconi, B. (2003). Re-examining politeness, face and the Japanese language. *Journal of Pragmatics, 35*(10–11), 1471–1506.

Rose, K. R. (2000). An exploratory cross-sectional study of interlanguage pragmatic development. *Studies in second language acquisition, 22,* 27–67.

Scollon, R., & Scollon, S. W. (2001). *Intercultural communication* (2nd ed.). Malden, MA: Blackwell Publishing.

Shardakova, M. (2005). Intercultural pragmatics in the speech of American L2 learners of Russian: Apologies offered by Americans in Russian. *The Journal of Intercultural Pragmatics, 2,* 423–451.

Spinelli, E., García, C., & Flood, C. E. G. (2009). *Interacciones* (6th ed.). Boston: Heinle, Cengage Learning.

Takahashi, T., & Beebe, L. M. (1987). The development of pragmatic competence by Japanese language learners of English. *JALT Journal, 8,* 131–155.

Tateyama, Y., Kasper, G., Mui, L., Tay, H., & Thananart, O. (1997). Explicit and implicit teaching of pragmatics routines. In L. Bouton (Ed.), *Pragmatics and language learning* (Vol. 8, pp. 163–77). Urbana, IL: University of Illinois at Urbana-Champaign.

Wenden, A. (1998). Metacognitive knowledge and language learning. *Applied Linguistics, 19,* 515–537.

Wildner-Basset, M. (1984). *Improving pragmatic aspects of learners' interlanguage.* Tübingen: Narr.

Chapter 7

Using Online Forums to Integrate the *Standards* into the Foreign Language Curriculum

Ana Oskoz, University of Maryland, Baltimore County

Introduction

Culture is a fundamental component of foreign language (FL) education, but achieving an understanding of different cultures beyond impressionistic and subjective accounts is still a slippery endeavor (Dubreil, 2006). Since their publication in 1996, the *Standards* have become a framework that has increasingly shaped the professional discourse (Aguilar-Stewart & Santiago, 2006; Ketchum, 2006; Lee, 1999; Polanski, 2004; Scott & Huntington, 2002, 2007; Weist, 2004; Yamada & Moeller, 2001). Yet, despite numerous references to the *Standards* in professional venues and FL textbooks, their actual application and integration into the college-level FL curriculum remains a challenge.

Technology—particularly Web-based applications—is ideally suited to provide an environment that supports such integration. In particular, discussion forums—online bulletin boards where anyone can read others' messages, write responses, raise questions, and expect answers—have provided an ideal environment for students to share knowledge and cultural perspectives. Face-to-face or synchronous online interactions offer little time for reflection; however, the time lag between reading and posting in an asynchronous online discussion forum provides time to "understand others' ideas and develop a detailed response or posting" (Meyer, 2003, p. 60). In contrast to other forms of asynchronous discussion, online discussion boards are inclusive environments that enhance collaborative discourse among larger groups of students. Widely used to enhance cultural development and connections (Furstenberg, Levet, English, & Maillet, 2001; Hanna & Noy, 2003; Lomicka, 2006), the discussion board has been instrumental in enhancing students' cultural reflections (Lamy & Goodfellow, 1999; Wildner-Basset, 2005). Though discussion boards have frequently been used to connect students from different cultures (Furstenberg et al., 2001; Hanna & Noy, 2003; Lomicka, 2006), there is also a valuable place for online forums within the domains of any FL classroom (Wildner-Basset, 2005).

This chapter describes an FL program at the University of Maryland, Baltimore County, that integrates both in-class and online discussions to reflect on and interpret a variety of documents and experiences. In particular, it focuses on how Intermediate Spanish I students used such interactions to explore, analyze, and reflect on cultural topics. We collected data while applying the five goals of the *Standards*: Communication, Cultures, Connections, Comparisons, and Communities. Subsequent analysis of the data showed that the online forums can become springboards for students to share, debate, and interpret information; to gain knowledge and understanding of other cultures; to reflect and make connections to additional bodies of knowledge; to compare and contrast the target culture with their own; and to participate in multilingual and multicultural communities. In particular, this study focuses on the extent to which online forums become spaces where students can develop an understanding of the target culture as defined by the *Standards*.

Literature Review

The *Standards* in Foreign Language Education

Byram's (1997, 2000) intercultural communicative competence (ICC) and the *Standards for Foreign Language Learning in the 21st Century* (1999, 2006) frameworks have provided directions for conducting intercultural studies as well as promoting cultural understanding in FL classrooms. Whereas studies examining ICC have focused on students' interactions among classes in other countries (Belz, 2003; Liaw, 2006; Lomicka, 2006; Müeller-Hartmann, 2006; O'Dowd, 2006; Schneider & von der Emde, 2006), the *Standards* provide a pedagogical framework specifically targeted to the needs of students in FL classrooms. As well as fostering direct interactions with target culture communities (Polanski, 2004; Yamada & Moeller, 2001), the *Standards* have suggested other goals, which include, among others, incorporation of knowledge from, and to, other academic disciplines and interpretations of a wide range of target culture documents and linguistic comparisons across languages. Practical research has confirmed the value of this approach (Abrams, 2002; Aguilar-Stewart & Santiago, 2006; Ketchum, 2006; Scott & Huntington, 2007).

The five goals are further subdivided into two or three standards each. The goal of Communication includes Interpersonal, Interpretative, and Presentational modes of interaction. In the Interpersonal mode, learners learn how to converse in culturally appropriate environments; in the Interpretive mode, learners understand and interpret written and spoken language; in the Presentational mode, learners focus on "the presentation of information, concepts and ideas in spoken or written modes" (p. 45). As Scott and Huntington (2007) pointed out, interpretation was previously understood as a solitary process; however, interpretation is now understood "as a process involving a (re)construction of meaning through interaction" (p. 4). In this mode learners discuss, analyze, explain, and interpret their own beliefs, experiences, and newly acquired knowledge with others.

Perspectives, practices, and products, among which there is a mutually influential relationship, are at the heart of Cultures, the second goal. The term *perspectives* is understood as the worldview, attitudes, and belief systems that frame what speakers of a language think and do (*Standards*, p. 45). *Practices* refers to the understanding of a society's patterns of behavior, what to do when and where. *Products* include both tangible and intangible manifestations, such as aesthetic expressions with or without a utilitarian purpose—literature, art, music, pottery, musical instruments, or functional objects used in everyday life. Though sometimes it is possible to identify particular products, there is often a blurred distinction between products and practices when pertaining to social, political, economic, or cultural institutions (*Standards*, p. 45). For example, the family or health systems are institutions that cannot be understood outside the societies in which they are established. It is also true that none of these elements—products, practices, and perspectives—are static; in fact, "[they are] constantly in flux and changing" (Lange, 1999, p. 60). This continuous evolution facilitates a journey of constant discovery for the learner.

The third goal, Connections, concerns the links students make either to other academic disciplines or to their personal interests. When studying a foreign language, learners apply information studied and acquired in other subject areas to the products and practices learned about the target culture; this application of information allows them to acquire new knowledge and perspectives (*Standards*, p. 56). The connections are further supported by the use of the Internet, which allows learners to seek out, analyze, and process material of interest at ease, and makes them better informed citizens of the world (Abrams, 2002; Lee, 1998).

Comparisons, the fourth goal, invites students to understand the concept of culture by comparing the products, perspectives, and practices of various cultures, as well as by analyzing and comparing the different linguistic systems. Although the concept of culture permeates all of the standards, the second standard of Comparisons is even more closely linked to the goal of Culture (Lange, 1999) because, as Fantini (1999) pointed out, the goal of Culture would be incomplete without "explicitly and systematically engaging in Comparisons" (p. 166). Finally, as posited in the Community goal, the needs of today's changing society and the possibility of worldwide instant communication require a skilled, multilingual workforce. The ability to communicate in another language for work or for leisure purposes enables students to better understand other cultures as well as to practice their languages skills.

Technology and the *Standards* in the Foreign Language Classroom

Since their initial publication in 1996, the *Standards* have been relatively absent in the college-level FL classroom curriculum. Yet, they have also been integrated through the use of literary texts (Aguilar-Stewart & Santiago, 2006; Ketchum, 2006; Scott & Huntington, 2002, 2007; Weist, 2004), traditional pen-and-paper pen-pals (Yamada & Moeller, 2001), video (Herron, Cole, Corrie, & Dubreil, 1999; Herron, Dubreil, Cole, & Corrie, 2000), ethnographic studies (Bateman, 2002), and tutoring services to the community (Polanski, 2004). Computer technologies such as the World Wide Web (Abrams, 2002; Dubreil, Herron, & Cole, 2004; Lee, 1998, 1999; Walz, 1998) or synchronous and asynchronous computer-mediated communication have also become tools to achieve standards-based classrooms (Abrams, 2002; Lee, 1999).

The integration of synchronous and asynchronous computer-mediated communication for cultural development is not a new concept (Dubreil, 2006; Ducate & Lomicka, 2005; Furstenberg et al., 2001; Lamy & Goodfellow, 1999; O'Dowd, 2006). From the wide range of synchronous and asynchronous tools, online forums provide "a critical common space in which [to] share and verify hypotheses and points of view, to ask for help deciphering meanings of words and concepts, and to constantly negotiate meanings and interpretations" (Bauer, deBenedette, Furstenberg, Levet & Waryn, 2006, p. 35). Moreover, students' use of online discussion forums has encouraged and enhanced their cultural reflections (Wildner-Basset, 2005). Participating in culturally focused discussion boards eases the process of developing "an awareness of other people's world views, of their unique way of life, and of the patterns of behavior which order their word" (*Standards*, p. 47). The time-delayed nature of online forums also allows students to bring in outside material and experiences (Kol & Schcolnik, 2008), creating an ideal environment for connected learning.

The collaborative interaction promoted by discussion boards supports a constructivist, learner-centered approach that develops learners' autonomy, as well as aids "the development of the learners' capacity for a more active, reflective, and self-directed approach to [...] learning" (Wenden, 1999, p. 2). The instructor is not the authoritative figure and sole distributor of knowledge, but is an open-minded facilitator of learning (Barnett, 1999) who guides and supports learners in the process of knowledge construction. Rather than being passive consumers of facts that merely reproduce the teacher's knowledge, learners become active contributors by dynamically participating in asynchronous online discussions; thus, they take responsibility for their own learning as they take part in the collaborative construction of knowledge (Dawson, 2006; Jonassen, 1994; McLoughlin & Lee, 2008; Weasenforth, Biesenbach-Lucas, & Meloni, 2002).

Use of the First Language

The *Standards* advocate the use of culturally appropriate ways for learners to engage with the target or second language (L2). Learners may interpret information available through the L2, or discover practices, products, and perspectives related to the FL; they may also reinforce knowledge of other disciplines through the L2, demonstrate growing linguistic understanding, and access information and forms of entertainment only available to the speakers of the target language. Yet, the *Standards* also state that learners "can use critical thinking skills in beginning language classes by conducting some tasks in English" (1999, p. 35). Though there is no doubt that the use of the first language (L1) might delay the extent to which students can achieve linguistic development in the L2, the use of the L1 allows learners to embark on a reflective process and to develop an early ability to hypothesize about different cultural systems. Novice and intermediate language learners need opportunities to engage in reflective interpretations and discussions (Abrams, 2002; Scott &

Huntington, 2007), and the L1 is the cognitive tool that allows them to achieve higher levels of cultural reflection and understanding (Antón, DiCamilla, & Lantolf, 2003).

An increasing number of studies have examined and confirmed the benefits of the use of the L1 in the FL classroom (Antón & DiCamilla, 1998; Belz, 2002; Chavez, 2002). In particular, some studies have recommended the use of the L1 to avoid the possible dominance by a group of individuals related to differing levels of proficiency (Bauer et al., 2006); others have allowed students with low L2 proficiency to use the L1 to encourage more sophisticated reflection and analysis (Abrams, 2002; Elola & Oskoz, 2008; Scott & Huntington, 2002, 2007). In this context, using the L1 enables students to express their views fully and in detail; it helps them formulate questions and hypotheses clearly, and to deal with complex, nuanced information unfettered by limited linguistic abilities (Bauer et al., 2006). Even when encouraged to use the target language, students may resort to their L1 to exchange "substantial ideas regarding their cultural inquiry" (Abrams, 2002, p. 144). Therefore, to move beyond content focused on utilitarian communicative needs—e.g., dining or entertainment activities—and to engage students in the level of critical thinking that allows them to be reflective, it is advisable to conduct activities primarily in the learners' L1 at the beginning and intermediate levels (Abrams, 2002; Elola & Oskoz, 2008; Scott & Huntington, 2007).

Methodology

The study was conducted during the spring semester of 2007. The objective was to examine the extent to which students, through their interactions with the online discussion boards, explored, analyzed, and reflected on different cultural topics. The aim was for students to investigate journals and Web sites and to reflect upon and share their discoveries about the target culture as well as their own culture(s). Students were asked to address, via the discussion boards, several topics initiated in the classroom. The data were subjected to a qualitative content analysis; however, because of space limitations, this chapter focuses on the quantitative than on the qualitative interpretations of students' comments.

Participants and Setting

The course in question was a third-semester, intermediate-level Spanish class of 20 students from the University of Maryland, Baltimore County. For the discussion board experience, which was completed as homework, the instructor decided to use small groups and randomly divided students into 5 groups of 4 students each to ensure all students were heard in the cultural discussions. Following the suggestions put forth by Arnold and Ducate (2006) and Weasenforth et al. (2002), each group had a leader who was in charge of starting, maintaining, and summarizing/ closing the cultural discussion, as well as 3 members who answered the various postings. The role of the leader rotated among all the group participants so that each student was the leader for one discussion board and a regular member for three discussions. Though all students could potentially see other groups' discussions (all the groups belonged to the course discussion board), students responded only to their own group members. The instructor provided the triggering prompt but did not participate in the online discussion. She told the students they were in control of the task and they could take the discussion in any direction they chose based on their own research.

Tasks

Students participated in 4 in-class and online discussions related to the chapter topics of the course textbook (bargaining, advertising, issues concerning the elderly, and urban versus suburban lifestyles; see Table 1). The textbook used for this class has some sections that deal with cultural comparisons by distinguishing

Table 1
Description and Aims of Tasks

Task	Title	Description	Aim
1	Bargaining	Students examine commerce in Spanish-speaking countries. Focusing on "bargaining," students investigate whether it is a customary practice, and if so, where and when.	Students reflect on commerce practices in Spanish-speaking countries and in the United States.
2	Publicity	Students research, read, and reflect upon the graphic and textual content in movies, music, and ads both in Spanish-speaking countries and in the United States.	Using movies and ads as a springboard, students discuss what these products say about a particular society.
3	The elderly	Students find information in journals and in Web sites about the elderly in Spanish-speaking communities. Students compare their findings to their knowledge and expectations regarding family life in the United States and Spanish-speaking countries.	Students discuss the concept of family, and the role of the elderly, in Spanish-speaking countries. Students also address the effect of modern life in traditional practices.
4	Living in the city	Students compare urban and rural settings in Spanish-speaking countries and in the United States. They examine common modes of transportation in Spanish-speaking countries and in the United States.	Students reflect on concepts of space and efficiency. They reflect on the economic, geographic, and historic causes of the differences that lead to the creation of various urban settings.

and reflecting on similarities and differences between the United States and several Spanish-speaking countries. Topics arising from the book were initially discussed in class, and all leaders responded to the same instructor-initiated prompt; however, students' cultural discussions tended to move in diverse directions according to the learners' interests and curiosity, or based on the information they gathered while researching the Internet, journals, or other sources.

Procedure

Each task took about 3 weeks to complete. At the beginning of each chapter, the instructor and students had an initial face-to-face in-class discussion related to the cultural topic. To continue the conversation, the instructor posted a prompt shortly thereafter based on the topic. In each prompt, students were encouraged to examine practices, products, and perspectives (*Standards 2.1* and *2.2*), make connections with their personal interests and other academic disciplines (*Standards 3.1* and *3.2*), and compare among cultures (*Standard 4.2*); only the prompt in task 1 asked students to comment on their experiences using the target language if they were bargaining in a Spanish-speaking area (*Standard 5.1*). (See Figure 1, pp. 100–101, for an overview of the standards.) The leader of each group answered the initial prompt and expanded the scope and depth of the discussion by seeking out additional information and then posting, explaining, and elaborating on the new information, as well as asking questions intended to elicit a critical and thoughtful response, thereby continuing the discussion. The group members also searched for additional information, then posted, described, elaborated, and asked further questions to keep the conversation going. At the end of the chapter, teacher and students discussed the asynchronous online comments and findings in their regular in-class discussions.

Data Analysis

The electronic postings made during the semester, which constituted the data for the study, were subjected to qualitative content analysis using the *Standards*. Given that most students used the L1, it was expected that standards related closely to the use of the target language would not be present in the resulting data analysis. As shown in Table 2, however, the data revealed the presence of other standards. For the goal of Communication, it was evident that students used the L1 to understand and interpret written and spoken language on a variety of topics. Under the goal of Culture, there were instances in which students exhibited an awareness of the relationship between practices and perspectives as well as between products and perspectives of the culture studied. For the goal of Connections, students appeared to broaden their knowledge of other disciplines through the foreign language and learned to recognize the distinctive viewpoints that are available through the foreign language. With regard to the goal of Comparisons, students revealed an understanding of the concept of culture by comparing their own culture with the target culture. Finally, for the goal of Community, students showed evidence that they were learning the language for personal enjoyment and enrichment.

Table 2

Descriptions and Examples of the Standards Found in the Data

Standard	Description	Example
Communication	**1.2** Students understand and interpret written and spoken language on a variety of topics.	"I also found a map of the metro in Madrid, which was very similar to the DC metro map. Not very exciting or anything, but just thought I'd put it in. http://www.metromadrid.es/acc_resources/pdfs/Plano_Metro_2008.pdf"
Cultures	**2.1** Students demonstrate an understanding of the relationship between practices and perspectives of the culture studied.	"Research has shown me that the families in Spain and in other Spanish-speaking countries feel a strong responsibility when it comes to caring about the elderly members of their family."
	2.2 Students demonstrate an understanding of the relationship between products and perspectives of the culture studied.	"I found that there are only 2.5 nursing home beds for every 100 elderly people in Spain."
Connections	**3.1** Students reinforce and further their knowledge of other disciplines through the foreign language.	"As someone who is heavily involved in the arts, I've tried to make a kind of 'working definition' for myself."
	3.2 Students acquire information and recognize the distinctive viewpoints that are only available through the foreign language and its culture.	"After what I read, I think the traditions in [Spanish-speaking] countries are a lot stronger than they are here."
Comparisons	**4.2** Students demonstrate understanding of the concept of culture through comparisons of the cultures studied and their own.	"The major difference that the United States has from many other countries is that there is very little to help the elderly. There is Medicaid and Social security, but unlike Spain, the government does not help the elderly as much. Still, most American elderly people do not live with their children; I believe that it is much more of a cultural difference that has been shaped by American ideals with the 'American dream' wanting to be fulfilled."

(*continued*)

Table 2
Descriptions and Examples of the Standards Found in the Data (continued)

Standard	Description	Example
Communities	**5.2** Students show evidence of becoming life-long learners by pursuing the study of language for personal enjoyment and enrichment.	"My sister and I became haggling fiends [by speaking Spanish]."

The unit of analysis used was the speech segment, which is defined as "the smallest unit of delivery, linked to a single theme, directed at the same interlocutor" (Henri & Rigault, 1996, p. 62); this analysis was also used by Arnold and Ducate (2006) to examine students' interactions on discussion boards. Previous studies found that boundaries are not always clear when analyzing different units (Lomicka & Lord, 2007; Rourke, Anderson, Garrison & Archer, 2001). Therefore, the following sentence "after what I read, I think the traditions in [Spanish-speaking] countries are a lot stronger than they are here" was coded as being representative of *Standard 3.2* (referencing to a new point of view learned from the readings) and *Standard 4.2* (comparison between Spanish-speaking countries and the United States). The researcher and a second coder independently analyzed all students' entries on the first discussion board for the presence of the *Standards*, reaching an inter-rated reliability score of 0.90. After this initial session, the researcher independently analyzed the remaining three discussion boards.

Results

Although learners' cultural perceptions might not be fully captured in the online forums, the online discussions still provide us with a window to observe learners' understanding regarding the products, practices, and perspectives, of different cultures. As the researcher collected evidence of students' connections between FL learning and other disciplines or interests, she was able to evaluate the extent to which the discussions are a forum for cultural awareness. The quantitative results of the discussion board analysis are presented here in the following order: (a) descriptive statistics of the discussion boards, (b) Friedman tests, and (c) correlations of the standards. With regard to the statistical analyses, because of the small sample size, nonparametric statistics were used. Given the low number of students in each group, the results need to be interpreted with caution. They do, however, provide some preliminary insights.

Descriptive Statistics

As shown in Table 3, not all standards were addressed in students' interactions. The two standards most evident in the data were *Standard 2.1* (171 instances, 39.86%) and *Standard 2.2* (112 instances, 26.1%); these percentages illustrate that the students' primary focus was on the goal of Culture, namely on the practices, products, and perspectives of the other culture as well as their own. The third most frequent standard addressed was *Standard 4.2* (105 instances, 24.47%). Fourth and fifth were *Standard 3.2* (23 instances, 5.36%) and *Standard 3.1* (11 instances, 2.56%) under the goal of Connections. For this goal students tended to make connections with their own interests rather than with other academic disciplines. *Standard 5.2* came sixth (6 instances, 1.39%), followed finally by *Standard 1.2* (0.23%).

Table 4 presents descriptive statistics for all of the standards that were represented in the data. Therefore, medians are provided in addition to means and standard deviations.

Table 3
Raw Numbers for the Standards Present in the Discussion Boards (DBs) (N = 4)

Standard	DB1	DB2	DB3	DB4	Total
Communication (1.2)	0	0	0	1	1 (0.23%)
Culture (2.1)	44	32	80	15	171 (39.86%)
Culture (2.2)	14	38	41	19	112 (26.1%)
Connections (3.1)	2	6	0	3	11 (2.56%)
Connections (3.2)	1	0	18	4	23 (5.36%)
Comparisons (4.2)	25	25	35	20	105 (24.47%)
Communities (5.2)	6	0	0	0	6 (1.39%)
Total	92 (21.45%)	101 (23.54%)	174 (40.56%)	62 (14.45%)	429 (100%)

Table 4
Descriptive Statistics for the Presence of the Standards in All the DBs (N = 4)

Standard	Median	M	SD	Range
Communication (1.2)	0.0	0.25	0.50	0–1
Cultures (2.1)	38.0	42.75	27.54	15–80
Cultures (2.2)	28.5	28.00	13.50	14–41
Connections (3.1)	2.5	2.75	2.50	0–6
Connections (3.2)	2.5	5.75	8.34	0–18
Comparisons (4.2)	25.0	26.25	6.29	20–35
Communities (5.2)	0.0	1.50	3.00	0–6

Table 5

Friedman Test Across the Standards Using Subscales (N = 4)

Standard	Mean Rank	X^2 (df)
Communication (1.2)	1.75	19.78 (6)**
Cultures (2.1)	6.25	
Cultures (2.2)	6.00	
Connections (3.1)	3.00	
Connections (3.2)	3.00	
Comparisons (4.2)	5.75	
Communities (5.2)	2.25	

**p < .01

Table 3 illustrates that some standards, for example, *Standards 2.1, 2.2,* and *4.2,* appeared more frequently than others did in the discussions. To determine statistically whether some standards were appearing more frequently than others, the Friedman test was applied (see Table 5). The Friedman test, a nonparametric test, is appropriate for assessing mean differences across multiple measures that are measured on the same subjects. For the current study, the "subjects" are the discussion boards and the "measures" are the frequencies with which each of the seven standards appeared. To conduct the Friedman test, first the frequency with which each standard appeared in each discussion was ranked so that standards that appeared more frequently in that discussion were given higher ranks, and standards that appeared less frequently were given lower ranks. The mean ranks (averaged across the discussions) for each standard are presented in Table 5. The Friedman test computes whether the mean ranks are significantly different across the 7 standards.

Table 5 shows the mean ranks and the chi-square statistic for the Friedman test which was significant, $X^2(6) = 19.78, p < .01$, indicating that the standards do not appear with the same frequency in the online discussions. The Friedman test does not allow for specific posthoc tests to pinpoint where these differences lie in the presence of the standards. Therefore, the Wilcoxon Sum Rank Test was used to compare pairs of standards for differences; this analysis did not show any of the differences as significant (i.e., $p < .05$). However, four sets of differences were found to be marginally significant (all *ps* = .07) as follows: (1) between Communication (*Standard 1.2*) and Cultures (*Standard 2.1*), Cultures (*Standard 2.2*), and Comparisons (*Standard 4.2*); (2) between Communities (*Standard 5.2*) and Cultures (*Standard 2.1*), Cultures (*Standard 2.2*), and Comparisons (*Standard 4.2*); (3) between Connections *(Standard 3.1)* and Cultures (*Standard 2.1*), Cultures (*Standard 2.2*), and Comparisons (*Standard 4.2*); and (4) between Connections (*Standard 3.2)* and Cultures (*Standard 2.1*), Cultures (*Standard 2.2*), and Comparisons (*Standard 4.2*). These marginally significant differences

Table 6
Spearman Correlations Between the Standards (N = 4)

	1.2	2.1	2.2	3.1	3.2	4.2	5.2
Communication (1.2)	1						
Cultures (2.1)	−.78	1					
Cultures (2.2)	−.26	.40	1				
Connections (3.1)	.26	−.80	−.20	1			
Connections (3.2)	.26	.40	.40	−.80	1		
Comparisons (4.2)	−.82	.95*	.63	−.63	.32	1	
Communities (5.2)	−.33	.26	−.78	−.26	−.26	.00	1

*$p \leq .05$

suggest that we might have found more evidence of Cultures (*Standards 2.1* and *2.2*) and Comparisons (*Standard 4.2*) than of Communication (*Standard 1.2*), Communities *(Standard 5.2)*, Connections (*Standards 3.1* and *3.2*) if we had had more students and more discussion boards.

As suggested by Fantini (1999), there are some standards closely linked to others, such as Comparisons and Cultures; thus, it was of interest to know whether there was any statistical correlation between these two or any of the standards. Table 6 presents Spearman rank correlations between all pairs of standards, which shows that only two correlations were statistically significant: Comparisons (*Standard 4.2*) and Cultures (*Standard 2.1*) were highly positively correlated ($\rho = .95$, $p = .051$), and Comparisons (*Standard 4.2*) and the two Cultures standards (*Standards 2.1* and *2.2*) combined were also highly positively correlated ($\rho = .95$, $p = .051$). The results of these correlations support Fantini's claims regarding the connections between Comparisons and Cultures, and in particular to *Standard 2.1.*

Discussion

Qualitative and quantitative analyses provided information about the extent to which discussion boards facilitate cultural discussions. The qualitative analysis revealed that the three most frequent standards addressed were the ones related to Cultures and Comparisons (*Standard 4.2*). Although the Wilcoxon Sum Rank Test did not indicate any significant differences ($p < .05$), the near-significant differences ($p = .07$) between the more frequent appearances of *Standards 2.1* and *2.2* and *Standard 4.2* when compared with the less frequent appearances of the rest of the standards illustrate a consistently higher prevalence of these three in the discussion boards.

With regard to Cultures, learners focused their discussion on the practices, products, and perspectives of the other culture. From the two standards included in this goal, while still addressing *Standard 2.2,* learners showed a tendency to focus on the target culture behaviors in everyday life (*Standard 2.1*). For example, in task 3 one group of students examined the topic of the scarcity of residential communities (product) for the elderly and considered the underlying beliefs and values that made that product almost nonexistent in Spanish communities (perspectives). They developed some understanding of the practice of grandparents living with or near the family by looking at it from the point of view of traditional Spanish values (perspectives). In keeping with constructivist views of learning, students demonstrated an awareness of the products, practices, and perspectives of the target culture, but they also understood that these customs were not static but rather dynamic, changing according to political and economical forces. As such, one student commented on the shift in family customs when he said: "[Latino] families aren't necessarily not taking care of their elders like in the past because they dislike traditions, but because of forces that are beyond their control, mostly economic." Through the interactive discussions, students engaged in a process of reflection and discovery that provided them with a dynamic picture of the family as an organization in constant flux (Lange, 1999).

Given that the concept of culture is integrated into the goal of Comparisons (Fantini, 1999; Lange, 1999), it was not surprising to find that the Comparisons (*Standard 4.2*) closely followed the two standards of Cultures. Learners often made comparisons between products, practices, and perspectives of the United States and the target culture(s). The connection between *Standard 4.2* and *Standard 2.1* is evident in the Spearman rank correlations. Although not significant, the moderate correlation between *Standards 4.2* and *Standard 2.2* suggests that there might have been significant results if there had been more students. Therefore, these results support Lange's and Fantini's claim that there is a close link between *Standard 4.2* and *Standards 2.1* and *2.2*. Though the comparison among cultures was constantly present in students' interactions, the linguistic comparison (*Standard 4.1*) was nonexistent. Learners' failure to address *Standard 4.1* was likely the result of communicating in the L1 rather than in the target language. It might also have been a result of the particular task that emphasized the comparisons of products, practices, and perspectives rather than linguistic comparisons.

Results for the Connections goal illustrate that students linked the tasks either to areas of their own interest or to other curricular disciplines. Whether students made more connections to other academic subjects or to topics of their own choice depended on the topic of the task. Task 2, for example, which focused on the world of publicity, elicited several connections to some students' majors in art or studies. For example, one student wrote "As a major, I can understand the need for a designer to want to make images that the public has not seen, and will be drawn to" (*Standard 3.1*). Task 3, however, which centered on the elderly, provoked more personal reactions, instigating students to search more widely for information that allowed them to recognize and learn about other viewpoints only available through the FL culture. For example, after reading about how elders are perceived in Spanish-speaking countries, students wrote comments such as "after what I read, I think it's clear that the 'typical' American family and Latino family have different ways of caring for their elderly," or, "Maybe the system is just designed for the caretaker to make all the decisions. That is an interesting situation, because in America, if we did not grant one patient's rights, it would be all over the news. And of course, someone would be sued!" Reading about practices different from their own provided the students with a new perspective of the world.

The goal of Communities was addressed by a few students who demonstrated the use of the target language for personal purposes in the target language community (*Standard 5.2*). When talking about *el regateo* (bargaining), several students commented on their experiences of using the target language for this type of economic transaction. One of them even commented on how not speaking the language could be a handicap: "Many, many times I saw travelers who spoke very little Spanish attempting to buy something from the vendors and paying the full price." The topic of *el regateo* was perfectly suited for demonstrating how the use of language can help achieve one's personal purposes, because it asked the students whether they had ever tried bargaining in a Spanish-speaking area. Given that several students had traveled to Spanish-speaking countries, such as Guatemala, Mexico, and Spain, or had lived in predominantly Spanish-speaking areas, it was not surprising that some of them could discuss real examples of using the L2 in the target language community. The three other tasks, however, did not involve the same level of interaction with the community, and thus students were less likely to show that type of language engagement.

The goal of Communication was the least represented in the discussion boards. Students' use of the L1 implied that they were reluctant to engage in conversations about providing and obtaining information, or expressing emotions, in the L2. Similarly, students' presentation of information, concepts, and ideas in the discussion boards was conveyed in their L1. Regarding interpretation, students were required to search for information in books, journals, and Web sites. The instructor did not specify whether the material should be in the L1 or the L2. Students, on their own initiative, searched Web sites written primarily in English, which echoes Abrams's (2002) remarks about students' preference for using L1 sources. The use of L1 Web sites can be questioned, however, because "decisions of what is and is not translated into English often has political and social implications" (*Standards*, p. 451). Nonetheless, students tend to seek out material that puts them in contact with new information and perspectives. Using L1 resources, therefore, should not in itself be regarded as detrimental to the cultural learning process. Undoubtedly, directly accessing cultural Web sites in the target language allows students to advance their knowledge of lexical items and idiomatic expressions; develop their reading skills and strategies; and obtain valuable, updated information that improves their understanding of cultural phenomena (Lee, 1999). Yet, unless closely guided by the instructor, students can become overwhelmed when confronted with a language they only partially comprehend. Therefore, provided that students still access reliable and current information, deemphasizing the use of the target language at lower proficiency levels will probably result in cultural gains.

In keeping with constructivist views, the combination of the time-delayed discussion board experience and Internet information retrieval empowered the students in the discovery of products, practices, and perspectives. Although the level of engagement with the task varied among the groups (one of the groups was not as culturally engaged in the discussion board as the other groups), by taking ownership of their own discussions, students became active researchers of the target culture. An excellent example of this occurred when the students engaged in a polemical debate regarding an advertisement that had been banned from the Spanish media. It was also the students who found that despite many of the elderly living with their families and actively contributing to the family well-being, "the biggest community for the elderly has a waiting list of over 20,000." Upon learning this statistic, the student who found this information questioned whether the elderly stayed home because they wanted to or because they lacked other alternatives. This question then propelled that particular student group into a process of discovery about current social practices regarding not only the elderly but also of their possibly stereotyped and static view of the "Hispanic family."

During these discussions, the instructor also became a student through reading the conversations and listening to her students, showing a shift from being an authoritative figure to an attentive one who was open to reconsidering her perceptions of both cultures. Despite the relevance of the instructor-as-student role, her position as architect, composer, and facilitator remains fundamental (Dubreil, 2006). In the class, the instructor needs to model behaviors, post further questions, and challenge students' conclusions to go beyond stereotypes or that which is simplistic. When discussing the banned advertisement designed by a famous Italian fashion house, students seized on the idea of Spain being a conservative country. The instructor's intervention was necessary for students to consider the causes of the Spanish government's actions, thus, challenging and reinvigorating students' discovery of the target culture.

Practical Suggestions

The use of online forums provided an environment that allowed students to engage in meaningful interactions in which they reflected upon practices, products, and perspectives of the target culture and their own. Yet, it is possible to achieve higher levels of cultural discussions. The following suggestions are outlined to increase the value of the online discussion board as a space for reflection and engagement, where students can better achieve the goals established by the *Standards*.

- Design online tasks that allow students to reflect upon practices, products, and perspectives, and compare among cultures. Provide tasks that encourage students to make connections with other academic disciplines and to their own interests. Students will understand that studying a second language strengthens their knowledge of other disciplines and provides them with a different perspective only accessible through the target language culture.
- Provide models for students on the types of discussions that lead to discoveries of the target language culture. By showing excerpts from

students' discussion board posts, along with examples including comparisons, connections, and discussions of different cultural aspects, students will understand what is expected in terms of their own discussions.

- Monitor and participate in the online discussions. Though learners still retain the overall control of the conversation, the instructor, maintaining the type of guided instruction typical of a constructivist teacher (Weasenforth et al., 2002), can model a coherent construction of meaning. In the discussions, challenge students to inquire beyond stereotypes by examining the underlying causes.

- Be flexible with the directions students take in the online discussions. Challenging prompts should be designed from the beginning of the semester to ensure that they are well integrated with the topics of the course (Weasenforth et al., 2002). However, in-class discussions might lead each group to pursue sub-topics of interest to them. While still keeping the task in mind, the instructor needs to be flexible and open-minded and even encourage new discoveries.

- Bring the students' online reflections to the classroom. While students are participating in the discussions, read their comments, share them with the class, and connect them to the in-class interaction.

- Communicate the expectations for the assignment by providing students with the evaluation criteria in advance. These should explicitly reflect the purpose of the online discussions.

Conclusion

The study presented in this chapter arose from the need to understand the effectiveness of the discussion board to enhance cultural communication as framed by the *Standards*. The analysis of students' interactions illustrates that, to varying degrees, utilizing the online discussion boards allowed students to: (a) examine practices, products, and perspectives of the target culture; (b) demonstrate understanding of the concept of culture through comparisons of the cultures studied and their own; (c) reinforce and further their knowledge of other disciplines through the discussion of the target culture; (d) present evidence of use of the target language for personal enjoyment; and (e) understand and interpret written language. Through their interactions in the discussion boards, students joined forces to discover, interpret, and reflect upon the target culture as well as their own.

Despite the positive results from the study, several limitations should be addressed in future studies. First, the small number of students provides an enlightening but still preliminary view of the potential of the discussion boards for cultural discussions. Further studies with larger groups of students would provide more generalizable results that can be applied in other contexts. Second, students in this study used the L1 for all their interactions and discussions. This choice meant that standards closely related to the use of the target language, such as *Standard 1.1* and *Standard 1.3*, were not evident in the data. Although we acknowledge the value of using the L1 at the elementary and intermediate levels, the use of the L2 at higher levels of instruction would provide additional data about the use of the target language in similar cultural discussions. More proficient students should be expected to use the target language to interact, search for, and read information as well as to present their findings. Third, the tasks described in this study required students to discuss practices, products, and perspectives within the target culture and to make comparisons across cultures. Other tasks could require students to make connections to their personal interests and academic disciplines. In addition to allowing the introduction of further social dimensions such as economic, geographic, or historic issues, making connections beyond the foreign language classroom will encourage deeper exploration of the dynamic concept of culture.

This study aims to add to the research that examines best practices for integrating the *Standards* in the FL classroom at the university level. As with the interpretation of conventional or unconventional texts, ethnographic studies, or pen-pal interactions, this chapter illustrates that discussion boards are another venue to promote meaningful interactions about cultural topics. Their time-delayed nature, which encourages reflection and allows learners to research and consult outside sources, makes them ideal settings for the discovery of the ever-changing nature of target cultures.

References

Abrams, Z. (2002). Surfing to cross-cultural awareness: Using Internet-mediated projects to explore cultural stereotypes. *Foreign Language Annals, 35*, 141–160.

Aguilar-Stewart, J., & Santiago, K. (2006). Using the literary text to engage language learners in a multilingual community. *Foreign Language Annals, 39*, 683–696.

Antón, M., & DiCamilla, F. (1998). Socio-cognitive functions of L1 collaborative interaction in the L2 classroom. *The Canadian Modern Language Review, 54*, 314–342.

Antón, M., DiCamilla, F., & Lantolf, J. (2003). Sociocultural theory and the acquisition of Spanish as a second language. In B. Lafford & R. Salaberry (Eds.), *Spanish second language acquisition. State of the science* (pp. 262–284). Washington, DC: Georgetown University Press.

Arnold, N., & Ducate, L. (2006). Future language teachers' social and cognitive collaboration in an online environment. *Language Learning & Technology, 10*, 42–66.

Barnett, M. A. (1999). Whose course it is? In M. A. Kassen (Ed.), *Language learners of tomorrow: Process and promise* (pp. 125–149). Northeast conference reports. Lincolnwood, IL: National Textbook Company.

Bateman, B. (2002). Promoting openness towards culture learning: Ethnographic interviews for students of Spanish. *The Modern Language Journal, 86*, 318–331.

Bauer, B., deBenedette, L., Furstenberg, G., Levet, S., Waryn, S. (2006). The cultura project. In J. A. Belz & S. L. Thorne (Eds.), *Internet-mediated intercultural FL education* (pp. 31–62). Boston, MA: Heinle & Heinle.

Belz, J. (2002). Identity, deficiency, and first language use. In C. Blyth (Ed.), *The sociolinguistics of foreign language classrooms* (pp. 209–248). AAUSC Issues in Language Program Direction. Boston, MA: Heinle.

Belz, J. (2003). Linguistic perspectives on the development of intercultural competence in telecollaboration. *Language Learning & Technology, 7*, 68–117. Retrieved February 8, 2007, from http://llt.msu.edu/vol7num2/belz/default.html

Byram, M. (1997). *Teaching and assessing intercultural communicative competence.* Clevendon, UK: Multilingual Matters.

Byram, M. (2000). Assessing intercultural competence in language teaching. *Sprogforum, 18,* 8–13.

Chavez, M. (2002). The diglossic foreign-language classroom: Learners' views on L1 and L2 functions. In C. Blyth (Ed.), *The sociolinguistics of foreign language classrooms* (pp. 163–208). AAUSC Issues in Language Program Direction. Boston, MA: Heinle.

Dawson, S. (2006).Online forum discussion interactions as an indicator of student community. *Australasian Journal of Educational Technology, 22,* 495–510.

Dubreil, S. (2006). Gaining perspective on culture through CALL. In L. Ducate & N. Arnold (Eds.), *Calling on CALL: From theory and research to new directions in foreign language teaching* (pp. 237–268). Texas State University: CALICO.

Dubreil, S., Herron, C., & Cole, S. (2004). An empirical investigation of whether authentic web sites facilitate intermediate level French language students' ability to learn culture. *CALICO Journal, 22,* 41–61.

Ducate, N., & Lomicka, L. (2005). Exploring the blogosphere: Use of web logs in the foreign language classroom. *Foreign Language Annals, 38,* 410–421.

Elola, I., & Oskoz, A. (2008). Blogging: Fostering intercultural competence development in foreign language and study abroad contexts. *Foreign Language Annals, 41,* 421–444.

Fantini, A. E. (1999). Comparisons: Towards the development of intercultural competence. In J. K. Phillips & R. M. Terry (Eds.), *Foreign language standards: Linking research, theories and practices* (pp. 165–218). ACTFL Foreign Language Education series. Lincolnwood, IL: National Textbook Company.

Furstenberg, G., Levet, S., English, K., & Maillet, K. (2001). Giving a virtual voice to the silent language of culture: The cultura project. *Language Learning & Technology, 5,* 55–102. Retrieved August 17, 2008, from http://llt.msu.edu/vol5num1/furstenberg/default.pdf

Hanna, B. E., & Noy, J. (2003). A funny thing happened on the way to the forum: Electronic discussion and foreign language learning. *Language Learning & Technology, 7,* 71–85. Retrieved August 17, 2008, from http://llt.msu.edu/vol7num1/pdf/hanna.pdf

Henri, F., & Rigault, C. R. (1996). Collaborative distance learning and computer conferencing. In T. Liao (Ed.), *Advanced educational technology: Research issues and future potential* (pp. 45-76). Berlin: Springer Verlag.

Herron, C., Dubreil, S., Cole, S., & Corrie, C. (2000). Using instructional video to teach culture to beginning foreign language students. *CALICO Journal, 17,* 393–429.

Herron, C., Cole, S., Corrie, C., & Dubreil, S. (1999). The effectiveness of a video based curriculum in teaching culture. *The Modern Language Journal, 84,* 518–533.

Jonassen, D. H. (1994). *Technology as cognitive tools: Learners as designers.* IT Forum Paper #1. Retrieved August 17, 2008, from http://it.coe.uga.edu/itforum/paper1/paper1.html

Ketchum, E. M. (2006). The cultural baggage of second language reading: An approach to understanding the practices and perspectives of nonnative product. *Foreign Language Annals, 39,* 22–42.

Kol, S., & Schcolnik, M. (2008). Asynchronous forums in EAP: Assessment issues. *Language Learning & Technology, 12,* 49–70. Retrieved June 9, 2008, from http://llt.msu.edu/vol12num2/kolschcolnik.pdf

Lamy, M. N., & Goodfellow, R. (1999). "Reflective conversation" in the virtual language classroom. *Language Learning & Technology, 2*(2), 43–61. Retrieved August 17, 2008, from http://llt.msu.edu/vol2num2/article2

Lange, D. L. (1999). Planning for and using the new national culture standards. In J. K. Phillips & R. M. Terry (Eds.), *Foreign language standards: Linking research, theories, and practices* (pp. 57–135). ACTFL Foreign Language Education Series. Lincolnwood, IL: National Textbook Company.

Lee, L. (1998). Going beyond classroom learning: Acquiring cultural knowledge via online newspapers and intercultural exchanges via on-line chatrooms. *CALICO Journal, 16,* 101–120.

Lee, L. (1999). Students' perspectives on the Internet: The promise and process of online newspapers and chats. In M. A. Kassen (Ed.), *Language learners of tomorrow: Process and promise* (pp. 125–149). Northeast conference reports. Lincolnwood, IL: National Textbook Company.

Liaw, M. (2006). E-learning and the development of intercultural competence. *Language Learning & Technology, 10*(3), 49–64. Retrieved February 8, 2007, from http://llt.msu.edu/vol10num3/liaw/default.html

Lomicka, L. (2006). Understanding the other: Intercultural exchange and CMC. In L. Ducate & N. Arnold (Eds.), *Calling on CALL: From theory and research to new directions in FL teaching* (pp. 63–86). CALICO monograph series, *v. 5.* San Marcos, TX: Texas State University.

Lomicka, L., & Lord, G. (2007). Social presence in virtual communities of foreign language (FL) teachers. *System, 35,* 208–228.

McLoughlin, C., & Lee, M. (2008). Future learning landspaces: Transforming pedagogy through social software. *Innovate, 4*(5).

Meyer, K. A. (2003). Face-to-face versus threaded discussions: The role of time and higher-order thinking. *JALN, 7,* 55–65. Retrieved May 30, 2007, from http://www.aln.org/publications/jaln/v7n3/pdf/v7n3_meyer.pdf

Müller-Hartmann, A. (2006). Learning how to teach intercultural communicative competence via telecollaboration: A model for language teaching education. In J. Belz & S. Thorne (Eds.), *Internet-mediated intercultural FL education* (pp. 63–86). Boston, MA: Heinle.

O'Dowd, R. (2006). The use of videoconferencing and e-mail as mediators of intercultural student ethnography. In J. Belz & S. Thorne (Eds.), *Internet-mediated intercultural FL education* (pp. 86–120). Boston, MA: Heinle.

Polanski, S. (2004). Tutoring for community outreach: A course model for language learning and bridge between universities and public school. *Foreign Language Annals, 37,* 367–373.

Rourke, L., Anderson, T., Garrison, R. D., & Archer W. (2001). Assessing social presence in asynchronous text-based computer conferencing. *Journal of Distance Education, 14,* 50-71. Retrieved June 9, 2007, from http://www.jofde.ca/index.php/jde/article/view/153/341

Schneider, J., & von der Emde, S. (2006). Conflicts in cyberspace: From communication breakdown to intercultural dialogue in online collaborations. In J. Belz & S. Thorne (Eds.), *Internet-mediated intercultural FL education* (pp. 178–206). Boston, MA: Heinle.

Scott, V. M., & Huntington, J. (2002). Reading culture: Using literature to develop C2 competence. *Foreign Language Annals, 35,* 622–631.

Scott, V. M., & Huntington, J. (2007). Literature, the interpretative mode and novice learners. *The Modern Language Journal, 91,* 3–14.

Standards for foreign language learning: Preparing for the 21st century. (1996). Yonkers, NY: National Standards in Foreign Language Education Project.

Standards for foreign language learning in the 21st century. (1999, 2006). National Standards in Foreign Language Education Project. Lawrence, KS: Allen Press.

Walz, J. (1998). Meeting standards for foreign language learning with world wide web activities. *Foreign Language Annals, 31,* 103–114.

Weasenforth, D., Biesenbach-Lucas, S., & Meloni, C. (2002). Realizing constructivist objectives through collaborative technologies: Threaded discussions. *Language Learning & Technology, 6*, 58–86. Retrieved June 9, 2008, from http://llt.msu.edu/vol6num3/weasenforth/

Weist, V. D. (2004). Literature in the lower-level courses: Making progress in both language and reading skills. *Foreign Language Annals, 37*, 209–223.

Wenden, A. L. (1999). Developing autonomous learners: Defining a new role for the second language teachers in the 21st century. In M. A. Kassen (Ed.), *Language learners of tomorrow: Process and promise* (pp. 1–27). Northeast conference reports. Lincolnwood, IL: National Textbook Company.

Wildner-Bassett, M. E. (2005). CMC as written conversation: A critical social-constructivist view of multiple identities and cultural positioning in the L2/C2 classroom. *CALICO Journal, 22*, 635–656.

Yamada, Y., & Moeller, A. J. (2001). Weaving curricular standards into the language classroom: An action research study. *Foreign Language Annals, 34*, 26–34.

Part Three

Literature and Culture:
Closing Divides

Chapter 8

A *Standards*-Based Framework for the Teaching of Literature Within the Context of Globalization

Jean Marie Schultz, University of California at Santa Barbara

Introduction: The Conjoining of the 2007 MLA Report and the Foreign Language Standards

The 2007 MLA report *Foreign Languages and Higher Education: New Structures for a Changed World* calls for a radical reconceptualization of the traditional advanced-level foreign language goal of replicating to the extent possible the language competency of the educated native speaker (p. 4). Taking into consideration the rapidly changing globally oriented world within which foreign language teaching and learning must now take place, the narrowly framed and often unrealistic goal for near-native speaking ability, which has hitherto driven language instruction and language policy, does not necessarily include the culturally sensitive critical evaluation skills necessary for learners to function within the global arena. Precisely because economic, scientific, and technological advancements, as well as international relations and emigration, have shifted, expanded, and blurred national borders, we no longer operate in a world characterized by notions of fixed national, ethnic, and linguistic identity. The MLA report is quick to note that linguistic outcomes need thus to be redefined in terms of "translingual" and "transcultural" competence, redefinitions that shift the emphasis of language learning to promote intellectual, linguistic, and cultural flexibility, thereby allowing learners "to operate between languages" (p. 4). This reconceptualization of language education is an ambitious one.

> In the course of acquiring functional language abilities, students are taught critical language awareness, interpretation and translation, historical and political consciousness, social sensibility, and aesthetic perception. They acquire a basic knowledge of the history, geography, culture, and literature of the society or societies whose language they are learning; the ability to understand and interpret its radio, television, and print media; and the capacity to do research in the language using parameters specific to the target culture. (MLA, 2007, p. 5)

As we can see from this description, the scope of translingual and transcultural competence is a broad one, which, at first blush, may seem daunting to foreign language professionals. Moreover, it complicates the already problematic role of literature within the foreign language curriculum (Schultz, 2001; see Belcher &

128

Hirvela, 2000). One of the MLA Ad Hoc Committee members has, indeed, gone so far as to put the teaching of literature seriously into question, stating that "the teaching of literature has become an end in itself" and a "triumph of historically dehydrated theory" (Michael Geisler as quoted in Jaschik, 2007). As we can note from the definition of the translingual and transcultural cited earlier, the final MLA report does not go as far as its one panel member. However, noting that only a minority of undergraduate foreign language majors continue on to advanced degrees in literature (p. 6), and as also suggested in the earlier definition of the translingual and transcultural, the report makes a strong case for a reconfigured, highly interdisciplinary language curriculum that resituates literature within larger essentially globally oriented contexts.

Given the current discussion within the humanities in general and within foreign language education in particular, language professionals may now well wonder how tangibly to respond to the curricular recommendations set forth in the MLA report and, within this context, how specifically to integrate literary texts into curricula, if, indeed, they should be integrated at all. Moreover, the *Standards for Foreign Language Learning in the 21st Century* (1999/2006) from which many language professionals take their cue for their curricula reflect a certain ambivalence as to the very use of literary texts. Literature, in fact, does not even figure into the core language of the Five Cs. Rather it can be inferred only from the expanded descriptions of the *Standards* that literary texts figure among the cultural products of a country, providing just one of the means by which to establish connections to larger communities. Noting that only 2 of the 34 sample Standards-based curricula presented in the *Standards* make explicit use of literature, Tucker (2000) makes the point that literary texts risk becoming marginalized in the various iterations of a *Standards*-based curriculum (p. 54). However, despite the fact that literary texts are not mentioned specifically, it is important to note, it is important to note that the *Standards* in no way exclude the use of literature. Based on the long-standing divide in some foreign language departments between literature and language faculty (Barnett, 1991; Byrnes, 1998; Schultz, 1991)—a divide that the MLA report addresses directly—the apparent neglect to mention literature in the *Standards* may at some point need to be redressed. Phillips (2007) notes that, in fact, the *Standards* constitute fundamentally a working document, many aspects of which "will continue to be submitted to research, experimentation, and refinement within the professional dialogue" (p. 4). She insists, moreover, that the *Standards* were not conceived to impose a specific agenda for language instruction. Rather, the Five Cs were broadly defined in terms of a philosophy of language education aimed to ensure that all students "develop and maintain proficiency in English and at least one other language" (*Standards*, p. 7). The *Standards* ultimately represent a significant step forward in language learning because they essentially move concepts of language education beyond a narrowly framed, primarily linguistically oriented understanding of language learning to an expansive view consisting of numerous interconnections with other disciplines, cultures, and communities. These interconnections form the basis for the basis for precisely the type of language education proposed in the MLA report. Phillips (2007) emphasizes that "the standards expanded the definition of foreign language education from one that addressed only communication to one that embraced other areas of the humanities, in other words, culture, literatures, cross-disciplinary studies" (p. 268). The mention of literatures here is significant, for within the context of the many disciplines of which cross-disciplinary studies consist, literature is accorded its own status within a *Standards*-based curriculum.

The Neglected Standards: Connections and Communities

For all their deliberate vagueness on the use of literature in the language classroom, the *Standards* allow for a significant amount of latitude in terms of approaches to literary texts. Addressing three of the Five Cs in conjunction with the teaching of literature, I point out in "The Gordian Knot: Language, Literature, and Critical Thinking" (2001) that "the philosophical and theoretical underpinnings of the *Standards* suggest a more dynamic use of literature than has been the case in the past" (p. 13). I go on to argue for an approach to literary texts in the language classroom that combines the methods of both reader-response and semiotic analysis to foster the development of learners' higher level critical-thinking skills. A reader-response view essentially capitalizes upon students' individual and experiential interactions with texts, gradually encouraging them to restructure their own experiences and eventually to develop a reflectively critical view of a given literary work and of the culture that helps produce it. The tendency toward subjectivity encouraged by reader-response approaches is counterbalanced by the more linguistically focused methods of semiotic criticism that encourage students to attend not only to the language system itself—lexicon, diction, syntax, grammatical constructions, and the like—but also to the role that these points play in creating meaning both as intended by the author of the text and as interpreted by the reader. I then further parse these two dominant approaches to texts in terms of the cultural, communicative, and comparative dimensions of the *Standards*, demonstrating how the use of literary texts addresses these three goals in dynamic ways in order to foster critical thinking through language learning.

Taking into consideration the MLA report call for an interdisciplinary and globally oriented reconfiguration of literature, it is telling that "The Gordian Knot brushes" over two of the *Standards*' categories—Connections and Communities—which, in fact, are essential for a reassessment of the role of literary texts in the context of globalization. These two categories in particular reflect the interdisciplinary, multiculturally, and the globally interactive dimensions of literature that are often ignored in the text-centered approaches of reader-response and semiotics. Rethinking the role of reader-response approaches with their inherent risk of self-referentiality, I subsequently revise my earlier position in "The Gordian Knot", asserting that "one of the shortcomings of reader response within a multicultural and multimodal context is that rather than recognize the essential otherness of texts from different cultures, it sees them essentially as extensions of the analyzing self" (Kern & Schultz, 2005, p. 384). Communicative approaches that feature literature but do so fundamentally as a stimulus for experiential discussion that quickly obfuscates the text itself, treating it "as little more than sources of comprehensible input and springboards for conversation and personal expression" (Walther, 2007, p. 8), also fall short in terms of advancing students' abilities to perceive meaningful associations within and outside the text. The Connections standard when applied to literature represents an attempt to redress solipsistic responses to texts by emphasizing the need for external referentiality. According to the Connections standard, language learning needs to be seen as a network of intersecting associations with other disciplines and as a means by which to acquire further knowledge about the world. Moreover, language study should help students "recognize the distinctive viewpoints that are only available through the foreign language and its cultures" (*Standards*, p. 9). The questions naturally arise, then, as to how literature should be handled to provide these distinctive viewpoints and as to what disciplines language teaching should turn, particularly when the ideals expressed in the interdisciplinary Connections standard may seem outside the realm of expertise of many language professionals.

The Connections Standard in a Globalized Language Curriculum

The realization of the Connections standard intersects to a significant degree with a globally oriented view of literary texts, for one of the hallmarks of literature is precisely the shifting and alternate points of view inherent in texts. As critics such as Eagleton (1983), Lukacs (1971), and Jameson (1981) point out, literature reflects in highly complex ways the cultures of which it is a product, as well as the contemporary culture's responses to it. In terms of the ideological underpinnings of a text, it is at the same time a partial reflection of the culture as it is but also of that culture as it would wish to be (Lukacs, 1971). In terms of readers who cannot help but interpret texts in light of their own concerns (Eagleton, 1983, p. 12), literature thus provides additional varying viewpoints. Contemporary interpretations of texts reveal ideological views that have shifted over time, as well as the often radically different views of the culture inherent in the foreign language reader's response to them. A case in point would be texts written during periods of colonization that reflected a positive view toward empire building and the imposition of European culture, a view that now is seriously called into question within critical analyses and within postcolonial texts (see Said, 1978, 1983). The multiple points of view that are always present in literary texts can thus do much to sensitize students precisely to the diverse and yet intersecting cultural perspectives targeted in the

Connections standard. Moreover, in terms of globally oriented language learning, literature also provides a way for students to tap into the cultures of marginalized groups for whom texts furnish a means by which to narrativize their utterances and thereby gain recognition (Jameson, 1981, p. 86). The current interest in colonial literature exemplifies the multicultural connections that the literary text can provide. For learners of French, for example, the incorporation of texts not only from France but also from Canada, Senegal, the Ivory Coast, Viet Nam, and Martinique helps readers come to grips with the many perspectives of multiculturalism and to form connections with cultures that are linked through a common French heritage but that are also distinctly different from one another.

The Connections standard encompasses not only the multicultural but also, as suggested earlier, the interdisciplinary, and here, too, literature can serve a facilitative role. Based on the existence of courses in many departments of language and literature that are team-taught with colleagues in departments of history, art history, film, and music, it is evident that interdisciplinary approaches play a well-established role in the humanities, a role that the 2007 MLA report suggests should be further encouraged but with still more carefully articulated educational goals. "A curriculum should consist of a series of complementary or linked courses that holistically incorporate content and cross-cultural reflection at every level" (p. 6). The complementarity of disciplines within the humanities thus multiplies in yet another way the cultural perspectives to which language students might have access. However, in that literature is essentially a verbal genre that makes use of language in an aesthetic mode, one that narrativizes human experience, it often goes beyond the objective language of history, which Jameson (1981) notes "is inaccessible to us except in textual form, or in other words, [...] can be approached only by way of prior (re)textualization" (p. 82). Literature also goes beyond the unspoken language of music and art by verbalizing the nonverbal. In short, literature helps readers process through language the lived-through experience of texts (Turner, 1996) and can therefore be partnered with other disciplines to foster the acquisition of knowledge from multiple perspectives.

Interdisciplinarity should not be limited to the humanities, however. To help students develop the transcultural and translingual skills they need in a complex and globally oriented world that makes use of multiple modalities for the creation and transmission of information (see Kern & Schultz, 2005), intersections with other fields must be explored further than has hitherto been the case. Courses that conjoin literature with the sciences, economics, mathematics, artificial intelligence, or biology can do much to help students understand in concrete ways not only the practical advantages of their language skills for acquiring specific knowledge but also the complex human dimension of the hard and social sciences that literature helps make accessible. One such pioneering interdisciplinary undergraduate course offered at the University of California at Santa Barbara explores the intricacies of memory by combining work in neurobiology with literary texts to provide a multidimensional understanding of the physiological and aesthetic mechanisms involved in remembering. In this specific case, the work in neurobiology and in literature provides students access to multiple discourse communities, both literary and scientific.[1]

The Communities Standard
and Globalized Literature

Literature, when integrated into an interdisciplinary language curriculum, thus not only helps to realize some of the goals inherent in the Connections standard but also provides students a means by which to access various cultural and discourse communities associated with their language of study (Gee, 1996; Kern & Schultz, 2005). Precisely because the literary text serves as a point of convergence for multiple discourses—the author's, the intended readership, the cultural underpinnings, the variety of interpretations over time and across other cultures—it serves implicitly as a point of entry to the Communities standard which, like the Connections standard, has perhaps not received the attention that it deserves. The Communities standard is glossed over not only in my 2001 article, "The Gordian Knot," but also, and perhaps more significantly, in the ACTFL volume *Foreign Language Standards: Linking Research, Theories, and Practices* (1999), which dedicates an entire chapter to each of the standards except for Communities. The lack of attention to the Communities standard is perhaps partly due to a superficial interpretation of the principle. Although the *Standards* clearly situate this C within the context of globalization by defining it as the ability to "participate in multilingual communities at home and around the world" (p. 9), the two subdefinitions, "students use the language both within and beyond the school setting" and "students show evidence of becoming life-long learners by using the language for personal enjoyment and enrichment" (p. 9), can be very narrowly construed. It is easy to imagine simply using the target language in the classroom and a student's interest in vacation travel to a country where the target language is spoken as fulfilling the Communities standard.

The Communities standard is far more complex than a superficial reading of the *Standards* might suggest, however. According to Thorne (2007), communities are defined in terms of membership, shared location, shared cultural practices and values, interpersonally meaningful relationships, collective goods and resources, commitment and reciprocity, a sense of identity, and sustained duration (Thorne, 2007; see also Wenger, 1998). Learning simply to communicate in a foreign language thus in no way ensures that an individual will be able to participate in a given community. Within the context of globalization, the Communities standard becomes still more complex and takes on a new sense of urgency. As the world becomes increasingly interconnected through technology, economics, and emigration, the ability to take part in various communities as an effective translingual and transcultural participant constitutes an essential and complex skill set to avoid marginalization through monolingualism. As Kern and Schultz (2005) note, "[t]he challenges of multiculturalism and multimodal forms of communication call for a revised definition of literacy [...] Literacy redefined must encompass complex interactions among language, cognition, society, and culture" (p. 383).

The fact that the interpretation of texts fosters the ability to make connections, to compare, and to communicate orally and in writing confirms the positive role that literature can play in providing students with some of the critical-thinking skills they need. Moreover, literature, with its potential to develop literacy skills, seen not just as reading and writing but also as multicultural literacy, can help students tap into the ideological underpinnings of the discourse community represented not only in the text but also in the array of interpretive responses to it generated by different communities. Ingeborg Walther closes her article "Ecological Perspectives on Language and Literacy" by providing the example of a student who had been required to memorize Rilke's poem "Herbsttag" in a German language class. Later during the course of an interview for an investment banking position in Germany to which the student was applying, the interviewer quoted from the poem. Without missing a beat, the student was able to complete the poem and got the job (Walther, 2007, p. 13). The importance of Walther's example is not so much the message that language learning through literature brings financial success, but rather that literature can serve as a bridge to a community different from that of the language learner by becoming the medium for shared experience. A literary education was very much a part of the interviewer's personal discourse community and identity. The Rilke poem granted the student honorary access to a part of that community.

The use of literature in conjunction with the Communities standard serves another role in language learning, however. Also noting the lack of attention to this particular standard, Magnan (2007) has focused on this C as providing environments that foster the acquisition of language. Although her emphasis is on Internet communication and participation in the often multilingual and international online communities inherent in chat rooms and games, her point that community participation is important to language learning is well taken. Swain (1985) has compellingly shown in her theory of output that interaction with others significantly enhances language learning, and particularly the development of communicative competence. Lave and Wenger (1991) go further by insisting that participation in communities of practice becomes a fundamental part of the learning process (see also Wenger, 1998). One of the problems for language learners, however, is access to the targeted community, access that is often blocked due to linguistic, discoursal, and cultural inadequacy.

Writing from an ecological-semiotic perspective, van Lier (2002) addresses precisely this issue of community participation, emphasizing the crucial role of deixis, of being able to anchor oneself to the world, of "grasping the world through language, and tying the self to the world, resulting in mind" as a crucial key to participation in a community (p. 153). van Lier elaborates on deixis as follows: "Deixis has several functions, the most important of which include indexing, referring, and naming. The indexical functions of language are instrumental in sorting out the world, [...]" (p. 152). Although van Lier emphasizes that it is through participation with other members of a community that a learner taps into the indexical plane of language, eventually moving into a more symbolic linguistic realm to gain community membership (p. 153), his work cannot help but support the role of literature as an ideal indexical medium, one that by definition is replete with signs made accessible through the conscious manipulation of language. In coming to terms with a literary text in a foreign language, learners are plunged into a culturally, historically, and linguistically rich sign system that makes salient the indexical function of language. To participate in the world of the text, readers must retrace the various references and interpret rhetorical features and aesthetic structures. As they do so, they understand on a deep level the cultural, social, and personal resonances that comprise the text. van Lier's deixis as an essential component of language acquisition and subsequent key to a new discourse community thus takes on added dimension when applied to literary texts.

> The most important key to becoming a member of a community is the indexing or deictic one, the one that allows for pointing, referring, and participating. It allows for the creation and use of relevant affordances and signs, but more importantly it is the workbench or desktop on which the learner may negotiate the free flow among signs and the construction of options for life. Without the deictic key, the learning person remains an outsider, but with that key an invitational culture of learning is possible, and learner may become a "signatory" to that culture. (van Lier, 2002, p. 154)

In essence, the literary text is a rich source of linguistic signs and language use that helps readers create a connection with the culture of the target language through reflective participation and a teasing out of multiple references. Through literature, readers fundamentally share in the discourse communities of the text, thus gaining at least partial access to these communities through their language study.

Based on the preceding discussion, it is clear that there is a striking overlap between the *Standards* document and the MLA report with regard to a new paradigm for language learning. Both documents clearly support a philosophy of foreign language instruction that goes beyond a self-referential view of the endeavor as narrowly defined by grammatical mastery, vocabulary acquisition, and even the abilities to speak, read, listen, and write correctly in the target language. These are all obviously fundamental goals of language learning, but goals that were previously limited to learning the language for its own sake without any particular connection to other disciplines, to any of the expansive views expressed in the Five Cs, or to notions of translingualism and transculturalism. The conjoining of the principles expressed in the *Standards* and in the MLA report calls for a paradigm of language learning that invites a redefinition of the role of the literary because, as argued earlier, the literary has the potential to do much to foster the learning outcomes promoted by both documents.

The Globalization of Literary Studies and the Implications of Language Teaching

In response to the effects of globalization, literary studies as a discipline in and of itself is being reoriented by its practitioners. Symptomatic of the reconfiguration of literature is the January 2001 volume of the *PMLA* dedicated entirely to the topic of "globalizing literary studies" (Gunn, 2001). In his introduction to the volume, Gunn writes about the ways in which the field of literature is changing.

> "As evidenced by a vast array of critical texts that traverse various national borders and frequently link the literary not only with the philosophical, the psychological, the religious, the political, the economic, and the legal but also with other media, such as the visual arts, music, sculpture, the dance, photography, and the cinema, literary studies has in recent years been resituated in ever more extensive (and extended) networks of meaning and significance in the present and in the past". (p. 16)

The interdisciplinary and cross-cultural resituating of literature in response to globalization is obvious in Gunn's assessment of the direction that literary studies is taking. The various articles in the *PMLA* volume refine in diverse and complex ways the implications of globalizing literary studies. Paul Jay (2001), for example, argues for a reorganization of literary studies that will move the field "beyond the outmoded nationalist paradigm ... and that highlight how during various periods literature has been caught up in ... multidirectional flows" (p. 42). Stephen Greenblatt (2001) emphasizes that "... literary history ... has ceased to be principally about the fate of the nation; it is a global phenomenon " (p. 53). In his article on the "cultural logic of global literary studies," Ian Baucom (2001) asks the question as to "whether globalization does and will entail the liberation or the erasure of difference " (p. 158). Finally, Wai Chee Dimock (2001) puts a distinctly linguistic and translation-oriented spin on his view of globalizing literature by noting that "Translation ... unsettles the native tongue ... alienates it, puts it into perspective, throws it into a linguistic continuum more turbulent and more alive than the inert lines of the geopolitical map " (p. 176). All of these authors intersect not only with each other but also with the positions of the MLA report and the *Standards* document in terms of the very multiplicity of implications of globalized literary studies and of the flexibility that globalization brings to the field. If the actual discipline of literature sees itself as irrevocably resituated in response to the forces of globalization, there are significant implications for the resituated use of literary texts within the foreign language curriculum as well. To avoid the "dehydration" of literature as an object of study in and of itself that Geisler criticizes (as cited in Jaschik, 2007), literary texts need to be repositioned to foster the communicative, cultural, comparative, connective, and community goals expressed in the *Standards*.

Literary Texts and Globalized Language Teaching

As the previous discussion suggests, imposing a fixed paradigm for the use of literature within a globally oriented language curriculum would constitute a move contrary to the spirit of the *Standards*, the recommendations of the 2007 MLA report, and globalized literary studies. Nevertheless, concrete efforts to reconfigure the literary component of curricula along global lines potentially provide insights into the effectiveness of such undertakings as well as material for research into language learning. In 2006 the Department of French and Italian at the University of California at Santa Barbara undertook such an effort in response to the needs of the university's Global Studies majors. The University of California at Santa Barbara, which is one of the leaders in shaping the emerging field of Global Studies, counts over 900 undergraduate majors, all of whom must study a minimum of 3 years of at least one language. The hope is, however, that students will have already completed at least 2 years of one language in high school and will come into the major prepared to do an additional year of upper division work, and then two more years studying another language. French, with its combined European and African, Caribbean, American, and Indonesian outreach, figures as one of the more popular languages among Global Studies majors. With the needs of these majors in mind, the Department of French and Italian developed an alternate French 6 course, French 6 Global Studies (French 6 GS).[2] French 6 is the final quarter of the three-quarter intermediate, 2nd-year French language series.

The French 6 GS reader consists of three thematic units designed to address the concerns of Global Studies students. The first unit, "La présence française en Afrique et les Africains dans les colonies française d'Amérique" (The French presence in Africa and Africans in the French colonies in America), provides students information on French colonial efforts, focusing primarily on Senegal and covering the historical and geographical dimensions of colonization and independence. The readings consist of four texts: the 1685 *Code noir* (Black Code) or set of laws promulgated under Louis XIV legislating the treatment of slaves in the colonies within the parameters established by the Catholic church, the 1766 encyclopedia article by Louis de Jaucourt entitled "Traite des nègres" (Negro trade), the 1848 decree abolishing slavery, and the 2005 speech by the French Ambassador to Senegal. These texts represent different genres that push the boundaries of what might be categorized strictly as literature, thus connecting with different disciplines: international relations, legal studies, and literary studies (the 18th-century *Enclopedia*). The approaches to these texts employed in the classroom are largely literary. Students are asked to compare the views on race and on slavery expressed in each document by using a close reading technique that helps them perceive the inherent contradictions in the *Code noir* in which slaves are treated both as human beings with a soul to be saved and as personal property on the same level as a piece of furniture. In addition, students compare the shifting historical views on slavery and race relations over time as expressed in the 18th and 19th and 21st centuries. Students are also encouraged to make connections between French and American viewpoints on the issue of slavery, thus tapping into still other types of cultural, comparative, and connective dimensions. Finally, the literary work done in this first unit of French 6 GS exposes students to a variety of discourses over time and across cultures, which helps them understand better some of the contemporary sociological issues that France faces today, particularly with regard to their roots in her colonial history. The unit closes with the film *Le bouillon d'Awara* (Awara soup) (Paes, 1996), which features the harmonious coexistence and intermingling of many cultures that share French as a common medium of expression.

The intensive work done on French–Senegalese relations, particularly in conjunction with the history of slavery, forms the knowledge base for the second unit of French 6 GS that focuses specifically on language issues. The unit entitled "Le français, 'langue marâtre', 'langue adoptive', 'langue adoptée'?" (French, "stepmother tongue," "adoptive tongue," "adopted tongue"?) is the most overtly literary of the three units and plays with notions of French as a language imposed from the outside, the "stepmother language" that cannot ultimately replace the speaker's native tongue but that perhaps the speaker has chosen as preferred medium of expression. The unit raises numerous questions regarding the various authors' attitudes toward second language use and bilingual identity. Is French, for instance, an adoptive language, one that is acquired through a process of adoption with all the implications of mixed codes, linguistic malleability, and shifting linguistic identity? Is French an adopted tongue, the language that the speaker chooses to appropriate? Why write in a second language and why French? The texts selected for the "langue marâtre" subsection include one of Nancy Huston's letters to Leïla Sebbar from *Lettres parisiennes: Autopsie de l'exil* (Parisian letters: Autopsy of exil) (1986) and an excerpt from Assia Djebar's *L'amour. La fantasia* (Love. Fantasia) (1985). Huston, who in ways rejects her Canadian and American heritage to embrace a French identity, speaks at length about her struggles to appropriate French, which will never entirely replace her native English, and about the ways in which the language she speaks, English or French, affects her sense of self. Her French identity is more reserved and less given to anger precisely because in French she lacks the automaticity of unmediated expression that takes over in an emotionally charged situation. Djebar (1985), for whom French represents a means of escape from certain repressive aspects of her Algerian world, nevertheless expresses ambivalence and even resentment toward her "stepmother tongue" that she speaks better than Arabic but that has separated her in significant ways from her cultural heritage. The "langue adoptive" section focuses on Mohammed Dib's *L'arbre à dires* (Tree for statements) (1988) that deals with his relationship to his mother tongue, Arabic, which forms an intimate part of his identity, and to French, which is imposed on him at school but which conjoins with his native Arabic to become a still more creative medium of expression. Finally, the "langue adoptée" section of the unit includes among others, an excerpt from Marjane Satrapi's *Persépolis* (Persepolis) (2000), Andrée Chedid's song "Je dis Aime" (I say love) (1999), and the rapper Mc Solaar's song "La concubine de l'hémoglobine" (The concubine of hemoglobin) (1994). For all of these writers and singers, French serves as the language of choice for expressing globally oriented content. For Satrapi, French provides a means by which to introduce the Iranian world to a French-speaking readership and by which to grapple with bicultural conflictual issues. In "Je dis Aime" (1999), Chedid combines images from both her Egyptian and French worlds to underscore her globally directed message of universal love as antidote to hatred. Mc Solaar's song (1994) in which he combines images of violence throughout the world makes significant use of code-switching to convey his opposition to the destructive forces of war, genocide, human rights violations, and ignorance (see Swaffar & Arens, 2005, p. 147 for a discussion of literature and rap). All of these writers, then, for whom French is not their native language, have adopted it for their creative work; but in so doing, they must also deal head-on with multiple issues of bilingual and bicultural identity and with their own struggles with a second language.

These struggles mirror to a certain degree the very struggles that the students enrolled in French 6 GS also face as they set about refining their language skills. In dealing with authors who overtly feature themes of linguistic appropriation and identity, students cannot help but reflect on their own relationships to French and on the extent to which their own cultural, linguistic, and ethnic identities take on new dimensions and nuances. In the course of coming to terms with the various texts in the "langue marâtre" unit, students engage in comparative work linguistically, thematically, and culturally. They make connections through the interdisciplinary intersections of literature with music, history, geography, and sociology. This work, in turn, prepares students to understand better and to share in the ideological underpinnings that form the bases of the various communities revolving around the French and Francophone world. As van Lier (2002) might put it, the texts hold some of the keys that potentially permit language learners access as honorary signatories to the communities represented therein.

The final unit of French 6 GS focuses on France's position within the European Union, and as such introduces yet other interdisciplinary connections to the course: political science, international relations, and international law. The unit is divided into two parts. In the first part, the readings concentrate on the formal structures of the European Council and on the implications of European Council law for French law. To illustrate the differences between the two legal systems, the students study a legal case involving inheritance rights for illegitimate children. Under both systems, estates are divided equally among the children of the deceased. However, under French law, illegitimate children receive only half of what would be their normal portion of the inheritance, with the other half divided among the legitimate children. Students read excerpts from the case of an illegitimate heir who appealed the decision of the French court before the European Council. The heir won his case and the French ruling was overturned. In dealing with this case, students draw on the skills of close reading, linguistic evaluation, and interpretation that they have developed and refined in their work with literary texts to come to terms with the legal arguments for both sides of the case. Moreover, students further develop both their oral and written communicative skills through the activities developed for the legal texts. Working in teams, students engage in debates reformulating the positions of French and European Council law; they write up their findings in either dialectical format or in mini-legal briefs modeled on the excerpts in the reader. In the second section of the third unit, students increase their knowledge of the European Union and French politics by studying the various treaties behind the current iteration of the European Union and by studying the political issues behind France's 2006 decision not to ratify the constitution. They read essays both for and against the ratification of the constitution; again, drawing on their skills with literary texts, students evaluate and compare the various positions and arguments. After this evaluative work, the students are asked to prepare their own position papers for both written and oral presentation. As we can see from the description of the these three units, the French 6 GS course thus provides just one example of an effort to resituate literary texts within an interdisciplinary framework that includes historical, legal, political, and musical texts.

Conclusion

Globalization as a concept has rapidly evolved over the course of the past 10 years. The term originally coined by economists and social scientists to categorize the spread of Western economic and cultural practices worldwide has essentially mutated into an ontological construct based on the convergence of sociological, economic, technological, cultural, scientific, environmental, and academic fields. As such, it cannot help but have a dramatic impact on many different disciplines, including literary studies, as we have seen, but also on language teaching and learning especially with its overtly cultural focus. However, as the 2007 MLA report as well as the 2001 *PMLA* issue on globalizing literary studies suggest, the resituating of literature within global contexts has rendered the construction of language curricula highly problematic because of the many directions and approaches possible as well as the depth and breadth of desired learning outcomes. Despite some dissension regarding the use of literature, the case for incorporating literary texts into the language classroom has clearly been made (Kramsch, 1993; Scott & Tucker, 2001; Swaffar & Arens, 2005), and language professionals have explored the ways in which the *Standards* might intersect with or inform literary approaches to language learning (Fantini, 1999; Lange, 1999; Schultz, 2001; Scott & Tucker, 2001; Tucker, 2000). Most discussions have concentrated on the three standards most easily associated with literature: Cultures, Communication, and Comparisons. However, within the context of globalization the Connections and Communities standards take on a new significance. The Connections standard pertains not only to the multiple viewpoints of literary texts but also to the multicultural and interdisciplinary functions, all of which are promoted in the MLA report and in the *Standards*. Likewise, the Communities standard highlights the power of literature to provide foreign language learners keys to the discourse communities represented in the text, inviting them to share at least partially in those communities. Thus, although the *Standards* are deliberately vague on the specific use of literary texts in the language curriculum, the Five Cs nevertheless provide flexible guidance for literature's role in globalized approaches to language instruction. This flexibility is, moreover, a crucial point because the rigidity of prescriptive approaches to texts would be contrary to the spirit of the *Standards* and the MLA report as well as to the need for a constant rethinking of the role of literacy and language in a globalized world. The *Standards* can thus be used to help shape a globally oriented approach to literary texts in the language classroom, one that situates texts in such a way as to promote precisely the kind of critical language awareness that transcultural and translingual competencies suggest.

Notes

1. The course on memory, "Memory: A Bridge Between Neuroscience and the Humanities" offered at the University of California at Santa Barbara, is team-taught by Professor Dominique Jullien of the Department of French and Italian and Professor Kenneth Kosik of the Department of Molecular Cellular and Developmental Biology.
2. The course was created by Dr. Pierre Bras working under the supervision of the author as principle investigator and with the help of Maryam Emami. Funding was obtained from the Office of Educational Development and the Dean of Letters and Science, Dean David Marshall. I would like to take this opportunity to thank all of the above for their efforts and their support.

References

Barnett, M. (1991). Language and literature: False dichotomies, real allies. *ADFL Bulletin, 22*, 7–11.

Baucom, I. 2001. Globalit, Inc.; or, The cultural logic of global literary studies. *PMLA, 116*, 158–172.

Belcher, D., & Hirvela, A. (2000). Literature and L2 composition: Revisiting the debate. *Journal of Second Language Writing, 9*, 21–39.

Byrnes, H. (1998). Constructing curricula in collegiate foreign language departments. In H. Byrnes (Ed.), *Learning foreign and second languages* (pp. 262–295). New York: The Modern Language Association of America.

Chédid, A. (1999). Je dis Aime. In *Je dis Aime* [CD]. France, European Union: Delabel.

Dib, M. (1988). *L'Arbre à dires*. Paris: Albin Michel.

Dimock, W. C. (2001). Literature for the planet. *PMLA, 116*, 173–188.

Djebar, A. (1985). *L'amour, la fantasia*. Paris: Lattès.

Eagleton, T. (1976). *Criticism and ideology*. London: The Thetford Press Limited.

Eagleton, T. (1983). *Literary theory: An introduction*. Minneapolis: The University of Minnesota Press.

Fantini, A. (1999). Comparisons: Towards the development of intercultural competence. In J. K. Phillips & R. M. Terry (Eds.), *Foreign language standards: Linking research, theories, and practices* (pp. 165–218). Lincolnwood, IL: National Textbook Company.

Gee, J. P. (1996). *Social linguistics and literacies: Ideology in discourses* (2nd ed.). London: Taylor & Francis.

Greenblatt, S. (2001). Racial memory and literary history. *PMLA, 116*, 48–63.

Gunn, G. (2001). Introduction: Globalizing literary studies. *PMLA, 116*, 16–31

Huston, N., & Sebbar, L. (1986). *Lettres parisiennes. Autopise de l'exil*. Paris: Barrault.

Jameson, F. (1981). *The political unconscious: Narrative as a socially symbolic act*. Ithaca, NY: Cornell University Press.

Jaschik, S. (2007). Dramatic plan for language programs. *Inside Higher Ed*. Retrieved January 2, 2007, http://www.insidehighered.com

Jay, P. (2001). Beyond discipline? Globalization and the future of English. *PMLA, 116*, 32–47.

Kern, R., & Schultz, J. M. (2005). Beyond orality: Investigating literacy and the literary in second and foreign language instruction. *The Modern Language Journal,* *89*, 381–392.

Kramsch, C. (1993). *Context and culture in language teaching.* Oxford: Oxford University Press.

Lange, D. L. (1999). Planning for and using the new national culture standards. In J. K. Phillips & R. M. Terry (Eds.), *Foreign language standards: Linking research, theories, and practices* (pp. 57–135). Lincolnwood, IL: National Textbook Company.

Lave, J., & Wenger, E. (1991). *Situated learning: Legitimate peripheral participation.* Cambridge: Cambridge University Press.

Lukacs, G. (1971). *The theory of the novel* (Anna Bostock, Trans.). Cambridge: MIT Press.

Magnan, S. (2007, February 23). *From national educational standards to language use.* Paper presented at the Berkeley Language Center Conference. University of California, Berkeley.

Mc Solaar. (1994). *La concubine de l'hémoglobine.* In *Prose combat* [CD]. Cohiba.

Modern Language Association. (2007). *Foreign languages and higher education: New structures for a changed world.* New York: The Modern Language Association of America. Retrieved from http://www.mla.org/flreport

Paes, C. (1996). *Le Bouillon d'Awara* [Documentary film]. France/Belgium: Tous Publics.

Phillips, J. K. (2007). Foreign language education: Whose definition? *The Modern Language Journal, 91,* 266–268.

Phillips, J. K., & Terry, R. M. (Eds.). (1999). *Foreign language standards: Linking research, theories, and practices.* Lincolnwood, IL: National Textbook Company.

Said, E. W. (1978). *Orientalism.* New York: Random House.

Said, E. W. (1983). *The world, the text and the critic.* Cambridge: Harvard University Press.

Satrapi, M. (2000). *Persépolis I.* Paris: l'Association.

Schultz, J. M. (1991). The role of writing mode in the articulation of language and literature classes: Theory and practice. *The Modern Language Journal, 75,* 411–417.

Schultz, J. M. (2001). The Gordian knot: Language, literature, and critical thinking. In V. M. Scott & H. Tucker (Eds.), *SLA and the literature classroom: Fostering dialogues* (pp. 3–31). AAUSC Issues in Language Program Direction. Boston: Heinle.

Scott, V. M., & Tucker, H. (Eds.). (2001). *SLA and the literature classroom: Fostering dialogues.* AAUSC issues in language program direction. Boston: Heinle.

Standards for Foreign Language Learning in the 21st Century. (1999/2006). National Standards in Foreign Language Education Project. Lawrence, KS: Allen Press.

Swaffar, J., & Arens, K. (2005). *Remapping the foreign language curriculum: An approach through multiple literacies.* New York: The Modern Language Association of America.

Swain, M. (1985). Communicative competence: Some roles of comprehensible input and comprehensible output in its development. In S. M. Gass & C. G. Madden (Eds.), *Input in second language acquisition* (pp. 235–253). Cambridge, MA: Newbury House.

Thorne, S. L. (2007). *Community as mediated participation in activity.* Paper presented at National Standards and Instructional Strategies for Foreign Language Learning Lecture Series, University of Wisconsin-Madison Language Institute, Madison, WI.

Tucker, H. (2000). The place of the personal: The changing face of foreign language literature in a standards-based curriculum. *ADFL Bulletin, 31*, 53–58.

Turner, M. (1996). *The literary mind.* New York: Oxford University Press.

van Lier, L. (2002). An ecological-semiotic perspective on language and linguistics. In C. Kramsch (Ed.), *Language acquisition and language socialization* (pp. 140–164). London: Continuum.

Walther, I. (2007). Ecological perspectives on language and literacy: Implications for foreign language instruction at the collegiate level. *ADFL Bulletin, 38*, 6–14.

Wenger, E. (1998). *Communities of practice: Learning, meaning, and identity.* Cambridge: Cambridge University Press.

Chapter 9

Incorporating the *Standards* into a 3R Model of Literary and Cultural Analysis[1]

Eileen Ketchum McEwan, Muhlenberg College

Introduction

The *Standards for Foreign Language Learning in the 21st Century* (1999, 2006) have significantly shaped the discourse of foreign language teaching by emphasizing the interdisciplinary nature of foreign language learning and providing a cohesiveness for language programs as a whole. The advances in foreign language teacher preparation at the K-12 level have been many, as graduates are expected to guide their teaching through standards-based methodologies and adhere to national and state standards documents. Following the initial development of national standards in the 1990s, initiatives were widened to include teaching standards for languages other than English designed by the National Board for Professional Teaching Standards (NBPTS), standards for new language teachers developed by the Interstate New Teacher Assessment and Support Consortium (INTASC), and new standards for foreign language teacher education programs established by the National Council for Accreditation of Teacher Education (NCATE). Indeed, this professionwide interest in standards-based teacher training has led to increased continuity across linguistic, curricular, and geographic boundaries.

However, the cohesiveness offered by the *Standards* does not seem to transfer across program levels; that is, it appears limited to K-12 language programs. The 1996 publication of the *Standards for Foreign Language Learning: Preparing for the 21st Century* resulted in many workshops, conferences, and meetings of academic associations to create awareness on the part of college faculty. Scholarly journals published numerous articles outlining specific projects for incorporating standards into a college curriculum, such as the *ADFL Bulletin's* two-part series in 1999 and 2000 in which 18 university professors evaluated the *Standards* document in relation to their own foreign language programs.[2] The 2006 edition of the *Standards* was expanded to include levels 13–16, with language-specific Progress Indicators for grade 16, to engage postsecondary language instructors in this national discussion. Though their goals of interdisciplinary connections, communication strategies, critical thinking, cultural knowledge, and linguistic understanding are clearly appropriate for college-level work, the *Standards* have yet to be fully embraced by postsecondary language professionals. The lack of communication between high schools and colleges regarding their individual curriculum and what their students know and can do at the end of their programs, often coupled with a certain disregard on the part of college language teachers for their colleagues in the high schools, has led many at the university level to ignore or superficially glance at the *Standards* without much application to their own teaching. In a 1998 ACTFL white paper, Welles argues:

> College faculty members need to be reminded that the production of the Standards represents the work of a range of foreign language professionals from elementary, secondary, and college levels and from several languages; that the usefulness of the Standards has been recognized by many in the field; and that the Standards are voluntary. Further, since the Standards are organized around the connections between language and culture, they provide a framework on which to build the competencies and accomplishments appropriate to college-level work in literature and other fields. (p. 9)

College professors ostensibly should become better informed about the *Standards* and recognize that they provide a foundation for curricular continuity that builds on what students have learned in high school, allowing for deeper levels of self-exploration and connections to other disciplines available on a university campus. Although valiant efforts have been made to apply the *Standards* to the college curriculum, a good number of language professionals in postsecondary education continue to ignore their value for progressive, process-based language learning.

Among reasons given for not considering the *Standards* when developing their curriculum, college-level faculty cite their lack of clarity concerning literature and grammar, typically the primary focuses of university foreign language programs. Rather than focus on form, as has been the case in traditional language instruction, the *Standards* (see this volume, p. xxii–xxiii) take a more holistic approach to communicative competence, including grammar as an understanding of how language works, "[s]tudents demonstrate understanding of the nature of language through comparisons of the language studied and their own" (*Standard 4.2*). Linguistic knowledge also appears within a cultural context, "[s]tudents acquire information and recognize the distinctive viewpoints that are only available through the foreign language and its cultures" (*Standard 3.2*), and as a productive function, "[s]tudents understand and interpret written and spoken language on a variety of topics" (*Standard 1.2*) and "[s]tudents use the language both within and beyond the school setting" (*Standard 5.1*). Indeed, the lack of precision here, the very flexibility of the *Standards* in regards to grammar, allows instructors to decide how they will teach grammar within this framework of cultural and communicative competence. As the document itself proclaims:

> In the past, classroom instruction was often focused on the memorization of words and grammar rules. The standards for foreign language learning require a much broader definition of the content of the foreign language classroom. Students should be given ample opportunities to explore, develop, and use communication strategies, learning strategies, critical thinking skills, and skills in technology, as well as the appropriate elements of the language system and culture. The exact form and content of each of these elements is not prescribed in

the present document. Instead, the standards provide a background, a framework for the reflective teacher to use in weaving these rich curricular experiences into the fabric of language learning. (2006, p. 32)

Likewise, the inclusion of literature within the *Standards* has been left somewhat vague, permitting the same type of flexibility in curriculum development and instruction. Although the reading skill is specifically mentioned in *Standard 1.2*, "[s]tudents understand and interpret written and spoken language on a variety of topics," the document does not specify what types of texts are appropriate. Rather, literature is relegated to the general category of cultural product, in that students are asked to "demonstrate an understanding between the products and the perspectives of the culture studied" (*Standard 2.2*). Welles (1998) bemoans this imprecision in the *Standards* by saying "While I believe that the study of foreign languages is not just for literature any more, I find it distressing that literary works are not more central to the Standards, at least as vehicles for teaching much of the culture and discourse underscored in the document" (p. 8). Only two of the sample learning scenarios, the readings of Diego Rivera and fairy tales, specifically refer to literature as the cultural product in question. Within the language-specific Sample Progress Indicators, literature is mentioned more frequently, such as for Arabic, grade 16, "[s]tudents share their reactions to literary texts and analyze them" (2006, p. 122), and can "read, analyze, and appreciate Arabic literature and poetry and discuss its role in expressing the beliefs and political views of their authors and the society or ideology they represent" (p. 131); for French, grade 12, "[s]tudents analyze the plots, characters, and themes in francophone literary works" (p. 244), postsecondary "[s]tudents read and analyze French-language literary works, such as poems, short stories, and novels" (p. 255); and for German, grade 12, "[s]tudents share their analyses and personal reactions to expository and literary texts (news articles, poems, and plays) with peers and/or speakers of German" (p. 298), and can "analyze the main plot, subplot, characters, their descriptions, roles, and significance in authentic texts" (p. 300). This brief list of examples demonstrates the inconsistencies among the various languages regarding the treatment of literature, as well as the lack of precision in the types of analyses required at each stage. As Holly Tucker (2000) pointed out in her analysis of the lack of literature within the *Standards*, "[t]he Standards project must find adequate ways to address specifically the needs and concerns of literature instructors. Otherwise, there is little hope for its integration into grades 13–16" (p. 55).

With this goal in mind I developed a method for analyzing literature and culture that addresses the needs of the *Standards*, while responding to the call by postsecondary language instructors for greater precision in linguistic and literary analysis in standards-based instruction. Designed to teach literature, language, and culture simultaneously at all levels of foreign language learning, this 3R Model acknowledges the interdisciplinary and process-building nature of the *Standards* while providing a flexible and specific set of strategies for foreign language instructors to use literature as a "vehicle" for teaching culture (Welles, 1998, p. 8). At the same time, my 3R Model recognizes the intrinsic value of literature in itself, helping students appreciate the literary techniques, the unique practices that point to a particular cultural perspective within a cultural product. Focusing on teaching the *process* of literary and cultural analysis—rather than the product—this 3R Model incorporates these practices and perspectives in a cyclical exploration of the literature of the target culture.

Using the *Standards* as a general framework, the 3R Model also relies on research in reading comprehension strategies to fill the gap left by the *Standards* regarding literary analysis techniques. Reader response theories, where "meaning is not in the written or spoken text, but in the dialogue between the learner and the text" (Kramsch, 1993, p. 177), allow for the flexibility and diversity of interpretation that underlie the *Standards* while creating a student-centered learning environment where the student can explore his or her own interest in the text. Furthermore, the burden of cultural expertise is transferred from the teacher to the student, creating unique interdisciplinary connections based on the students' own background knowledge. For example, a student with expertise in dance might have a different interpretation of a particular poem than a student majoring in history or anthropology. Indeed, "reading is a complex process that involves many variables, including the interaction between the reader (where the old information is stored) and the text (the new information). The reader not only deciphers new words but also thinks about how the text relates to what the reader already knows" (Brantmeier, 2001, p. 326).

Schema theory, introduced originally in 1932 by Sir Frederick Bartlett in his book *Remembering,* has evolved in second language acquisition research to emphasize the role of background knowledge in the relationship between reader and text. Schema theorists posit that the text does not contain meaning in itself, but its meaning is derived from an interactive process between the reader's background knowledge and the cultural clues in the text, that signal the reader to activate certain slots of information in their brains. Schemata, or "active organization of past reactions, or past experiences" (Bartlett, 1932, p. 201), have particular significance for foreign language learners because readers must not only activate the appropriate background knowledge when interpreting a text, but they must also determine what cultural information is lacking for an adequate understanding of the text. As explained by Carrell (1988),

> Not only is the reader's prior linguistic knowledge ("linguistic" schemata) important and level of proficiency in the second language important, but the reader's prior background knowledge of the content area of the text ("content" schemata) as well as of the rhetorical structure of the text ("formal" schemata) are also important. (p. 4)

Therefore, methods must be devised to help foreign language students recognize what type of information they are missing, acquire that knowledge, and interpret the text in light of those new findings.

3R Model: Recognize-Research-Relate

My 3R Model follows this research in reading comprehension by helping students uncover their prior linguistic, content, and formal schemata while providing strategies for filling in the necessary gaps that will allow them to understand the relationship between the practices and perspectives of a literary text. Divided into three stages—Recognize, Research, Relate—the 3R Model focuses on helping the students recognize textual clues and trigger their previously existing background knowledge, research new and relevant information, and relate the new and prior knowledge back to the text. As presented in Figure 1, this method can be best envisioned in a triangular format, each stage simultaneously informing and expanding upon the others in a cyclical analysis of literature, language, and culture.

Figure 1
The 3R model

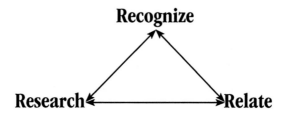

In the first stage, *Recognize,* students are asked to identify linguistic and literary elements in a text, such as particular words, images, metaphors, expressions, rhythmic patterns, and geographic references, that might reflect the target culture. This stage will essentially guide the students' analyses of the text, because it reveals any prior knowledge that the students might have about linguistic and literary practices of this culture, while also uncovering any stereotypes that need further investigation throughout the analysis. For lower-level students, language may pose the greatest difficulty for interpreting the text; therefore, instructors might want to begin by generating a list of unfamiliar words with the students, leading to a discussion of which words might be specific to that target culture. In an upper-level class, students may have fewer questions about particular words in the text, yet a similar discussion might follow in which the students discuss those words that seem to reflect the cultural context of the author. Following this exploration of vocabulary, instructors might ask students to consider literary elements of the text, teaching the students literary analysis techniques while permitting flexibility in the students' responses. In essence, the 3R Model asks that the instructor be solely responsible for teaching the students general literary analysis skills, providing a framework that the students can explore on their own in the following stages. It is the students' individual interpretations that allow for a rich understanding of each text, based on the unique schemata and personal interests each student brings to the analysis.

After having identified the linguistic and literary practices/elements of the text, the students then progress to the *Research* stage in which they explore the underlying cultural perspectives of the text, investigating the visible and invisible culture that might lead to the linguistic and literary choices made by the author. Based on the lists generated in the *Research* stage, students choose a topic of interest to explore further, either in groups or individually. Once again, the instructor serves as a guide in this process, suggesting specific resources and research techniques that will help the students become independent, lifelong learners. This stage teaches students not to become complacent learners, not to be satisfied with one answer or viewpoint, but to use multiple sources and arrive at their own informed interpretation of the subject in question. Resources might include databases of literary and cultural articles (such as the *Modern Language Association Bibliography* and JSTOR), region-specific dictionaries (e.g., the *Lexique du français au Sénégal* for Senegalese texts, Québécois-Anglais dictionaries for Québécois authors), videos (possibly videos of West African dance, musical ceremonies, or informational videos about daily life in the particular cultural region), Internet sites, and native informants (keypals from the target culture, in-class guest speakers). The multitude of resources on a college campus provides opportunities to develop many interdisciplinary connections, relying on colleagues in dance, history, music, anthropology, and film departments, for example, to assist the students in their explorations. These interdisciplinary connections can be quite valuable in a small college, where foreign language departments often struggle for funding or recognition of the many of roles they play. In larger universities, such relationships might set the foundation for a Languages Across the Curriculum program. Depending upon the amount of time devoted to each text, students research their topic for a week or two, meet with their groups periodically to discuss their findings and then present their information back to the class at the end of that time. In this way, the students can share the knowledge they have acquired to approach the text with similar schemata, while maintaining a specific expertise in their analyses.

In essence, the *Research* stage targets several standards, namely Communication, Connections, and Communities. In particular, the students practice the Communication standards in that they "provide and obtain information, express feelings and emotions, and exchange opinions" (*Standard 1.1*), as well as "understand written and spoken language on a variety of topics" (*Standard 1.2*) if using resources in the target language. The Connections standards are met through the interdisciplinary research the students conduct, helping them to "reinforce and further their knowledge of other disciplines through the foreign languages" (*Standard 3.1*) and "acquire information and recognize the distinctive viewpoints that are only available through the foreign language and its cultures" (*Standard 3.2*). Finally, the Communities standard directs the students to "use the language both within and beyond the school setting" (*Standard 5.1*), an objective they gain by incorporating Web resources, keypals or e-mail correspondents, and their group discussions of their findings outside of class. To ensure that the groups use the target language in these discussions, instructors might have students e-mail their conversations in a chat-room or discussion board format using Blackboard or WebCT. These research strategies will hopefully engage the students and help them become lifelong learners by "learning to use the language for personal enjoyment and enrichment" (*Standard 5.2*).

Once the students have completed their *Research* stage, they will return to the text in the final *Relate* stage, in which they make links between the literary and linguistic elements identified in Stage 1 with the newly acquired schemata from Stage 2. At this point, students might reconsider their lists to see if any elements should be removed or added based on what they have learned about the target culture, thus demonstrating the triangular nature of the 3R Model. By rereading the text, students might note new literary elements that reflect the realities of the culture they have researched. Following this somewhat superficial reading, students then conduct a close analysis of the text, reexamining the language, images, rhythm, expressions, and so forth that they recognized previously in light of the new cultural knowledge they have acquired. Deviations from the cultural norms are of particular interest here, in that such variations allow the students to understand the importance of the individual in understanding culture, specifically the manner in which each writer chooses to follow or disregard established literary or linguistic practices. For example, a folktale from West Africa (consider Bernard Dadié's "Le pagne noir") may begin with "Il était une fois" (Once upon a time), a standard opening line for French folktales, thereby portraying an author's acceptance of and adherence to European cultural standards.

In the *Relate* stage, students analyze the "relationship between the practices and perspectives of the culture studied" (*Standard 2.1*) in the text at hand, as well as consider this text in relation to other texts they may have read from that culture. In effect, the 3R Model can be used throughout an entire semester, comparing and contrasting texts and authors within one culture, as well as across different cultures, to understand the "distinctive viewpoints that are only available through the foreign language and its cultures" (*Standard 3.2*). Students may research the same topic throughout the semester, allowing for comparisons of how different authors vary their treatment of this cultural element, or they may choose to select new research topics with each text, thereby expanding their content schemata in diverse arenas. The *Relate* stage also includes a reflective investigation of the students' own culture, helping them to understand their own distinct viewpoints "through comparisons of the cultures studied and their own" (*Standard 4.2*).

When designing a course or unit with the 3R Model, one must begin by establishing the goals to determine the number of texts and length of time to devote to each text.

Goal 1: Cultural Comparisons

If one hopes to allow cultural comparisons within one culture as well as across cultures, one needs to include several texts from a single target culture. For a 15-week semester course, 3 weeks per text should be sufficient: 1 week for the Recognize phase and preliminary research of a topic, another 2 weeks for Research and the final analysis in the Relate phase. Otherwise, if time is limited within the semester, the instructor may want to choose a broad theme (such as colonization) and select one text from various cultures that treat that subject. The instructor can decide at that point how many weeks to devote to each text, keeping in mind that it requires at least 2 weeks for a solid textual and cultural analysis using this 3R Model. One may also decide to vary the students' literary experiences and choose texts with various cultural elements from a diverse range of cultures.

Goal 2: Variety of Genres

The instructor may decide that students should learn to recognize different genres within and across cultures, thereby comparing how different cultures approach, for example, the writing of folktales. Therefore, text format needs to be considered, as well as how many texts of that particular genre from each culture. Again, depending on how many texts one chooses to treat, one may use this 3R Model over an entire 15-week semester or as a 6-week unit on genres of Francophone literature—covering three texts of three different genres—within a larger framework of literary analysis.

Goal 3: Depth of Research

Instructors need to decide the length of time to give students to research each text (usually 1 or 2 weeks is sufficient), as well as whether the students should alter their subjects with each text or continue the same topic throughout the unit or course.

Goal 4: Linguistic Competence

The choice of texts is crucial, because students need to be able to grasp the basic meaning of the text, while challenging their linguistic skills to allow for language learning along with literary analysis skills. Short texts, such as poems and folktales, are effective for lower-level classes (e.g., François Sengat-Kuo's poem "Ils sont venus" or Birago Diop's folktale "Les mamelles"). Novels and texts with complicated formal structures may be useful in upper-level classes to develop the students' linguistic competency while expanding their formal schemata in complex texts.

Overall, these goals target the development of the students' linguistic, content, and formal schemata while meeting the goals of the *Standards*, as has been demonstrated in the presentation of the 3R Model. However, the 3R Model can be best understood through application to a specific text, Léopold Senghor's (1964) "Femme noire" (Black woman), a poem with relatively simple language and structural elements for lower-level students, as well as complexity of meaning that will challenge upper-level students (see http://www.franceweb.fr/poesie/senghor1.htm for the full version of this poem).

Analysis of "Femme noire"

Recognize

At first glance, "Femme noire" does not appear much different than any traditional poem from French or European literature; that is, the poem is divided into stanzas and based on established rules of versification, including rhyme and line structure. In fact, the poem bears a slight resemblance to the European sonnet by its organization into three stanzas followed by a short *renvoi* at the end. Educated in French schools while growing up in colonized Senegal and later attending high school and university in France, Senghor was undoubtedly exposed to the rigid rules of European classical verse. Indeed, Senghor admits to having imitated many poets from French literary history, yet for the most part found his influences in the poetry of African writers: "Je confesserai même ... que j'ai beaucoup lu, des troubadours à Paul Claudel. ... La vérité est que j'ai surtout lu, plus exactement écouté, transcrit et commenté des poèmes négro-africains" (I will even confess ... that I read a lot, from the troubadours to Paul Claudel. ... The truth is that I especially read, more precisely listened, transcribed, and commented on negro-african poems) (1964, p. 157).[3] Therefore, in the *Recognize* stage, when students are asked to find any structural elements in the text that seem reflective of a sub-Saharan African cultural perspective, they may point out the repetitions of "Femme nue" (nude woman), "Femme noire" (black woman), and "Femme obscure" (dark woman), given that these repetitions seem essential to the poem's rhythm. Sophisticated readers would notice the poem's resemblance to French poetry and may want to pursue that idea further in their research, perhaps investigating the European influence on Senghor's (or Senegalese) literary and linguistic practices.

The first area in which an African difference seems significant to this poem pertains to the language. The linguistic elements of "Femme noire" reflect an African cultural reality due primarily to Senghor's use of French terms specific to an African context. Mona Mikhail (1971) describes Senghor's use of language in this way: "His use of such expressions as 'sombres extases du vin noir,' 'femme obscure,' 'tamtam sculpté,' 'peau qui se moire,' revolutionizes the French language by the addition of the African context and ennobles Black beauty" (p. 69). For this reason, Senghor's poem is quite effective for students approaching sub-Saharan African poetry for the first time, given that the language is somewhat familiar while the underlying meaning requires further analysis of the culture. Terms such as "savane" (savanna), "Vent d'Est" (East wind), "princes du Mali" (princes of Mali), and "gazelle" denote elements particular to an African culture, while words such as "femme noire," "vin noir" (black wine), "la nuit de ta peau" (the night of your skin), "ta peau qui se moire" (your skin that shimmers), and "cendres" (ash) are terms from standard French to allude to the darkness of African skin. Senghor's use of the word "tam-tam" refers to a specifically African instrument for which a French translation "tambour" would not suffice in conveying the cultural significance of the term. André Kapanga (1992) refers to this practice as lexical transfer, in which "lexical items from the source language are transferred into the language of the discourse" (p. 330). According to Kapanga, African writers employ both deliberate and nondeliberate strategies to enrich standard French into an African variety that more accurately represents their cultural reality:

> Given that the language in which they have chosen to express themselves cannot properly impart many social, cultural, political, geographical, and psychological realities of their world, these writers have no other choice but to innovate their medium of communication by using processes such as borrowing, calqueing, foregrounding, and outright coining of lexical items or expressions. Thus, these linguistic processes are in fact used to convey the beliefs, affiliations, customs, and cultural allegiances that typify the various communities to which the writers belong, a reflection of the Africanness of the French language and contextual realities of Africa. (p. 76)

Indeed, for students of French, this poem—and others from Francophone sub-Saharan Africa—offer a rich opportunity to explore the distinct viewpoints of a particular variety of French, thereby developing their understanding of how linguistic practices uniquely reflect the cultural perspective of the author.

Beyond language, "Femme noire" contains distinguishing rhythmic qualities that may indicate an African cultural context. Most notably is the repetition of the words "Femme nue, femme noire" or "Femme nue, femme obscure" at the beginning of each stanza. Presented as a type of refrain, these verses are the shortest in the text and serve to structure the poem in a cyclical pattern: "Femme nue, femme noire" begins the first and last stanzas, whereas "Femme nue/noire, femme obscure" represents the first line of the two middle stanzas. The repetition of these brief lines sounds like a recurring beat and alludes to a certain oral or musical quality in African literary traditions. The significance of these repeated lines is further emphasized by the fact that these are the only lines that contain a balanced rhythmic structure; the remaining 14 lines vary in length from 17 to 30 syllables. Hence, the return to "Femme nue, femme noire/obscure" at the start of each stanza presents a leitmotif of words, imagery, and sounds that provides a structure to the poem that is otherwise lacking in formal versification.

The images of the African woman woven within this rhythmic framework reinforce the structure of the poem by following a cyclical progression of metaphors pertaining to birth, death, and rebirth. In the first stanza, Senghor focuses on beauty and life-giving qualities of the woman as mother: "Femme nue, femme noire / Vêtue de ta couleur qui est vie, de ta forme qui est beauté! / J'ai grandi à ton ombre; la douceur de tes mains bandait mes yeux" (Nude woman, black woman / Clothed in your color which is life, your form which is beauty! / I grew in your shadow; the sweetness of your hands bandaged my eyes). Students might remark in these lines that Senghor evokes the universal image of the woman as mother, yet with a characteristic difference: it is her color—her blackness—that provides life and protection for the poet. The images alter somewhat in the second and third stanzas where the woman becomes "obscure," no longer the protective mother but a lover whose body is compared to the "sombres extases du vin noir" (somber ecstasies of black wine), the "Savane aux horizons purs / savane qui frémis aux caresses ferventes du Vent d'Est" (Savanna of pure horizons / savanna trembling under the fervent caresses of the East wind), "Huile que ne ride nul souffle, huile calme aux flancs de l'athlète, aux flancs des princes du Mali" (Oil unwrinkled by winds, oil smooth on athletes' thighs, on the thighs of the princes of Mali), and a "Gazelle aux attaches célestes" (Gazelle with celestial attachments). Following a common trope of comparing women to nature, the metaphors in Senghor's poem pertain particularly to an African context. The references to the "savane," the "Vent d'Est," Mali, and a gazelle with celestial attachments would certainly trigger the students' curiosity regarding the African nature of these descriptions. Moreover, the celestial connection with the African woman seems reinforced by references to her such as the "chant spirituel de l'Aimée" (spiritual song of the lover) and her skin described as "les perles sont étoiles sur la nuit de ta peau" (pearls are stars on the night of your skin). Students may also notice the striking image of "vin noir," placing even greater emphasis on the woman's blackness because of this uncommon combination. Furthermore, the African woman is a "bouche qui fai[t] lyrique ma bouche" (mouth that makes my mouth sing), a familiar theme in Western literature of the woman as muse for the poet, while surrounded by other more African images. However, she is also a "Tam-tam sculpté, tam-tam tendu qui gronde sous les doigts du vainqueur" (Carved tam-tam, tense tam-tam, grumbling under the fingers of the conqueror). This conspicuous African image might raise insightful questions to explore in the *Research* stage regarding the tam-tam, its role in social contexts, who the "vainqueur" might be, and so forth. Such interplay of cultural references may be useful for students in understanding how Francophone literature often contains a mélange of literary traditions—both Western and non-Western—that the author chooses to include or alter into his or her own perspective.

In the final stanza, the images of the black woman evolve in concurrence with the end of her life. She becomes a "beauté qui passe" (passing beauty), yet a "forme que je fixe dans l'Eternel" (form that I fix in eternity) due to the poet's description of her. The theme of the flight of time and the poet's ability to render his subject immortal is certainly not unique to Senghor or African literature, yet Senghor conceives of a new manner in which to present this common theme. He tells his "femme noire" that he must act quickly to sing her beauty "avant que le Destin jaloux ne te réduises en cendres pour nourrir les racines de la vie" (before a jealous fate reduces you to ashes to nourish the roots of life). For Western poets, death usually represents the end of a linear conception of life; whereas in Senghor's text, death becomes an opportunity to renew life, hinting at a circular conception of life that students may want to research in the following stage of analysis.

Research

Using the lists of language, rhythm, and images that the students recognize as perhaps reflective of a Senegalese cultural context, the instructor or students may then establish groupings or categories of ideas to research. For this poem, several themes seem to emerge: (a) the insistence on blackness or Négritude ideals, (b) African music, (c) the link between the African woman and nature, and (d) the link between the African woman and the spiritual world. Clearly, the initial evocation of "noir" in the title, along with the constant reiteration of blackness throughout the poem, underlines the Négritude movement of the 1930s in Paris, of which Senghor, Léon Damas, and Aimé Césaire were the forerunners. Students researching the Négritude movement would discover that these writers essentially defined a new "prise de conscience" (coming to awareness) concerning the suppression of African cultural values. Senghor himself defines Négritude as "the awareness, defence, and development of African cultural values" (1965a, p. 97). Indeed, the Négritude writers sought to establish a literature purely based in African traditions through a "retour aux sources" (return to the source), an Africa free of Western influences. With this knowledge in hand, the students can better understand Senghor's insistence on the blackness of the woman's skin as a new vision of beauty from African eyes.

The Négritude movement also placed renewed emphasis on the cultural elements that Senghor portrays in his poem, such as African music as illustrated through the metaphor of the tam-tam. Research into the role of the tam-tam in African cultures might reveal how it is traditionally used in almost all aspects of daily life: to communicate messages throughout the village, to accompany ceremonial events such as entry into adulthood and marriages, to assist workers in accomplishing their tasks through rhythm and song, and to provide harmony for dancers and storytellers. However, with the arrival of the European colonizer, the tam-tam was forsaken as many of these African rituals were replaced by Western practices of religion, work, and social relations. Thus, Senghor's return to the tam-tam as a cultural metaphor in "Femme noire" reinforces the ideals of the Négritude movement by reestablishing the origins of his culture from beneath the forced assimilation of European cultural practices.

Moreover, students researching African music might discover that Senghor himself insists that the role of music in African cultures goes beyond simple accompaniment or pleasure to represent the heart of the African spirit, an inescapable rhythm that guides the African writer in composing his or her text. In Senghor's words, "Les poètes nègres … sont, avant tout, des 'auditifs', des *chantres*. Ils sont soumis tyranniquement à la 'musique intérieure', et d'abord au rythme" (Black poets … are, above all, auditory, bards. They submit tyrannically to an interior music, and first of all to rhythm) (1964, p. 161). Without rhythm, the image in any African literary text is incomplete, for "l'image ne produit pas son effet chez le Négro-africain si elle n'est pas rythmée" (the image doesn't produce its effect for a Negro-African if it isn't rhythmic) (Senghor, 1965b, p. 60). According to Mikhail (1971), Senghor's depiction of feminine beauty is indeed much more active than the portraits found in French literature:

> In French presurrealist tradition, feminine beauty is most often defined by abstraction of forms and their harmony. The woman is pictured as a rested posture, fixed as a work of art. With Senghor, she is rhythm, sound and smell. She is the "tam-tam sculpté," a drum that vibrates under "les doigts du vainqueur." (p. 66)

Therefore, the repetitions and rhythmic structure of "Femme noire" directly underscore this link between rhythm and image, this return to an image of African beauty both as a portrait of femininity and as a renewed literary tradition that both rejects and retains European influences.

Further renewing these African literary practices, the link between the woman and nature, particularly within an African context, clearly distinguishes this poem from French literary traditions. Indeed, the relationship between the African woman and the Earth is not unique to Senghor but a common theme throughout African literature, "the woman as guardian of traditions, the strong Earth-Mother who stands for security and stability" (Rushing, 1979, p. 19). Since traditional sub-Saharan African communities were primarily agricultural, many African societies linked the fertility of women with the fertility of the earth, nurturing a type of "sacred cult" of women in African cultures (Mikhail, 1971, p. 63). Thus, in many sub-Saharan African cultures, a woman must bear children to gain social status in the community. In her study of women in Dakar, Solange Faladé (1963) concluded that for an African woman, "to be a mother not only ensures the stability of her marriage, but also confers respect upon her as a woman" (p. 224). The bond between mother and child in African societies is traditionally very strong, as the child accompanies his or her mother in all of her daily tasks from the moment he or she is born until the age 6 or 7. Carried on her back, the child experiences the rhythms of the mother's movements in unison with her, reinforcing the fundamental rhythm that underlies the African spirit. Thus the mother as life-giver, protector, and link to nature as seen in Senghor's "Femme noire" is encompassed by the African perspective of her role as mother.

The African woman's role as mother also relates to the belief in the link between women and the spiritual world in sub-Saharan cultures. Students investigating the religious belief systems of sub-Saharan Africa might discover that the woman is traditionally considered the intermediary between the earthly and celestial worlds. According to traditional African religious beliefs, each newborn child receives the spirit of his or her ancestors to continue the family lineage. The woman, the source of this new life, thereby has a direct connection to the ancestors as the receptacle for the spirit sent by the ancestors. Moreover, upon death, one's life does not end but is transformed and carried into the spiritual world of the ancestors. As A. Raphaël Ndiaye (1986) explains this belief in the cycle of life, "Mourir n'est pas s'évanouir dans la ténèbre d'un abîme sans fond, mais devenir 'souffle d'ancêtre', présence profonde et légère à laquelle on officie, ou qui intègre parfois le corps d'une femme féconde pour pouvoir renaître" (To die is not to fade into the darkness of a bottomless abyss, but to become the "ancestor's breath," a profound and light presence where one presides, or that sometimes integrates into the body of a fertile woman in order to be reborn) (p. 135–136). Therefore, the dying "Femme noire," the incarnation of traditional African values, returns to the ancestors and the celestial world from which she came, but her spirit will continue to live and nourish the new Africa to come.

Although the resources and information presented here are primarily literary references, other types of resources would allow for a more multisensory and interdisciplinary perspective on the themes chosen for this poem. As stated earlier, a university campus would provide additional dimensions by consulting with colleagues in women studies, dance, music, and history departments, for example, to provide lectures for the students on their fields of expertise. For "Femme noire," an interactive African drumming demonstration might be effective as well, showing the students how the tam-tam not only accompanies the woman in her movements but also guides her, as the rhythm of the poem creates and is created by the image of the African woman. Another possibility might be a specialist in African art who could show the students portraits that correspond to the image Senghor describes, providing a visual representation to complete the mental illustration his metaphors present. In sum, the primary goal of the *Research* stage is to acquire background knowledge about the target culture by connecting with other disciplines, thereby arriving at a multifaceted perspective with which to approach the text in the final stage.

Relate

In the *Relate* stage, the students apply their collective and individual background knowledge back to the text, creating a unique interpretation that relies on the particular schemata they choose to incorporate into their analyses of the poem. Thus, each class might arrive at new interpretations due to the subjects of research that they develop and the literary and linguistic practices they elicit from the text. For example, knowledge of the Négritude movement would allow the students to understand Senghor's use of vocabulary that focuses on the blackness of the woman's skin. The protection afforded by the "ombre" (shadow) and blackness of the mother's skin, the emphasis on black being life ("ta couleur qui est vie"), the sensual qualities of the black woman and her intoxicating qualities as a "vin noir"—all these elements have a more profound meaning as a reinforcement and glorification of the African cultures. The fact that she is naked, the pure essence of beauty, rings of the "retour aux sources" proclaimed by the Négritude movement. The poet sings of her beauty and fixes her for eternity so as to render the African culture that she represents immortal, unable to be effaced once again by the European colonizer. The musical references, such as the tam-tam, "ta voix grave de contralto" (your low contralto voice), "le chant spirituel" (the spiritual song), and "Je chante ta beauté qui passe" (I sing your passing beauty), emphasize Senghor's belief in the inextricable link between rhythm and images. Furthermore, the association between the African woman and the tam-tam—"tam-tam qui gronde sous les doigts du vainqueur"—underscores Senghor's perspective of her as the incarnation of African cultural values, the communicator who portrays these messages to the rest of the world as does the tam-tam within African villages. Perhaps the "vainqueur" is Senghor himself, who fashions his "Femme noire" into the rhythmic image he would like to portray in his message of Négritude. Knowledge of the important link between the woman and the Earth in her life-giving role as mother, combined with her relationship with the celestial world as a connection to the ancestral spirits, would allow the students to understand more fully the images that abound in the poem relating to both earth and sky. Expressions such as "Terre promise" (promised land), "fruit mûr" (ripe fruit), and "savane" in the first half of the poem transform into metaphors that link her to the celestial world in the second half, such as "gazelle aux attaches célestes," "la nuit de ta peau," and the "soleils prochains de tes yeux" (nearby suns of your eyes). Aware that sub-Saharan African cultures view the woman as the intermediary between these two worlds, students might better comprehend the transformation that occurs quite subtly within the poem and perhaps point out other expressions and images that relate to this cultural perspective. At the end of the poem, she returns to the Earth to nourish "les racines de la vie"—a renewal that reflects not only the traditional African viewpoint of the cycle of death and rebirth but also suggests Senghor's perspective of the rebirth of African literary traditions through his portrayal of the "femme noire." As summarized by Rushing (1979), "What is being hymned is woman's closeness to the earth (the repository of the spirits of the ancestors), her biological connections to the rhythms of birth, growth, and death, and her proximity to traditional African culture in a world increasingly besieged by Western mores" (p. 21). Hence, before these Western influences can reduce her to "cendres," Senghor creates a poem lauding the beauty of the African woman that links sub-Saharan African cultural literary practices and perspectives, providing a model for the Négritude writers to follow.

Although this illustration of the 3R Model focuses on a Francophone sub-Saharan text, its openness and flexibility clearly allow its application to literature from any language and any level. The lack of precision within the *Standards* in fact prescribes such a methodology, and the 3R Model thereby follows that example by providing a framework of analysis that can be adapted to each instructor and group of students. Furthermore, the student-centered nature of the 3R Model removes the burden of expertise from the teacher to the students, making this model extremely useful for beginning language instructors and their supervisors by providing continuity within language programs.

Conclusion

At a time when colleges and universities are increasingly under scrutiny to provide evidence of the effectiveness of their foreign language programs through assessable goals and outcomes, it is becoming ever more important for postsecondary educators to familiarize themselves with the national standards and the ways they can be used for curricular innovation and reform. In essence, the *Standards for Foreign Language Learning in the 21st Century* provide the necessary program goals that can be adapted to each language program while establishing common outcomes within often disparate foreign language departments. A new generation of *Standards*-educated students is arriving on college campuses and it is time to calibrate the goals—particularly those of cross-cultural understanding, linguistic accuracy, and literary analysis—to meet these students' expectations and build on their experiences. As Dorothy James (1998) recommends, "[i]nstead of worrying about whether *Standards*-based students will be adequately prepared to take our college-level courses, we would be better advised for our own sakes to worry about how to prepare ourselves to teach *Standards*-educated students" (p. 5). It is not a matter of lowering our expectations, as James goes on to say, but rather of taking the skills and knowledge of the *Standards* seriously. The 3R Model presented here demonstrates strategies to strengthen the rigorousness of the *Standards* to match a college-level curriculum, with close analyses of literary texts combined with interdisciplinary cultural acquisition. Hopefully such a model, combined with other *Standards*-based approaches that are sure to emerge in the next few years, will convince postsecondary foreign language educators that they must adapt their curriculum to incorporate and build upon the capabilities students acquired through K-12 *Standards*-based programs. Indeed, the survival of college foreign language programs may be determined by their ability to attract and retain students with the kinds of competencies outlined in the *Standards*.

Notes

1. Portions of this article are derived from my doctoral dissertation, "Through western eyes: A model of literary and cultural analysis for teaching francophone Sub-Saharan African literature" (UW-Madison, 2002), under the direction of Sally Sieloff Magnan and Aliko Songolo.

2. See *ADFL Bulletin 31*(1), 70–87 and *ADFL Bulletin 31*(2), 59–79.

3. All translations are my own.

References

Bartlett, F. C. (1932). *Remembering: A study in experimental and social psychology.* Cambridge: Cambridge University Press.

Brantmeier, C. (2001). Second language reading research on content and gender: Challenges for the intermediate curriculum. *Foreign Language Annals, 34*(4), 325–333.

Carrell, P. L. (1988). Introduction: Interactive approaches to second language reading. In P. C. Carrell, J. Devine, & D. E. Eskey (Eds.), *Interactive approaches to second language reading* (pp. 1–7). Cambridge: Cambridge University Press.

Dadié, B. (1955). *Le pagne noir.* Paris: Présence Africaine.

Diop, B. (1961). *Les contes d'Amadou Koumba.* Paris: Présence Africaine.

Faladé, S. (1963). Women of Dakar and the surrounding urban area. In D. Paulme (Ed.), *Women of tropical Africa* (pp. 217–229). Berkeley: University of California Press.

James, D. (1998). *The impact on higher education of standards for foreign language learning: Preparing for the 21st century. ACTFL White Paper.* Yonkers, NY: American Council on the Teaching of Foreign Languages.

Kapanga, A. M. (1993). Discourse strategies in francophone African literary works. *Francographies, 2,* 121–130.

Kramsch, C. (1993). *Context and culture in language teaching.* Oxford: Oxford University Press.

Lexique du français au Sénégal. (1979). Dakar: Nouvelles Editions Africaines.

Mikhail, M. (1971). Senghor, women, and the African tradition. *Rackham Literary Studies, 1,* 63–70.

Ndiaye, A. R. (1986). *La place de la femme dans les rites au Sénégal.* Dakar: Nouvelles Editions Africaines.

Rushing, A. B. (1979). Images of black women in modern African poetry. In R. P. Bell, B. J. Parker, & B. Guy-Sheftall (Eds.), *Sturdy black bridges: Visions of black women in literature* (pp. 18–24). New York: Anchor Press/Doubleday.

Sengat-Kuo, F. (1971). *Fleurs de latérité.* Paris: Présence Africaine.

Senghor, L. S. (1964). *Poèmes.* Paris: Editions du Seuil.

Senghor, L. S. (1965a). L'esprit de la civilisation ou les lois de la culture négro-africaine. *Présence Africaine, 8–10,* 51–65.

Senghor, L. S. (1965b). *Prose and poetry.* London: Oxford University Press.

Standards for foreign language learning in the 21st century. (1999, 2006). National Standards in Foreign Language Education Project. Lawrence, KS: Allen Press.

Standards for foreign language learning: Preparing for the 21st century. (1996). Yonkers, NY: National Standards in Foreign Language Education Project.

Tucker, H. (2000). The place of the personal: The changing face of foreign language literature in a standards-based curriculum. *ADFL Bulletin, 31*(2), 53–58.

Welles, E. (1998). Standards for foreign language learning: Implications and perceptions. *ACTFL Newsletter, 11*(1), 7–9.

Chapter 10

Teaching Culture: The *Standards* as an Optic on Curriculum Development

Katherine Arens, University of Texas at Austin

This chapter offers an experiment designed to challenge the typical language-and-literature department and its claims to teaching culture, claims that are often vague about what they actually require to be taught and learned. This experiment extends the logic contained in a document rarely referred to in postsecondary academe, namely the *Standards for Foreign Language Learning in the 21st Century* (2006), originally published in 1996 with grants from the U. S. Department of Education and the National Endowment for the Humanities. The framework in the *Standards* has provided common benchmarks for developing curricula that are well articulated across the K-12 levels and for teacher training, while remaining largely unnoticed in postsecondary contexts.

Yet the *Standards* overtly redefine the whole enterprise of language learning, particularly by describing language as a set of interlocking literacies, including pragmatic, social, and cultural domains that go beyond language alone. These literacies are also well suited, therefore, to aid in a rethinking of postsecondary curricula. Traditional foreign language (FL) classrooms at the postsecondary level have all too often defined culture as a set of facts: the names, dates, social roles, artifacts, historical memories, and/or similar pieces or patterns of knowledge that individuals within a culture need to know. The *Standards* suggest an opposing view: that culture may be profitably defined as a field of cultural practices, signifiers, and knowledge (with language in the narrower sense serving as only one set of elements in it) and that learning a culture means not only acquiring its knowledge base, but also the strategic competencies needed to function within it.

Defining culture as a pragmatic field structured like a language but functioning in more dimensions is not willful. The sociologist Pierre Bourdieu (1991) uses the term *field* to refer to any site or region within which a group acts, communicates, and evolves its characteristic knowledge and identities. That site is also furnished with a tradition of institutions, group behaviors, pragmatic practices, discourses (verbal and otherwise), ideologies, and a characteristic knowledge base. Once populated and furnished, Bourdieu's field functions like a chessboard on which individuals act to produce, manage, or reproduce knowledge; signify affects and identities; negotiate meaning; and reinforce or challenge positions. The site thus sponsors a culture with a distinct set of native (or indigenous) resources and functions.

Bourdieu's model of a field challenges us to rethink *learning language* as *learning culture* on such a field because it suggests that culture must be understood not only in terms of the resources available to a native speaker (writer and reader) but also in terms of the history, traditions, and resources that affect how such speakers function in social systems, construct and assert their identities, and manage pressures from history and infrastructure. That is, citizens of such fields must be literate in the culture(s) of their site, not just their languages. They must, for instance, be able to handle the pragmatic details of an interview situation (dress, posture, tone of voice, manners) as well as the linguistic ones. The *Standards* contain within them a parallel to Bourdieu's analysis of the relation of history, semiotic systems, identity, and social-pragmatic competence, although they have, to this point, been read principally as descriptions of language to be taught, rather than as more encompassing socio-pragmatic challenges.

That is, most implementations of the *Standards* have read them as applying to language in the way that formal linguistics might, as defining domains in which language functions in the narrow sense. The experiment proposed here will be a rereading of the *Standards* to argue that they apply to a more encompassing model for learning, especially for teaching and learning culture as a set of semiotic systems revealed in the pragmatic choices made by members of a cultural community in a particular field of culture.

The present chapter will experiment in rereading the *Standards* to reclaim a definition of learning culture that is compatible with Bourdieu's insights. Such a rereading may be considered a falsification of the *Standards'* original intent, but I will claim instead that it is necessary, if we are to be able to construct a culture-based curriculum, rather than a language-based one. In what follows, I will construct an imaginary—but necessary—rereading of the *Standards* as referring to culture literacies and strategic sociocultural competence rather than to language.[1] Defining forms of cultural literacy as outcomes appropriate to specific curricula, in turn, will require us to abandon the traditional image of culture as a split between "big C" (high culture) and "litte c" (popular culture) and their attendant class reification, and to embrace the full range of sociolinguistics and other social sciences (especially sociology and anthropology, but also cultural geography, critical discourse analysis, and epistemological critiques of identity politics), beyond the formal linguistics of communication that has been an almost exclusive benchmark for curricular development to date. My experiment, therefore, challenges how the *Standards* have been read and implemented overall.

This rereading of the *Standards* will proceed in sequence with each discussion prefaced by a rewriting, and by examples of what each new standard might mean within local pragmatic constraints imposed by the institution that delivers it and the learners who progress through it. All curricula must function by implementing benchmarks locally, not in the abstract, and by setting benchmarks for levels in terms of local learner-centered, or learning-to-learn-centered criteria.

The rewriting of the *Standards* that I propose is not just an academic exercise or a falsification of an important curricular tool. Rather, this speculative exercise is, I believe, critical for our ability to critique current curricula for their limited visions of what learning language might mean, just as it points to what learning culture might imply in a typical undergraduate major. What emerges most clearly is that the typical undergraduate language curriculum takes a very narrow definition of linguistics/language behavior, often conflating how language functions as part of culture (*Standards 1–3*) with how culture manipulates those functions or with how individuals manage them (*Standards 4* and *5*, respectively)—functions of language exerted as a system occupied by individuals, conflated with those at play on the more abstract field of culture.

The *Standards* taken as a guide to teaching culture, in contrast, stress how acts of language parallel and are conflated with other systems of culture. If these systems are to be taught in a series of developmental levels in a curricular sequence, then that sequence must be defined with more careful attention to a specific target field in the C2. Teaching culture in the foreign language curriculum, as we shall see, can no longer mean simply taking up texts in various media and genres that represent second culture (C2), its history, and its current events and tastes. Texts need to be approached as elements in cultural networks that implicate not only language acts, but also a broader social-science view of culture, including anthropological and sociological systems, its sociology and social-semiotics, organized power structures (institutions, groups, policies), and the social-psychology and identity politics of individuals within it. Texts are not only sources of linguistic knowledge and cultural facts but are also representations of how culture is created and how it functions; they must be engaged not only for language and elements of content, but also as strategic interventions on the field of culture—as examples of how knowledge is produced, circulated, and managed.

Let us now turn to the experiment itself, namely rereading the *Standards* to think through how culture might be understood, theoretically and practically, to render it teachable, and to foster learning with assessable outcomes.

Defining Culture as a Domain of Learning: Applying the *Standards*

The Five Cs of the *Standards* are framed to highlight language use and acquisition, but they also imply how learners need to function between cultures—between their culture of origin, (here referred to as a C1) and a culture or cultures in which they wish to participate (a C2, or C3). At the same time, the *Standards* cannot be seen as providing stable or inflexible benchmarks for appropriate language acquisition; they are neither a method nor a grading scale. Instead, they function something more like Bloom's taxonomy,[2] characterizing stages in a typical learning sequence with progressive demands to be met by learners as they move from beginning to advanced levels. Curricular development, therefore, must project how learners learn in a sequence of levels of instruction, each with characteristic goals and tasks furthering the overall goal (in this case) of fostering culture literacy.[3] The levels in the sequence will not be defined around the presumed difficulty levels of the material (books, tasks, and media) presented to learners, but rather in light of how individual learners evolve both culture-based knowledge and pragmatic competencies to navigate cultural sites (in age and socioculturally appropriate fashion).

In the most pragmatic terms, developing a culture curriculum requires that a curriculum designer realize that the traditional L2 curriculum is actually a subset of the desired C2 curriculum, because culture, from the perspective of an individual learner, is a domain of performances executed within a community using various symbolic systems. The learner of that culture needs to understand and practice not only verbal language but also languages or patterns of markers through which individuals recognize, occupy, claim, and assert their personal positions within the group; produce products and effects; and join within a space of ethics and affects. Learning culture in this framework thus explicitly includes learning language and the facts used within the disciplines of history, anthropology, sociology, or the like. Yet, such a curriculum must do more; it must focus on the more encompassing dimensions of culture literacy, requiring that learners be exposed to and practice in community-based practices on the field of culture chosen as the curriculum's target, as well as knowledge of the material conditions conditioning such interactions. The curriculum's goal must be understood as teaching the socially, historically, and politically conditioned performances enacted by individuals within the space of a given C2 community and its understanding of the world it occupies (its field).

The *Standards'* Five Cs—Communication, Cultures, Connections, Comparisons, and Communities—already make this connection, defining a literacy in language as a set of literacies in several domains of culture. Reading them as a key to culture rather than language alone, however, suggests that each of these domains can be construed more broadly as sites of culture in their own right—an option by no means at odds with the original intent of the *Standards*. Reaching a culture literacy, however, will by definition require more than language-based tasks on the part of the learner.

How the *Standards for foreign language learning in the 21st Century* might be understood as "Standards for the study of culture" requires us to address norms of cultural performance, not just communication, and the extended reading I am offering here may, in fact, be an unacknowledged dimension of the *Standards* project. Each *Standard* category highlights a domain of experience, information, and strategic competencies that learners need to engage (in the form of verbal expression and beyond). They define how L1 speakers confront a C2, acquiring perspectives on culture as the way that individuals are interpolated into definable, legible, social identities and manage a shared lifeworld. Culture makes the world comprehensible and manageable for a group of people who identify with one another; it is a field within which all epistemological production and consumption of meaning (concrete or abstract, conceptual or material) take place.

At the same time, the rereadings highlight logical and content relations that are implicit in the original language *Standards* but which emerge as critical in a curriculum necessarily structured around content beyond language. Learners of a C2 (rather than a more simply defined L2) need to learn how to communicate within a cultural field but also how to produce, assert, and manage multiple pragmatic, procedural, or strategic knowledge within that field, only some of which are language based. These learners must learn not only to acquire language from culture capsules, films, texts, or other artifacts representing a particular C2—an activity that is essentially passive when it comes to cultural literacy, even as it fosters identification and practice of language literacies—but they must also conceptualize various content domains as managed fields constituting culture, all of which require very specific forms of performance, some cognitive, social, or anthropological, as well as linguistic.

To make the case for such a rereading requires a note about a concept that is implicit in the original *Standards*. The well-known graphic representation of the *Standards* shows the Five Cs as interlocking domains within the field of language, however none of these domains places the same cognitive demands on learners. As the *Standards'* numbers increase (both in ordinals and in decimal places underneath the ordinals), they describe increasingly more complex acts of language use, requiring progressively more complex cultural logics. Overall, the linear numbered form of the *Standards*, when seen as applying to a comprehensive field of culture, actually outlines a kind of developmental learning sequence, inscribed in learning models such as Bloom's Taxonomy (1956). Such sequences stress that learners move from comprehension to production, or from recognition and replication to application, and then creation/origination, in ever-increasing degrees of logical and fact-management difficulty—a move from being acted upon to controlling interactions. On the field of culture, they stress how knowledge and agency might be enacted through language and other symbolic forms.

Construed logically, the *Standards* fall into three groups overall, with the first two—Communication and Cultures—representing very basic competencies of an individual language learner, centered around that learner's point of view, or what he or she understands and deals with on his or her own terms. The Connections standard represents a shift of frame from the learner's point of view to his or her contact with another cultural frame of reference, both as managed by particular communities (*Standard 3.1*), and in general, as the prototypical space of the other, as a formal domain (*Standard 3.2*). The final two standards—Comparisons and Communities—refer explicitly to cross-cultural frameworks and strategic competencies, stressing the learner's ability to discriminate and negotiate between, and thus to compare, two frames of reference, the C1 and a target C2. Thus they also point to strategies for performance and identity politics necessary to join a C2 public, both in its own context (*Standard 5.1*) and for the learners to assert their own purposes (*Standard 5.2*)—again, a hierarchy of difficulty in social self-assertion and control.

Let us now turn to the hypothetical "Standards for the study of culture" proposed here to continue this process of redefinition.

Standard 1 for Language and Culture

COMMUNICATION (original)
Communicate in Languages Other than English

Standard 1.1: Students engage in conversations, provide and obtain information, express feelings and emotions, and exchange opinions.

Standard 1.2: Students understand and interpret written and spoken language on a variety of topics.

Standard 1.3: Students present information, concepts, and ideas to an audience of listeners or readers on a variety of topics.

COMMUNICATION (reread)
Perform Within the Pragmatic and Sociocultural Communication Norms of a Target Culture

Standard 1.1: Students engage in culturally specific and demographically appropriate acts of communication.

Standard 1.2: Students understand and interpret a variety of communication acts in written and spoken forms in terms of the implications of available positions, forms, and norms for production/acting.

Standard 1.3: Students learn to enact a variety of culturally appropriate acts to engage audiences/groups/communities with correct pragmatics.

In the original, *Standard 1* speaks of communication, subsequently nuanced into three types of communication, namely Interpersonal, Interpretive, and Presentational. (See p. xxii for an overview of the Standards.) Yet within the field of culture, these three types of communication represent different logical problems, with a clear hierarchy of cognitive and social complexity, if not necessarily in language complexity. *Standard 1.1* characterizes communication in general, referring not just to interpersonal situations, but particularly to student-centered language use in everyday life frameworks. *Standard 1.2* adds the challenge of interpretation within communication situations, stressing the learners' comprehension of a diversity of language fields and an ability to assert some type of authority over the act of communication. *Standard 1.3* moves to nuanced situations for language production based on what is comprehended—that is, to written or spoken language-based performances aimed at an audience, and hence clearly bounded by a network of social and cultural expectation, a complex social performance rather than more personal performance. Thus *Standard 1.3* also differs from *1.1* in an important way: Whereas *1.1* speaks of how an individual contacts other individuals, *1.3* is focused on communication for specific purposes and hence to the authority of the communicator within a specific community. In this sense, what seem to be more or less equivalent domains of language use within a linguistic framework emerge as nuanced across a specific hierarchy of social production/performance, in which interpersonal expression is easier to control and negotiate than is communication aimed at a particular group, with its supporting institutions and values. Seen within the field of culture, then, communication is a complex social performance based on language as well as other systems of communication, including gestures, postures, clothing, and other sign systems or semiotic markers.

If one extrapolates from these definitions to construct a curriculum that focuses on acts of communication as part of cultural competence and literacy rather than on language, then the first decision that must be made is what community (-ties) a group of learners are supposed to be joining. That decision will identify appropriate social identities for the learners within the C2, and hence what negotiation of roles and content will figure prominently in learner-appropriate acts of communication; it will foreground what language markers will need to be practiced for those learners to be able to insert themselves into a C2 culture's communications. Are the learners trying to participate in the C2 as full members, after a certain period of study? Or are they being prepared to be students in that C2, professionals who need to participate principally in various disciplinary communities within the C2, or tourists or other kinds of general consumers of that culture? The answers to these questions generally correlate strongly with an institution's mission statement and the demographics of their students. If learners in that curriculum plan to study abroad, they first need pragmatic communication skills (everyday language, general knowledge about how communities are structured in the C2), and then they must acquire more specialized academic/professional communication skills (how to read and write academic prose, make the kinds of presentations expected of a C2 student, etc.). However, if those learners plan to undertake internships in specific C2 industries, they will require different sets of pragmatics and semiotics because their social and professional goals will require different acts of communication— not just different vocabularies, but entirely different patterns of interactions and the tools to assert very different social identities.

These decisions about what C2 domain a learner is likely to join, in turn, will condition the texts and artifacts brought into the curriculum as the contents of appropriate cultural knowledge supporting acts of communication. If a vast majority of the learners in a curriculum go abroad to study chemistry or engineering or to interact with engineers during internships, for example (as the University of Rhode Island's German students are very likely to do[4]), then class time should be spent explaining how German labs are organized to equip learners to deal with these learning goals. The curriculum designer must target which domains of culture are of primary importance to the students' identities as models for their communication, not just those that may interest them. Where the original *Standard 1.1* concentrates on learner-centered language use, the reread Standard 1.1 takes as its starting point the identification of a discrete locus as the target for cultural communications to be modeled and practiced throughout the curriculum as the bases for language development—this particular curriculum's entry into learning culture, including its language, its semiotics, nonverbal communication patterns, and other pragmatic systems.

Once those types of communication are specified, the learner can practice a basic repertoire of age and demographically-appropriate acts that mark him or her as a member of that community, often in analogy to those from the C1. Social pragmatics, rather than a stylized representation of the native speaker, will drive additional choices of language resources. The new Standard 1.2 probably represents an intermediate level of such a model cultural curriculum. To fulfill its requirements, learners must not only perform basic communication acts represented in the target domain of the C2 field but also be able to grasp what they imply as culturally situated acts of communication. Interpretation requires sensitivity to networks of social forms, and thus to a specific form of sociocultural literacy—to how a message is received, not just how an individual chooses to structure it. To fulfill the demands set by this standard, a curriculum must compel a learner to active engagement in recognizing, discriminating, and enacting sociocultural pragmatics as implicating individual identity within a C2.

The suggested new Standard 1.3 moves even further along this path (and probably toward advanced levels of curricula), adding to prior requirements that learners not only understand the social pragmatics of communication but also produce them to assert cultural identity. To negotiate identity, authority, and position within a culture, a learner must monitor acts of communication in more than one dimension, and to practice various cultural positions within the chosen site, ranging from authority/empowered to disempowered social roles, polite to colloquial speech, verbal to nonverbal norms for communication (tone of voice, body language, etc.). In other words, this standard refers to, what Pierre Bourdieu would identify, as the symbolic power of language (1991).

Overall, the new Standards 1.2 and 1.3 would be critical to a curriculum's attention to cross-cultural literacy, requiring (especially at the intermediate and advanced levels) attention to problems of language literacy (register, complex language use, politeness, etc.) but also to factors considered to be part of anthropological, sociological, or cultural networks. Linguists typically subsume such issues under the category of pragmatics, namely that which defines a communication community and conditions its judgments about who belongs, who is successful, and the like. Yet reframed as an appeal to how culture may be learned, Standards 1.2 and 1.3 would require learners to have systematic knowledge about communication norms and networks of the C2, not just of its language.

The reframed Communication standard thus projects a very specific vision of how to structure the learning of the communication patterns of culture in a curriculum, starting with a targeted community or set of communities that students who complete a 4-year undergraduate curriculum might be interested in joining. At the earliest levels, they will be presented with materials exemplifying the C2's cultural patterns, initially primarily for comprehension and explicit language acquisition. They will then move through the pragmatics of language- and culture-based identity politics (based on history and values) within the C2 community. In this way, Language becomes part of this culture field, not only an expression of it. Thus, students learn how to respond to a person in terms of his or her specific location and within specific groups.

An utterance can only be deemed correct if it accounts for the fact that speaking to a friend in general is characterized by different language and gestural practices than speaking to a friend in temple or church. Likewise, formal communication in a lab setting is different than in an office setting because of diverse interpersonal and institutional constraints and social interactions.

If the field of culture, rather than the field of language, is the main focus for a curriculum, then these issues mean more than mere nods to cultural consciousness-raising or a community's identity. A learner must master cultural logics, not just linguistic ones—how individuals act, feel, negotiate, and believe within their C2 communities, professions, and goals, not just how they speak. Learners first must learn to match acts of cultural communication to situations (as *Standard 1.1* would insist), then at intermediate levels compare how forms of communication are chosen and enacted (*1.2*), and then produce such acts, in appropriate language and with appropriate cultural content (*1.3*).

Standard 2 for Language and Culture

CULTURES (original) **Gain Knowledge and Understanding of Other Cultures**	CULTURES (reread) **Gain Knowledge and Understanding of Other Cultures' Characteristic Structures and Points of View (Other= Alternate Groups, Times, Cultures).**
Standard 2.1: Students demonstrate an understanding of the relationship between the practices and perspectives of the culture studied.	**Standard 2.1:** Students demonstrate an understanding *about the cultural situations* studied, relationship between the epistemological practices and perspectives of the culture, as situated in particular, comprehensible sites. (Implies: knowledge of the social and pragmatic roles attributed to performer, audience, etc.).
Standard 2.2: Students demonstrate an understanding of the relationship between the products and perspectives of the culture studied.	**Standard 2.2:** Students demonstrate an understanding of the relationship between the products and perspectives of the *genre* studied *within the context of "otherness."* (Implies: knowledge of the artifacts, codes, practices, etc., that can be considered meaningful, used to create patterns of meaning and of the communities, groups, and institutions that can claim authority).

The *Standards* optic rests on the premise that language exists in more than one dimension. When it is reframed to speak of the field of a C2, standards other than Communication assume more urgency, because a C2 also implicates specific knowledge bases, not just forms of communication. A culture curriculum, therefore, must give just as much systematic attention to *Standard 2* as it does to the first, building up social and historic codes as systematically as language.

To be sure, *Standard 2* for language targets language as implicated in culture knowledge, beyond language as (self-)expression and joining communities. A hypothetical Standard 2.1 for the study of culture must do more to build a learner's culture literacy. Again, this reframing reveals a tacit hierarchy. The original

Standard 2.1 focuses on comprehension and replication—the ability to identify, for example, when formal or informal speech is called for, and how to use that speech to get information—and thus on who does what and how within a C2. *Standard 2.2*, in contrast, refers to a more complex cognitive negotiation—a more complex culture literacy—asking how particular artifacts of culture fit into its mindset and context, and what forms of incidental knowledge they convey within their C2 community.

These *Standards* can again be rewritten to direct the focus of a curriculum to the field of culture itself rather than to the culture of a C2's language. Standard 2 for the study of culture stresses the social and epistemological functions correlated with roles available within a specific C2 community, and the interests that are associated with them, namely the material facts and situations of a culture that an individual who registers as a culturally literate community member can negotiate. The learner has to learn not only the difference between formal and informal speech, but also what domains of formal culture exist in the target C2. This historical-cultural map of the targeted C2 culture that has more information than just the tag "formal" or "informal" does in sociolinguistics because it will include, for instance, the dress code and cultural expectations associated with each domain.

Again, there is a tacit alignment of Standard 2.1 with beginning levels of instruction, when learners need practice in matching roles and knowledge to the C2 site that is their curriculum's goal. They need to understand what lab assistants do in a French lab, and if (and how) those acts may be structured differently than in the C1; they need to consider what kinds of information they must have at their fingertips to seem credible, and if (and how) that information is stored, retrieved, parsed, or controlled differently than it would be in a lab in the U. S.

A reframed Standard 2.2 requires more complex insight into how particular practices (social, knowledge-based) are implicated into a culture's perspectives. That is, the individual learner would come to comprehend culture not just as a web of performances (e.g., a lab as sponsoring particular acts that produce knowledge that can be judged in various ways). That learner must also see how such performances can be mobilized to meet, appeal to, and even influence audiences' expectations, using various content elements from the culture, marked with appropriate semiotic choices. This Standard 2.2 thus emerges as requiring a learner to negotiate both the content and the context of culture consciously, not just to perform within its norms.

Note that this reframed standard still requires learners to acquire facts from the C2 (and, in the case of a site like a lab, not the traditional facts about history and cultural monuments). Yet in a culture curriculum, the arrangement and valuation of those facts within the C2 need to be objects of explicit instruction, and the essence of cultural literacy, not just knowledge. In a curriculum designed for students who will become lab interns in France, for example, the history of French chemistry might be much more important than French political history as reference points for the chemistry community and its interactions. In other words, this standard reframes the study of culture in almost Foucauldian terms, stressing how material culture, history, and semiotic resources work in systems with their own information value. Understanding a C2, then, means understanding its patterns; a language-centered curriculum fosters that understanding through explicit instruction in language, whereas a culture-centered curriculum does so through explicit instruction in language and other C2 systems simultaneously.

Standard 3 for Language and Culture

CONNECTIONS (original) Connect With Other Disciplines and Acquire Information	CONNECTIONS (reread) Connect With Other Social Perspectives/Communities and Acquire Information
Standard 3.1: Students reinforce and further their knowledge of other disciplines through the foreign language.	**Standard 3.1:** Students reinforce and further their knowledge of other cultures through materials (artifacts, codes, etc.) made for the C2, in terms of structured cultural interactions and strategies for knowledge production (Implies: not just facts, but cognizance of how the facts are put together distinctively).
Standard 3.2: Students acquire information and recognize the distinctive viewpoints that are only available through the foreign language and its cultures.	**Standard 3.2:** Students acquire information about and recognize the distinctive viewpoints about society and culture through materials (artifacts, codes, etc.) made for the C2, in terms of structured cultural interactions and strategies for knowledge production (Implies: ability to identify texts, etc., put together for C2 in terms of that culture's pragmatics).
	[**Standard 3.3:** Producing in different structured communication situations according to those conventions to instantiate self as a "speaking subject" within that culture.]

The third foreign language standard is most often associated with content-based instruction—with classrooms that use learners' existing knowledge and interests to drive the language learning. The original *Standard 3.1* stresses that a successful learner must use the FL to learn specific content areas; *Standard 3.2* stresses differences between source (a learner's C1) and target (C2) contexts that render such content intelligible.

What is often overlooked in this standard is that it shifts perspective radically away from what is modeled in *Standards 1* and *2*. It does not model language in pragmatic use as communication (*Standard 1*), or what the language in use correlates with or reveals about that C2 (*Standard 2*). Instead, *Standard 3* stresses disciplines—specialized language communities that have their own rules and that manage their own domains of language differently than does the language of a culture on the street. Therefore, this set of standards targets pragmatic competence and effectiveness within a specialized community, not within the C2 in general. The most common example might be found in the existence of separate curricula for classes like Business German or Spanish for the medical professions, which explicitly acknowledge that language is used distinctively in these disciplines, with its own rules and structures for knowledge.

As a standard for studying culture, then, the Connections standard refers less to communication or the knowledge base of a culture, and more to questions of disciplinarity and the sociology of knowledge, especially in a transnational context. The new Standard 3.1 models the strategic competencies involved in importing knowledge from a C2 back into the C1; it points to what a learner wants to know or acquire from the C2 and what competencies that learner will need to bring that information into the C1. A learner has to understand, for example, what the boundaries between religion and politics are in a culture, or what marks gender identity, before data on what it means to be religious or to be a woman can make sense and be negotiated. That learner might need to know how the discipline of linguistics is configured in Germany before texts on linguistics written in German make sense within the C1.

The new Standard 3.2 again moves from comprehension to production, pointing to the need for active comparison between specific knowledge communities in the C1 and the C2, without relying on false generalizations or stereotypes from the C1 imposed uncritically on the C2. There is no Standard 3.3 in the original, but within the framework of a culture-centered curriculum, there might be, for example, a requirement to produce a performance of some sort that corresponds to the framework of the C2 (e.g., plan a business meeting or an exhibition as the C2 would, accounting for the differences in that performance and one designed for the learner's C1). According to this definition a learner aiming at a lab internship ought to be able not only to describe lab practice in the target culture as a distinctive site for knowledge production, but also to use professional data from those labs, understanding the conditions and implications of their production and circulation.

The reframed Standards 1, 2, and 3 (Communication, Culture, and Connections) outline basic strategic literacies involved when a learner from a C1 learns to engage a C2. They suggest what kinds of pragmatic performances are required of an individual (in terms of communication skills, cultural knowledge, and the logical abilities to move between two variants of any one discipline or closed community). The curriculum designed to foster such cultural literacies will stress an individual learner's ability to perform within a C2, to know its distinctive reference points, and to compare structures and situations of the C2 (especially specialized communities or disciplines) with respect to those from the C1.

Standards logics, however, do not deal only with how an individual functions interculturally. The fourth and fifth categories, in fact, speak explicitly to issues of abstract or professional reasoning and thus to different problems to be negotiated across culture boundaries.

Standard 4 and Standard 5 for language and culture:

COMPARISONS (original)
Develop Insight into the Nature of Language and Culture

Standard 4.1: Students demonstrate understanding of the nature of language through comparisons of the language studied and their own.

Standard 4.2: Students demonstrate understanding of the concept of culture through comparisons of the cultures studied and their own.

COMPARISONS (reread)
Develop Insight Into the Nature of Semiotic Systems in Relation to Culture as Expression of Group Interests

Standard 4.1: Students demonstrate understanding of cultural semiotics by comparing the same cultural function in two cultures or as made for two different audiences.

Standard 4.2: Students demonstrate understanding of the concept of culture through comparisons of C1 and C2 communities enacting culture.

COMMUNITIES (original)
Participate in Multilingual Communities at Home and Around the World

Standard 5.1: Students use the language both within and beyond the school setting.

Standard 5.2: Students show evidence of becoming life-long learners by using the language for personal enjoyment and enrichment.

COMMUNITIES (reread)
Participate in Communities Associated with Cultures

Standard 5.1: Students understand cultural groups, their semiotics, and their social functions both within and beyond the school setting (as a scholarly concept, for readers, in bookstores, as guilds, as agents of social knowledge, etc.).

Standard 5.2: Students show evidence of becoming life-long cultural agents by identifying how to engage a cultural locus / community of experts to enhance personal and professional enjoyment and enrichment.

Despite the fact that these two standards prescribe different settings for language use, *Standards 4* and *5* are closely related to culture learning; both describe aspects of field-independent thinking about culture, rather than pointing to the pragmatics of individuals entering a C2 (field-dependent thinking). The original *Standard 4* focuses not just on knowledge derived from specific communities in the C2, as in *Standard 3*, but specifically on what it means to shift between cultures. It requires the learner to be able to compare language in the abstract. *Standard 4.1* thus requires that language function be considered in more than pragmatic terms—that the learner understand the nature of language rather than its uses alone. Its parallel Standard 4.2 performs similar work in asking a learner to compare not just the form but also the content of two cultures' language acts.

If reread for the study of culture, this standard would require learners to compare systems from the C1 and the C2 in a general cultural context, not only as referenced to an individual's performance. Standard 4.1 suggests that learners must learn to situate their acts of understanding vis-à-vis a specific audience and its power/value relations on knowledge. Standard 4.2 pinpoints the kinds of technical analysis practiced by experts, including analyses that factor in how scholarly or critical discourses compete or reinforce each other. Overall, Standard 4 speaks to the field of culture in Bourdieu's terms, defined as a literacy focused on abstract generalizations rather than on the management of concrete contexts. The learner, therefore, understands practices within a cultural field as acts that make communities work and enable individuals to act.

If, for example, a C2 curriculum is designed to help learners engage the culture of science and scientists, then they will have to understand not only how scientists function, but also how technical reports are written, how they are presented in the typical colloquia, how they are evaluated for journals, and how they are defined as the legendary "minimum publishable unit" for professional success. These analyses thus converge with analyses of abstract social power at play in a cultural field.

In Standard 4, a learner must confront and understand networks as abstracts; in Standard 5, in contrast, that learner must understand these abstracts as potentially linked to power on the field of culture. That reframed Standard 5 for languages, the Communities standard, focuses not on how systems characterize the field of culture in the abstract, but rather on the communities which uphold and function with them. The original *Standard 5* speaks first of language communities "within and outside the school setting" (*5.1*), and then of a learner's active world engagement (*5.2*). Transposed into benchmarks for a culture-based curriculum, this standard defines conditions for the possibility of identity politics or performativity, including how power is structured and localized (Standard 5.1) and deployed or deployable (Standard 5.2). These standards point, for example, toward another side of learning science by requiring the C2 learner to go out, locate, and engage real C2 communities, and then to practice negotiating positions within them. Thus, where a language-centered curriculum focuses on the linguistic resources required for an individual to deliver a standard speech in an appropriate register, a culture-centered one will also point to the power differentials involved in attendant Q&A sessions and social gatherings as the speechmaker tries to assert a role as expert.

Reframed Standards 4 and 5 thus move beyond the acts, words, signs, and other cultural systems at play, and into the realm of disciplines as particular fields within culture that sponsor distinct performances. What this implies can be clarified by reference to models for learning like Bloom's Taxonomy (or in any of its many successors after 1956). Learning happens not only in the cognitive domain but also in affective and psychomotor ones—as abstracts, as part of individual minds, and through the body. Moreover, that learning proceeds from comprehension—not only acquiring knowledge and attesting comprehension of that knowledge but also applying it to production namely, analysis, synthesis, and evaluation of how systems work. These characteristic acts of knowledge are also acts of culture by means of language, not just language acts.

If an undergraduate major curriculum is defined around language alone, or by taking culture up as content elements ancillary to language, it can often lack explicit address to the upper levels of learning as defined by Bloom's, or to the complex culture negotiations expressed in Standards 4 and 5. Taking acts of culture rather than language as the center of such a curriculum will also help implicate the learner's affective and psychomotor domains of learning, not only their cognitive ones.

The Curricular Implications: The Value of a Heuristic

The five reread standards outlined here make the case for the study of culture as a very different enterprise than the familiar language-based curriculum. To construct a curriculum that satisfies the demands outlined by these reread standards will clearly require a different planning strategy, focused not just on the bottom-up learning enshrined in many undergraduate language sequences (particularly in lower divisions) but also on large patterns in the field of culture that emerge in pragmatic negotiations and abstract systems alike.

The first decision required in a revised planning process, as already noted, must be what culture (cultural locus, group, institution, site) will be targeted as reachable, desirable, and feasible—or absolutely necessary—for learners to look toward as their target in the field of a C2. That decision speaks directly to what a particular student group will do with its language competence—from tourism (meeting people on an everyday level) and familiar forms of self-expression (what students do in the C2) to professional purposes (internships, professions) and employment (institutional behaviors). In this sense, all language learning will best be seen as language for special purposes, requiring learners to acquire distinctive patterns of competence or cultural literacy. How far an individual learner will progress toward that C2 competence will depend on where the learners start, the available resources and timeframe, the specific outcomes deemed desirable, and the kind of literacy possible for a specified student population to achieve (comprehension or production, everyday or expert).

After particular domain(s) of a C2 is (are) specified as targets for a curriculum, then appropriate texts must be chosen as models of the literacies to be taught, practiced, and learned. Some of those texts will be conventional readings (from books or from the web); others must model performances with the target culture's various sign systems, including clips from movies that simulate interpersonal interactions, newsreel footage documenting how individuals interact with events or institutions, literary texts modeling expressive language, newspapers for everyday registers of topical language, and scholarly texts for more complex registers of language on the same topics.

Depending on the C2 domain targeted, a culture curriculum may not even use much literature, or film, or music. A curriculum focusing on the culture of science, for example, will need to identify models not just for scientific language but also for how scientific communities operate—their languages, their uses of text, their social markers, and the like. In consequence, that curriculum need not necessarily even address the kind of colloquial language used in feature films, nor the extended bodies of prose represented in a novel; rather, it might use a scene in a laboratory from a film or novel including scientists as characters, representing that culture and the situations in which its scientific knowledge is produced and transacted. In terms of the *Standards* framework, a curriculum targeting the C2's science communities will heavily emphasize the Communities, Cultures, and Connections standards, rather than Comparisons—operating first and foremost within pragmatic frameworks in which scientists need to collaborate rather than theorize about how collaboration differs in the two cultures.

As an alternate example, if a culture curriculum is to be designed to prepare a group of students to study art in Paris, it must structure its tasks to meet the criteria set by the hypothetical culture standards just outlined. To fulfill the Communications standard, it must not only practice verbal communication but also other forms of communication particular to the art student environment in Paris. Those forms of communication might include the study of how teachers correct art students; the language of art criticism; editing symbols; abbreviations for colors, tools, and canvas; and grading scales. They must also include the semiotic systems that support the verbal communications within the art-teaching environment or that are used at this particular site to transfer information in culture-specific ways. For instance, it might be critical in that environment to know if physical dimensions are given in width-height order, or the reverse, to know how to count to 10 on fingers in the order used by Europeans, how loudly it is appropriate for superiors and inferiors to speak, or that paper sizes are given in terms like A4. The art community requires fluency in these systems of communication (semiotic, only incidentally verbal).

The Culture standard's optic on that curricular decision requires intensive study of the specific social formations, institutions, practices, and attitudes associated with the practice of art in the C2. What does a studio setup look like? What tools are available, and what are they called? What status do various media have? What products are known as "professional grade"? What acts of professional communication are needed—art tours or interviews? Exhibition catalogues or videos? Where does one buy art supplies? How do galleries, museums, and exhibition spaces work? What are copyright laws or tax laws associated with the ownership, purchase, or sale of art, each of which affects attitudes about connoisseurship? What are the periods associated with art history study?

The Connections standard will require learners in this model curriculum to practice deciphering not only the language of the C2, but also its artifacts. What does it mean if art criticism exists in mainstream newspapers, or only on the radio? What kinds of information are found in standard reference books? What kinds of production, performances, and interactions define an artist in the C2, and why? Can an artist launch a painting (sell it, advertise it) in the C2 using tactics other than persuasive speech or a gallery show? On the more abstract level, the Comparisons standard demands that a learner be able to provide explicit commentary on what is the same or different about being an artist in the C1 and the C2. The Communities standard requires practica—that a learner practice actually negotiating an artist's identity within the C2 context.

This curriculum also requires specific attention to text choice so that the chosen domains of culture are modeled for learners who need to see what acts of culture can be produced, comprehended, or circulated in engagements within a C2. Tasks fostering Communications standard learning require authentic models from the C2, for example, so that not just language choice, but also social conventions and sites are rendered comprehensible. The artist TV interview, for example, has a different form in Europe than it does on U.S. talk shows. What a catalogue of art supplies looks like in two cultures may be different; the formal description of a painting in any era has specific formulae that must be mastered. Greeting patrons may involve different kinds of social interactions that can be modeled by reference to scenes from movies or feature video stories of art openings. A learner confronts these models by looking not only for specific features of language for art purposes but also for the appropriate body language to use when approaching art clients, and/or the semiotics of art marketing.

The Culture standard requires a curriculum to focus on artifacts produced by and for the C2, and especially for the attitudes held by their users; the Connections standard requires that the learner differentiate art markets in the C2 from those in the C1. The Comparisons standard requires students to set up and present, not just comprehend, formal comparisons of artifacts, identities, acts of communication and self-expression, and user domains; the Communities standard implies that comprehension and knowledge be correlated with pragmatics of action, behavior and attitudes by individuals who wish to not only to know the C2 but also to function within it. Implementing such activities will thus require a curriculum designer to pay strict attention to multiple elements of a culture's literacy.

Assessment emerges here as a critical guarantor of such a curriculum's integrity. A learner in a culture curriculum as just sketched should never assume that full credit be granted for an utterance or performance in terms of grammatical correctness and/or content correctness alone. Tasks conforming to the Communications standard must, for instance, be assessed not just in terms of grammatical correctness but also as successful sociocultural negotiations—factoring in pragmatics, not just grammar, and including semiotic systems beyond language.

Culture and Connection standards set requirements that can only be met and assessed when learners figure out how and when to use reference books, not just if they know particular items of information. Culture standard tasks focus on content knowledge about the C2; Connections standard tasks, focus on performances about the C2, usually within the C1 context. Comparisons standard tasks factor in the sites on which activities occur, their cultural history and conditioning (habits and values, the negotiation of cultural bias, and hence issues of rhetorical organization and effectiveness). Communities standard tasks move learners toward critical and scholarly activities that will mark them as members of specialized communities, set off from the general public.

A curriculum can meet such goals only when it is structured comprehensively, starting with beginning levels and continuing into the upper division; such goals can be met only in a curriculum that starts with beginning levels and continues into upper divisions, not accepting any fundamental disjunction between lower- and upper-division learning.[5] This kind of curriculum will require new publicity about the implications of the foreign language major, once it is construed as more than a gateway to study abroad. Students will have to be assessed not only for language but also for competence in pragmatics and sociolinguistics, history, demographics, and domains of social practice; correct sentences, informational prose and reports in the form of culture capsules, and polite conversation must yield to the kinds of sophisticated performances that exist outside the sheltered environments of classrooms (including research and professional-level writing); personal expression must recede behind problem solving; and assessment needs to factor in the kinds of social power and position issues that are the preferred topics of today's upper-division curricula.

Some Conclusions: From a Culture Curriculum to Cultural Studies

In this chapter I have outlined representative challenges inherent in developing a culture curriculum, while arguing that the language curricula as presently constituted must surrender their willful isolation within the typical postsecondary institution and redefine themselves as fostering interdisciplinary learning in the humanities—as the kind of cultural studies curriculum that does not yet exist.

To define what might fill this gap, the MLA Ad Hoc Committee on Foreign Languages recommended, in May 2007, that the goal of language learning sequences must be made more ambitious, encompassing translingual and transcultural competence. Yet, in a recent set of reactions to that report published in *The Modern Language Journal*, Chad Wellmon summarizes the problem inherent in that recommendation, noting that even as we embrace cultural studies we have not redefined how language might be seen as key to cultural studies: "We have taken on culture as or object of analysis but have only now begun to consider what the *formal* and *functional* aspects of language might have to do with such a study" (Wellmon, 2008, pp. 293–294). He continues:

> Instead of embracing the amorphous imperatives of *interdiscipli-narity* and simply promoting interdepartmental collaboration, the report begs questions of disciplinarity.... Foreign language departments organized around national literatures or a vague notion of cultural studies are not in a position to pursue translingual and transcultural competence as a pedagogical goal.... Ultimately, I wonder if the authors of this report are imagining a cultural/ language studies field that would be a more radical cultural studies with a linguistic emphasis ... [which] would have to encourage constant attention to the particularities of how languages function and mean with respect to particular cultures. (p. 295)

Circumstance seems now to require that we take up culture, and hence a different logic, as the focus adequate for a newly conceived language curriculum. The rereading of the *Standards* presented here suggests that a language-based culture curriculum ought to teach not only language but also the space within which individuals exercise identity and agency, with respect to their target C2's distinctive use of artifacts and materiality, gesture, taste and power, politics and identity with their various faces. Such recommendations, however, also contain in them a covert threat, namely that the language teacher as traditionally defined may no longer have much credibility if that teacher cannot connect language learning to other specific content domains to construct an interdisciplinary and intercultural project of learning within the undergraduate curriculum of an institution.[6]

This statement might sound as if I were recommending that the foreign language curriculum converge with cultural studies as defined from a social science perspective:

> Arising amidst the turmoil of the 1960s, cultural studies is composed of elements of Marxism, new historicism, feminism, gender studies, anthropology, studies of race and ethnicity, film theory, sociology, urban studies, public policy studies, popular culture studies, and postcolonial studies: those fields that focus on social and cultural forces that either create community or cause division and alienation. (Guerin, Labor, Morgan, Reesman, & Willingham, 1999, p. 240)

Yet cultural studies have another dimension, derived from French structuralism, as Jonathan Culler underscores in discussing its "double ancestry" "culture as an expression of the people and culture as imposition on the people" (Culler, 1997, p. 44). That approach to cultural studies clearly converges with the study of language as part of the field of culture. Yet today's cultural studies has all too often been identified as synonymous with interdisciplinarity,[7] as Wellmon noted, or restricted to studying cultural artifacts as reflecting power relations—as products of the culture's value systems, reproducing its ideologies and marginalizing individuals. In rereading the *Standards for foreign language learning* in the 21st Century as "Standards for the study of culture," I have argued that the *Standards* can counter this trend as well, modeling how to accomplish a synthesis of linguistic and cultural studies proper.

Overall, that work has not been accomplished in present reading and implementations of *Standards*-based learning. Some linguistic approaches to curriculum development have begun to take on the challenge of structuring a curriculum around notions of culture, perhaps the most widely known of which is outlined by Claire Kramsch (2000). Yet Kramsch's model remains resolutely wedded to the domain of discourse analysis, stressing almost exclusively the role of the speaker/writer in joining culture through language rather than asking what specific demands a chosen domain within a C2 will force onto language. She does not move to reclaim the logics of culture that create such speakers/writers, nor how semiotics or domain-specific knowledges intertwine with speakers' identities or with language itself. Finally, she neglects the analyses of power that are the purview today of what is called critical discourse analysis, a politically engaged form of the sociolinguistics of texts in all genres and media, associated with names like Norman Fairclough (1992), Teun A. van Dijk (1997), and Ruth Wodak (1989).

Critical discourse analysis (CDA) is centrally concerned with issues of social power within groups, and with identity politics enacted through language.

However, as a linguistics-based model for analyzing culture, even CDA lacks attention to a feature that the present chapter has identified as critical within a culture curriculum, namely the role of local knowledge in specialized groups, as producing affects associated with individual identities. Beyond CDA, there are few contemporary linguistic approaches to culture that model specialized domains of knowledge as central to culture. One exception is Anna Wierzbicka (2003), who has discussed in several volumes how words open out a lifeworld, thus making linguistic analyses of critical usages into culture analyses, albeit focused on how language creates a space of meaning that may be politicized, not on individual identities.

The *Standards* project, however, has the potential to move us beyond these existing linguistic models, just as it has moved us past cultural studies, to show how "translinguistic and transcultural" language learning might be staged and practiced. Perhaps the *Standards for Foreign Language Learning in the 21st Century* offer a more comprehensive model for teaching and learning than has to date been acknowledged, embedding language in the cultural field and not only within domains of linguistic performance.

Notes

1. Note that I use the term *culture literacy* to apply to these multiple semiotic systems and how they work, not *cultural literacy*, which has been most frequently applied to being able to participate in one's C1. Arens (2008) offers one model for a possible curriculum reconceived in terms of one kind of culture literacy rather than language, taking genre as a reference point. Swaffar (2006) offers a parallel reconceptualization of a curriculum articulated across levels of communicative competence.

2. Bloom's Taxonomy (1956) has been realized in many forms. For an overview of early ones, see: http://www.nwlink.com/~donclark/hrd/bloom.html> [accessed 30 September 2007].

3. See Byrnes (2005) for a brief overview of what this kind of literacy involves.

4. For information on the Rhode Island program, see Grandin (2000)].

5. For information on the Georgetown curricular reform as such an extended curricular sequence, see Byrnes (2005).

6. See the commentary by a dean on the position of language teaching that does *not* join the major curriculum: (Lariviere 2002).

7. This problem is documented all too clearly in volumes on the state of my own discipline, German studies, by Denham et al. (1997), McCarthy and Schneider (1996), Brandhauer et al. (2005), or Hohendahl (2003). More problematic is a widespread assumption: "Cultural studies can become merely an intellectual smorgasbord in which a critic blithely combines fascinating texts and objects in response to other texts and objects without adequately researching and explaining what makes a 'culture' in the first place" (Guerin et al, 1999, p. 244).

References

Arens, K. (2008). Genres and the standards: Teaching the 5 C's through texts. *German Quarterly, 81*, 35–48.

Bloom, B. S. (1956). *Taxonomy of educational objectives, Handbook I: The cognitive domain*. New York: David McKay Co., Inc.

Bourdieu, P. (1991). *Language and symbolic power*. Cambridge, MA: Harvard University Press.

Brandhauer, A., Boss, B., Dunne, K., Mehigan,T., Möllering, M., & Veber, M. (Eds.). (2005). *New directions in German studies: A Context of interdisciplinarity*. Dunedin, New Zealand: University of Otago Department of Languages and Cultures, German Section.

Byrnes, H. (2005). Literacy as a framework for advanced language acquisition. *ADFL Bulletin, 37*, 11–15.

Culler, J. (1997). *Literary theory: A very short introduction*. Oxford: Oxford UP.

Denham, S., Kacandes, I., & Petropoulos, J. (Eds.). (1997). *A user's guide to German cultural studies*. Ann Arbor: University of Michigan Press.

Fairclough, N. (1992). *Discourse and social change*. Cambridge, UK, Cambridge, MA: Polity Press.

Grandin, J. M. (2000). Languages across the curriculum in the context of higher education reform. In M.-R. Kecht & K. von Hammerstein (Eds.), *Languages across the curriculum: Interdisciplinary structures and internalized education* (pp. 3–13.). Columbus, OH: National East Asian Languages Resource Center, et al.

Guerin, W. L., Labor, E., Morgan, L., Reesman, J. C., & Willingham, J. R. (1999). *A handbook of critical approaches to literature* (4th ed.). Oxford: Oxford University Press.

Hohendahl, P. U. (Ed.). (2003). *German studies in the United States: A historical handbook*. New York: Modern Language Association of America.

Kramsch, C. J. (2000). *Context and culture in language teaching*. Oxford: Oxford University Press.

Lariviere, R. W. (2002). Language curricula in the universities: What and how? *The Modern Language Journal, 86*, 244–246.

McCarthy, J. A., & Schneider, K. (Eds.). (1996). *The future of germanistik in the USA: Changing our prospects*. Nashville, TN: Vanderbilt University Department of Germanic and Slavic Languages.

Modern Language Association of America. (2007). *Foreign languages and higher education: New structures for a changed world*. New York: The Modern Language Association of America. Retrieved from http://www.mla.org/flreport

Standards for foreign language learning in the 21st century. (1999, 2006). National Standards in Foreign Language Education Project. Lawrence, KS: Allen Press.

Swaffar, J. (2006). Terminology and its discontents: Some caveats about communicative competence. *The Modern Language Journal, 90*, 246–249.

van Dijk, T. A. (1997). *Discourse studies: A multidisciplinary introduction*. London, Thousand Oaks, CA: Sage Publications.

Wellmon, C. (2008). Languages, cultural studies, and the futures of foreign language education. *The Modern Language Journal, 92*, 292–295.

Wierzbicka, A. (2003). *Cross-cultural pragmatics: The semantics of human interaction* (2nd ed.). Berlin, New York: Mouton de Gruyter.

Wodak, R. (1989). *Language, power, and ideology: Studies in political discourse*. Amsterdam, Philadelphia: John Benjamins.

Contributors

Heather Willis Allen (Ph.D., Emory University) is Assistant Professor of Second Language Acquisition and French at the University of Miami where she also directs the French Basic Language Program. Her research interests include motivation and language learning during study abroad, TA development, and literacy- and genre-oriented approaches to language instruction. She has published articles in *Foreign Language Annals* and the *NECTFL Review* and has forthcoming articles in the *French Review*, the *Journal of Studies in International Education*, and *The Modern Language Journal*. hallen@miami.edu

Katherine Arens (Ph.D., Stanford University) is Professor of Germanic Studies, Comparative Literature, and Women's and Gender Studies at the University of Texas at Austin. Her research interests include curriculum development for content-based instruction, Germanophone intellectual and cultural history since 1740, and cultural theory. With Janet Swaffar, she has published *Remapping the Foreign Language Curriculum* (Modern Language Association, 2005). k.arens@mail.utexas.edu

Elizabeth B. Bernhardt (Ph.D., University of Minnesota) is the John Roberts Hale Director of the Language Center at Stanford University and Professor of German Studies. She specializes in second-language reading, teacher preparation, and staff development. Her book, *Reading Development in a Second Language* (Ablex, 1991), was awarded the MLA's Mildenberger Prize as well as the National Reading Conference's award for excellence in literacy research. ebernhar@stanford.edu

Eva Dessein (M.A., Vanderbilt University) is in the Ph.D. program in French at Vanderbilt University where she is specializing in second language acquisition and applied French linguistics. Her research focuses on the development of second culture competence in a study abroad setting. She is particularly interested in the ways study abroad experiences can promote the emergence of a multicultural identity. eva.dessein@vanderbilt.edu

Lisa DeWaard Dykstra (Ph.D., University of Iowa) is an Assistant Professor of Spanish and Second Language Acquisition at Clemson University where she also directs the Spanish General Education Program. Her research interests include linguistic politeness and the acquisition of interlanguage pragmatics by American learners of Spanish and Russian. With J. Liskin-Gasparro and E. Beesley, she has published an article in the *AP Spanish Special Focus on Writing* (College Board, 2007). ldykstr@clemson.edu

Eileen Ketchum McEwan (Ph.D., University of Wisconsin–Madison) is an Assistant Professor of French at Muhlenberg College in Allentown, PA, where she specializes in Québécois and Franco-American literature and cultures, as well as 17th- and 18th-century French literature. Her research interests include Francophone literature and second language acquisition, in particular the cultural and linguistic differences between varieties of French within the Francophone world. She has recently published articles in the *French Review, Foreign Language Annals,* and a chapter in an upcoming volume entitled *Love and Death in French and Francophone Women's Lives* (Cambridge Scholars Press, 2009). ketchum@muhlenberg.edu

Alice Miano (M.A., UCLA) is a lecturer in Spanish and Coordinator of the Spanish language program at Stanford University. She is currently completing her doctoral dissertation, *"¡Quiero estudiar!* Mexican Immigrant Mothers' Participation in Their Children's Education—and Their Own," at UC Berkeley. In addition to immigrant families' interaction with the U.S. education system, her research interests include second language acquisition, bilingualism and language maintenance, literacy and biliteracy. alimiano@stanford.edu

Rachel Nisselson (M.A., Vanderbilt University) is a Ph.D. candidate in French at Vanderbilt University. Her dissertation, "Forgetting the Future: Memory and the Future of Israel/Palestine in 20th- and 21st-Century Francophone Literature," focuses on the works of several French-speaking authors who treat the Israeli-Palestinian conflict. Her interests in second language acquisition include the use of inner speech in the idea generation phase of foreign language writing. rachel.e.nisselson@vanderbilt.edu

Ana Oskoz (Ph.D., University of Iowa) is an Associate Professor at the University of Maryland Baltimore County (UMBC). Her research interests include the integration of Web 2.0 technologies in the foreign language classroom, such as the use of wikis to enhance second language writing or blogs to develop intercultural communication. She has published articles in the *CALICO* journal, *Foreign Language Annals*, and a chapter in the edited volume *El español a la luz de la lingüística: Preguntas y respuestas* (Cascadilla, 2008). aoskoz@umbc.edu

June K. Phillips (Ph.D., The Ohio State University) is Professor and Dean Emerita of Arts and Humanities at Weber State University (UT). She served as President of the American Council on the Teaching of Foreign Languages in 2001, chaired the Northeast Conference on the Teaching of Foreign Languages in 1984, and was a trustee for the Center for Applied Linguistics. She was project director for the design of the Foreign Language Standards and co-chaired the development of Standards for FL Teacher Education Programs that are approved by NCATE. She is currently directing a federally funded project to assess the impact of the standards a decade after publication. jphillips@weber.edu

Jean Marie Schultz (Ph.D., University of California, Berkeley) directs the French Language Program at the University of California at Santa Barbara. Her research interests include foreign language literacy, with an emphasis on writing, the teaching of language through literature, and most recently interdisciplinary approaches to language teaching within the context of globalization. She has published articles in *The Modern Language Journal*, the *French Review*, and *AAUSC* volumes, as well as chapters in a number of edited volumes. She has recently published the intermediate French textbook *Réseau: Communication, Intégration, Intersection* (Prentice Hall, 2010). jmschultz@french-ital.ucsb.edu

Virginia M. Scott (Ph.D., Emory University) is Associate Professor of French and Applied Linguistics at Vanderbilt University where she has served as the French language program coordinator and chair of the Department of French and Italian. Her research interests include the role of literature in second language development, bilingual studies, and approaches to classroom practice. She has recently published articles in *The Modern Language Journal, The French Review,* and *Foreign Language Annals.* Her most recent book, *Double Talk: Deconstructing Monolingualism in Classroom Second Language Learning* (Prentice Hall, 2010), examines language development and language use in the classroom. She is currently working with a federally funded task force to assess the influence, impact, and future directions of foreign language standards. virginia.m.scott@vanderbilt.edu

H. Jay Siskin (Ph.D., Cornell University) is Professor of French at Cabrillo College, where he also serves as Chair of the World Languages Department. His research interests include questions of identity in the pedagogical setting and the cultural context of foreign language teaching. He edited the 2007 volume in the AAUSC series titled *From Thought to Action: Exploring Beliefs and Outcomes in the Foreign Language Program.* The chapter in the current volume is excerpted from his forthcoming book, *Language Teaching and Learning: 100 Years of Precepts and Practices* (Yale University Press). hjsiskin@mac.com

Robert M. Terry (Ph.D., Duke University) is Professor of French, Emeritus, having retired from the University of Richmond in May 2008. His research interests continue to be foreign language teaching methodology, reading, and writing. He has published several textbooks as well as articles in *Foreign Language Annals,* the *French Review,* and the *Canadian Modern Language Review.* He was President of ACTFL in 1994 and served two terms on the ACTFL Executive Council. He is currently Articles Editor of the NECTFL *Review.* rterry@richmond.edu

Guadalupe Valdés (Ph.D., Florida State University) is the Bonnie Katz Tenenbaum Professor of Education at Stanford University. She specializes in language pedagogy and applied linguistics. She has carried out extensive work on maintaining and preserving heritage languages among minority populations since the 1970s. Her last book, *Developing Minority Language Resources: The Case of Spanish in California* (Valdés, Fishman, Chavez & Perez, Multilingual Matters, 2006) examines Spanish language maintenance and instruction in both secondary and postsecondary institutions. gvaldes@stanford.edu

AAUSC

The American Association of University Supervisors, Coordinators, and Directors of Foreign Language Programs

Purpose

Since its inception in 1980, the AAUSC has worked to:

- Promote and improve foreign and second language education in the United States
- Strengthen and improve foreign language curricula and instruction at the postsecondary level
- Strengthen development programs for teaching assistants, teaching fellows, associate instructors, or their equivalents
- Promote research in second language learning and development and on the preparation and supervision of teaching assistants
- Establish a forum for exchanging ideas, experiences, and materials among those concerned with language program direction

Who Can Join the AAUSC?

Membership in the AAUSC is open to anyone who is interested in strengthening foreign and second language instruction, especially, but not exclusively, those involved with multi-section programs. The membership comprises teachers, supervisors, coordinators, program directors, faculty, and administrators in colleges and universities that employ teaching assistants. Many members are faculty and administrators at undergraduate institutions.

How Do I Join the AAUSC?

Please fill out the following application for membership, and send it with annual dues to Robert Davis, or join online at *www.aausc.org.*

Dues (including yearly volume)

Regular .... $25.00/year, $40.00/two years
Student .... $15.00/year, $25.00/two years

Please make checks payable to:
Robert L. Davis, Secretary/Treasurer, AAUSC
Department of Romance Languages
University of Oregon
Eugene, OR 97403 USA
(541) 346-0956 phone
(541) 346-4030 fax
rldavis@oregon.uoregon.edu
www.aausc.org

AAUSC Application for Membership

New ☐   Renewal ☐

Name _____

School Address _____

_____

City _____ State _____ Zip _____

Telephone (work) _____

Fax _____

E-mail _____

Home address _____

City _____ State _____ Zip _____

Telephone (home) _____

Languages taught: Arabic ☐   Chinese ☐   ESL ☐

French ☐   Italian ☐   Japanese ☐   Portuguese ☐

Russian ☐   German ☐   Spanish ☐   Other ☐

Are you a: Teacher ☐   Program Director ☐

Dept. Chair ☐   Graduate Student ☐   Other ☐